INTERNATIONAL NIETZSCHE STUDIES

Nietzsche has emerged as a thinker of extraordinary importance, not only in the history of philosophy but in many fields of contemporary inquiry. Nietzsche studies are maturing and flourishing in many parts of the world. This internationalization of inquiry with respect to Nietzsche's thought and significance may be expected to continue.

International Nietzsche Studies is conceived as a series of monographs and essay collections that will reflect and contribute to these developments. The series will present studies in which responsible scholarship is joined to the analysis, interpretation, and assessment of the many aspects of Nietzsche's thought that bear significantly upon matters of moment today. In many respects Nietzsche is our contemporary, with whom we do well to reckon, even when we find ourselves at odds with him. The series is intended to promote this reckoning, embracing diverse interpretive perspectives, philosophical orientations, and critical assessments.

The series is also intended to contribute to the ongoing reconsideration of the character, agenda, and prospects of philosophy itself. Nietzsche was much concerned with philosophy's past, present, and future. He sought to affect not only its understanding but also its practice. The future of philosophy is an open question today, thanks at least in part to Nietzsche's challenge to the philosophical traditions of which he was so critical. It remains to be seen—and determined—whether philosophy's future will turn out to resemble the "philosophy of the future" to which he proffered a prelude and of which he provided a preview, by both precept and practice. But this is a possibility we do well to take seriously. International Nietzsche Studies will attempt to do so, while contributing to the understanding of Nietzsche's philosophical thinking and its bearing upon contemporary inquiry.

—Richard Schacht

Nietzsche and the Transcendental Tradition

Nietzsche and the Transcendental Tradition

MICHAEL STEVEN GREEN

University of Illinois Press

URBANA AND CHICAGO

∞ This book is printed on acid-free paper.

Library of Congress Cataloging-in-Publication Data
Green, Michael Steven.
Nietzsche and the transcendental tradition / Michael Steven Green.
p.   cm. — (International Nietzsche studies)
Includes bibliographical references and index.
ISBN 0-252-02735-3
1. Nietzsche, Friedrich Wilhelm, 1844–1900. 2. Neo-Kantianism.
I. Title. II. Series.
B3317 .G722   2002
193—dc21   2001005761

To Kiersten

Contents

Acknowledgments

Many of the ideas in this book reach back to my doctoral dissertation, which I wrote at Yale in the late 1980s, and my first debt of gratitude is to those who helped me through that process. These include my Doktorvater, Karsten Harries, and a number of people who were graduate students in philosophy at Yale at the time, particularly Sarah Buss and Mark Migotti. I would also like to thank the Deutsche Akademische Austauschdienst, which supported my research in Berlin for a year from 1987 to 1988, and the Stiftung Luftbrückendank Berlin, which did the same during 1990. While in Berlin, I participated in a seminar for Nietzsche-Doktoranten run by the late Wolfgang Müller-Lauter. I would like to express my gratitude to him and to the seminar's other participants, particularly Martin Bauer, for their helpful advice concerning some of my arguments. My very heartfelt thanks also go to Günter Abel of the Technische Universität, an insightful interlocutor and a good friend, and to Roswitha Paul-Walz of the Technische Universität for her warm welcome and helpfulness.

I wrote the first draft of what are now the first, fourth, and fifth chapters of this book as a philosophy professor at Tufts University in 1991–93. I would like to thank a former colleague at Tufts, Stephen White, for providing me with a number of ideas that I made use of in the final chapter, and the other members of the philosophy department for creating an exemplary setting within which to do philosophy. The Stiftung Luftbrückendank Berlin again provided me with generous research support in Berlin during the summers of 1991 and 1992.

In 1993, I quit my job at Tufts to go to law school. At the time I was unsure about whether I was going to return to academia, but shortly before leaving for New Haven, Richard Schacht asked to look at my manuscript for the new Nietzsche series he was founding. Both he and the reader for the University of Illinois Press, Brian Leiter, offered invaluable advice concerning improvements. In addition to inspiring me to simplify and clarify my often impenetrable prose, it is largely to address their concerns that I added the material on Afrikan Spir in what are now the second and third chapters. I don't like to think about what this book would have looked like had they not exerted their influence on it.

Unfortunately I didn't return to the manuscript until almost six years had passed—after a career as a law student and a lawyer. Remarkably, Richard Schacht and the University of Illinois Press stuck with me during those six years. I finally finished the book as a law professor, and I want to express my gratitude to my current home, the School of Law at George Mason University, and its Center for Law and Economics, for cheerfully supporting me while I worked on a project utterly unrelated to the law. Two of my colleagues at George Mason, Frank Buckley and Peter Berkowitz, provided helpful comments on a draft. Thanks also go to the School of Law at King's College London for providing me with a home while completing the final editing of the manuscript, during my sabbatical leave from George Mason.

I also owe a debt of gratitude to the following people: Maudemarie Clark, for her support and advice over the years and for providing a wonderful model of what a clear and careful study of Nietzsche is like; Ric Brown, Mark Cohen, Robin Small, Friedrich Ulfers, and Greg Whitlock, for their criticism and encouragement concerning a portion of this book that I presented at a meeting of the Friedrich Nietzsche Society at Cambridge University in September 2001; Thomas Brobjer, for his careful recommendations concerning the chapters on Spir's influence on Nietzsche; Karen Schutjer, for her help with translating some problematic passages from Nietzsche's notebooks; Matt Mitchell, Terry Sears, and Dick Martin of the University of Illinois Press, for their extensive help and infinite patience; and Koethi Zan and my former employer of Paul, Weiss, Rifkind, Wharton, and Garrison, for providing free legal advice concerning book contracts.

Abbreviations

Below are the abbreviations I use for referring to Nietzsche's writings; for complete publication information, see the bibliography. All references to Nietzsche's works will be to section number unless otherwise noted.

AC   *The Antichrist*
AOM   *Assorted Opinions and Maxims*
BGE   *Beyond Good and Evil*
BT   *Birth of Tragedy*
D   *Daybreak*
EH   *Ecce Homo*
GM   *On the Genealogy of Morals*
GS   *The Gay Science,* 1st ed.
GS2d *The Gay Science,* 2d ed.
HA   *Human, All Too Human*
KSA   *Sämtliche Werke: Kritische Studienausgabe* (see appendix 2)
PTG   *Philosophy in the Tragic Age of the Greeks*
TI   *Twilight of the Idols*
TL   "On Truth and Lies in a Nonmoral Sense"
WP   *The Will to Power* (see appendix 1)
WS   *The Wanderer and His Shadow*
Z   *Thus Spoke Zarathustra*

Introduction

1. Nietzsche and the Culture Wars

In 1990, while I was living in Berlin, I often worked in the philosophy library at the Free University in Dahlem, further down the red (now the green) subway line from my apartment in Friedenau. One day, while making the trip to Dahlem and reading through my dog-eared copy of *The Will to Power,* I noticed across from me a rather thin, nervous man in his mid-thirties, who was eyeing both me and my book rather strangely. He suddenly jumped up and tried to pull it out of my hands.

Had it been any other book I would have let him take it. But this wasn't just any book. Much of it was underlined and highlighted, the margins were filled with notes, and it bulged with strips of paper on which I had jotted down ideas and marked particularly important pages. I was not going to let go of it without a fight. For a remarkably long time—close to a minute—we struggled, trying to pull or twist the book out of one another's grip, while the other people in the subway car stared at us in passive silence. Finally it became clear to him that I was not going to give it up. He sat back down, adopting an expression as if nothing had happened at all. I slumped back into my seat, panting and cursing. He got out at the next stop.

This bizarre incident is not *that far* out of keeping with Nietzsche reception in general, which has always been abnormally passionate and vituperative. For the first seventy years or so it was Nietzsche's ethics that was the center of controversy. For Alfred Bäumler (1937) and other Nazi interpreters of Nietzsche's thought, his ethics provided a philosophical legitimization of Nazi eugenics, anti-Semitism, and authoritarianism. A movement worthy of respect in Germany had to have its philosopher, and Bäumler decided that Nietzsche would be the Nazis'.

Against Bäumler was Walter Kaufmann (1974) and other "soft" Nietzscheans, for whom freeing Nietzsche from the taint of Nazism was something like the final battle of World War II. The image of Nietzsche that emerges from Kaufmann's writings is of someone who is not only not anti-Semitic but a liberal and a democrat to boot. The more disturbing aspects of his ethics turn out to be mere metaphors. Nietzsche doesn't really advocate the cultivation of strength at the expense of the weak, it seems, only a Freudian sublimation of the passions. The Übermensch would not look out of place in the Princeton philosophy department.

If one were to choose between Bäumler's and Kaufmann's interpretations, one would, of course, choose Kaufmann's, which does far greater justice to Nietzsche's writings. But why make such a choice? To recognize that Bäumler was not *one hundred percent wrong* about Nietzsche does not make one a Nazi sympathizer; it does not even make *Nietzsche* a Nazi sympathizer. It only means recognizing that there is much about Nietzsche's ethics that is troubling.

Since the 1960s or 1970s, Nietzsche's views on truth and knowledge have become the focus of a new proxy war. A good deal of postmodernist skepticism about truth can be traced to Nietzsche's influence (Rorty 1989, 27–29). The literature generated by this strand of Nietzsche reception is heterogeneous, but the general idea is that Nietzsche intended to liberate us from stifling or inhibiting structures of thought, particularly those employed in the natural sciences; that he praised playfulness, creativity, and aestheticism in our interpretation of the world; and that he embraced paradox or self-contradiction as not merely inevitable but the very point of the philosophical enterprise.[1] According to the most extreme examples of this literature, Nietzsche sought to liberate us from truth itself and from the hegemonic and culturally chauvinist forces standing behind claims of truth.

In response, there is now a large and growing literature intent upon rescuing Nietzsche from the taint of irrationalism and cognitive irresponsibility, most notably by philosophers who work within the analytic tradition.[2] Although here too the interpretations of Nietzsche differ, the general idea is that he was not a critic of the goal of truth—indeed, he took his own views to be true. Instead, Nietzsche sought to provide a philosophical understanding of truth that is naturalistic and nonmetaphysical in outlook. Nor was Nietzsche an enemy of science—he wanted *more* scientific rigor and self-discipline, particularly in the study of man himself, which for too long had been a refuge for fantasy and self-deception.

As this essay will show, there is a good deal in these analytic readings of Nietzsche that I think is correct. However, much of this literature gives one the feeling that the issue is no longer understanding what Nietzsche has to say on these matters—it is instead the vindication of reason and rigorous argumentation in academic discourse in general. To concede that Nietzsche himself questions the possibility of truth is to give aid and comfort to the enemy: to legitimize in some way the barbarians who have taken over comparative literature and English and have now set their sights on philosophy.

To understand Friedrich Nietzsche, we need to stand back from the culture wars. It is important to remember that he wrote in late nineteenth-century Germany. His exposure to philosophy primarily came from two sources. He knew a great deal about ancient philosophy, especially Plato and the pre-Socratics, by virtue of his philological training. And he had read a number of philosophers in the nineteenth-century Neo-Kantian tradition, such as Schopenhauer, Friedrich Albert Lange, Gustav Teichmüller, and Afrikan Spir. It is to these writers that we should primarily look to understand what Nietzsche was talking about, not Derrida or Foucault and not Tarski or Quine.

This is not to say that we cannot arrive at an understanding of Nietzsche that has relevance for contemporary debates about truth. Nor do I want to suggest that Nietzsche's thoughts cannot overlap sufficiently with the work of current philosophers to make comparisons between the two enlightening. To the contrary, I will myself offer such comparisons. But the starting point for any interpretation of Nietzsche must be the traditions within which he worked. Furthermore, the desire to protect the academy should not blind one to the passages where Nietzsche claims that science falsifies the world or that cognition is impossible. For, as I will argue, such passages can be found everywhere in his writings. We should instead try to understand these passages and see how they can coexist with those where Nietzsche expresses a respect for truth.

This essay will attempt to make sense of Nietzsche's views on truth and knowledge by looking at him from the perspective of the Kantian tradition of transcendental idealism.[3] In particular, I will look to the writings of the philosopher Afrikan Spir, whose book *Denken und Wirklichkeit* was an extraordinarily important influence on Nietzsche's thought, and who offers an important bridge between Nietzsche and Kant. By drawing on the detailed arguments in Spir, we can make sense of Nietzsche's more cryptic and elliptical formulations.

The picture of Nietzsche that will emerge is of someone firmly grounded in the Neo-Kantian tradition. If Nietzsche's thought has relevance for current philosophical and cultural debates it is only because this tradition does so as well. To the extent that our interests are different, we should look elsewhere for our intellectual hero.

2. Naturalism and Normativity

My interpretation of Nietzsche is not organized around a particular position but around a *problem* that, I will argue, stands at the heart of the transcendental tradition in epistemology and generates the variety of epistemological positions that one finds in Nietzsche's writings. I hope to show that there is a strong thematic unity to Nietzsche's thought despite its inconsistencies.

The problem is the tension between two ideas. The first is *naturalism.* I take naturalism to be the demand that explanations of what human beings do be causal, that they be confirmed empirically, and that they be seamlessly integrated into our theories of nature as a whole. An *antinaturalist* approach to epistemology would be an account of human judgment in noncausal and nonempirical terms.[4] It would appeal to faculties not subject to deterministic laws (that is, faculties that are free in an incompatibilist sense) and having no causal connection with anything in nature. A good example, which will be explored later in this essay and which provided a model of antinaturalism for Nietzsche, is Kant's account of descriptive and moral judgment.

I once asked Ken Gemes, an analytic philosopher who himself has more than a modest interest in Nietzsche, what accounts for the sympathy for Nietzsche that one often finds among philosophers trained in the analytic tradition. Professors who have devoted their academic life to problems in modal logic and truth-functional semantics and who would never dream of reading Heidegger or Derrida often have an interest in and some opinions about Nietzsche. Gemes said that it is because Nietzsche, unlike most other continental philosophers, "respects the causal order." I agree. Nietzsche is fundamentally a naturalist.[5] He identifies the goal of "translat[ing] man back into nature" (*BGE* 230) as a distinctive element of his philosophical method. Like any good naturalist, Nietzsche rejects explanations that appeal to religious or otherworldly entities and forces (*D* 86). Indeed, his naturalism sometimes reaches remarkably reductive levels, for example, when he identifies religious and intellectual transformations with changes in diet (*GS* 134; *GM* 3:17).

Nietzsche's approach to epistemological issues is no different. His epistemological naturalism goes beyond emphasizing the role of sensation in knowledge to providing naturalistic accounts of human judgment itself. At times these accounts bear a strong resemblance to Hume; at other times they sound much like evolutionary epistemology (*GS* 111; *WP* 480, 494, 507).[6]

It is this naturalist, antimetaphysical Nietzsche that appeals to members of the analytic tradition. What then explains Nietzsche's appeal to postmodernists, for whom naturalist interpretations of the world are not cognitively privileged and the concepts relied upon by natural science are among those restrictions from which Nietzsche sought to liberate us? There is ample material to satisfy them as well.

At points, Nietzsche argues that the world is something that we make rather than discover and that it admits infinite possibilities of interpretation. Rather than privileging naturalistic and scientific explanations, Nietzsche argues that the concepts upon which they depend—including causality, substance, space, and time—*falsify* the world. Furthermore, as interpreters of Nietzsche such as Heidegger (1986) and John Richardson (1996) have emphasized, Nietzsche is inclined toward apparently metaphysical accounts of the world, in terms of the will to power or "becoming" (see also Schacht 1983, 187–89). Nietzsche's metaphysics of the will to power is offered, somewhat tentatively in his published works and more wholeheartedly in his notebooks, or Nachlaß, as an attempted explanation of what the world is like in its *intelligible character,* that is, independent of scientific and empirical explanations of it (*BGE* 36; *KSA* 11:40[53]). Furthermore, this apparently metaphysical account is often presented by Nietzsche with a self-conscious awareness of its incoherence. Rather than being a straightforward theory about the world, it looks as if the contradictions in the will to power are its very message.

There are, it seems, two Nietzsches. I will argue that this second, seemingly postmodern Nietzsche has its source in the tension between naturalism and a second idea, which stands at the heart of the transcendental tradition in philosophy: If our judgments are true or false, this cannot be solely because of what *is* the case about them. It must also be because of what *ought* to be the case about them. That a judgment is true or is false is a *normative* fact about that judgment.

The normativity of truth is evident in what I take to be a very clear and simple requirement for judgments to be true or false, a requirement once again drawn from the Neo-Kantian tradition within which Nietzsche worked. Our judgments cannot be true or false unless they apply *concepts.* We can, with Kant, think of concepts as rules for mentally associating objects and of a judgment as applying a concept to an object in the sense that the judger sees the object as appropriately associated with the other objects that fall under the concept.[7] When I judge something to be green, I see it *as green,* that is, as appropriately associated with those other objects that fall under the concept *green.*

If, when lumping objects together under the word "green," I am *not* acting in a rule-bound fashion—if I lump things together the way I do under a term, like "frob," that has no meaning (not even an idiosyncratic one that I have assigned to it)—then it is not possible for my judgment that something is green to be true or false. Concepts are the *oughts* through which the truth or falsity of judgments comes into being.

There is a conflict between naturalism and the normative character of truth because a naturalistic account of our judgments is able to do without normative facts, and so truth, entirely. Perhaps the best example of this problem is Hume's account of causal judgments. Hume understands these judgments naturalistically as the habitual associations of events that result from observing their constant conjunction. This makes the concept of causality unnecessary, because our judgments will proceed according to these habits whether or not we have such a concept. All that matters is that I do associate events, not that I ought or ought not to associate them.

Hume's "solution" to the problem is to deny that we have any concept of the causal. We cannot *think* about causality; instead we merely associate events on the basis of habit. These associations are as meaningless as those that might coalesce around the word "frob." Because causal judgments are not *about* anything, they cannot be assessed according to the norm of truth. Hume offers in the place of truth more pragmatic reasons to affirm our causal judgments, in particular the role that habit or custom plays in our lives.

Why then is there a tension between naturalism and truth, rather than simply the triumph of the former over the latter? The problem is that it seems impossible to understand our judgments as not bound by the norm of truth. The very act of naturalistic explanation appears to be bound by this norm. Consider, once again, Hume's account of causal judgments: this account is itself causal. Hume argues that if one has observed the constant conjunction of two events, the idea of the antecedent event will *cause* the idea of the consequent. To be consistent, Hume would have to admit that his account of causal judgments is itself neither true nor false. And yet it appears to be presented to us *as true.*

The conflict is even more serious than it seems because it extends well beyond causal judgments. Hume, of course, does not think that *all* judgments are noncognitive. He allows for the existence of a cognitive space within which true and false judgment can proceed and from which causal judgments are excluded. For example, we can make true judgments about our sensations. In doing so, however, Hume is insufficiently comprehensive in his naturalism. In particular, he does not examine the naturalistic causes of judgments about sensations but instead simply identifies a sensation with a judgment about it.[8] But once they are naturalized, judgments about sensations look no more sensitive to empirical concepts than causal judgments were to the concept of causality under Hume's account.

I will argue that the radical, postmodernist nature of Nietzsche's epistemologies proceeds from the fact that he naturalizes *all* of our judgments, including the empiricist's favored judgments about sensations and other foundational judgments in the natural sciences. As a result, Nietzsche casts doubt upon the possibility of any truth, including the truth of the very naturalism that motivates his philosophy. In a sense, Nietzsche thinks that naturalism is insufficiently naturalistic because it assumes the ability to make truthful judgments about nature, and it is only on the basis of a non-naturalistic conception of human judgment that such truthful judgments are possible. The position that Nietzsche is inclined toward is, paradoxically, a form of naturalism in which naturalism cannot be thought.

In denying that cognition[9] is compatible with naturalism, Nietzsche shows himself to be strongly influenced by Kantian and Neo-Kantian accounts of objectively valid judgment. For Kant, a judgment cannot be true or false if it proceeds through Humean laws of association. Only necessary and atemporal mental associations can say anything about the world. Contingent laws of association merely carry the mind blindly from one image to another.

Furthermore, like others in the transcendental idealist tradition, Nietzsche believes that the non-naturalistic presuppositions for thought can be drawn out of the very objects about which one thinks. If one is able to describe the world at all, one must apply to it concepts of "being"—including substance, causality, absolute space, and absolute time—that are incompatible with the change and plurality shown by the senses. As a result, there are latent contradictions—the Kantian antinomies—within our descriptions of the world. Kant argues that the antinomies show that empirical reality is transcendentally ideal. In contrast, Nietzsche, under the influence of Spir, argues that the antinomies show that these descriptions of the world are necessarily false.

Finally, in an attempt to provide an account of reality that does not rely upon problematic concepts of being, Nietzsche at times offers a theory of absolute becoming that does violence to practically every fundamental conception we have about the natural world. A world of absolute becoming is without substances and causal relations, within which things happen at no particular rate of time and things exist in no particular place.

It is in these reflections that the postmodernists see their Nietzsche. I agree with the postmodernists that such theories, which alternatively deny the possibility of cognition and claim that it falsifies the world, are present in Nietzsche's thought. Indeed, they make up the bulk of his reflections on epistemological matters.

But the lesson to draw from this radical strand of Nietzsche's philosophizing is not that our judgments about the world should be a matter of play and aestheticism or that science should be abandoned. As analytic readers of Nietzsche emphasize, when making his own judgments about the world and particularly man's place in it Nietzsche is scrupulous, deadly serious, and by and large naturalistic. The dominant theme in his ethics, for example, is the evaluative consequences of a naturalization of our evaluations. Getting these naturalistic accounts right—being a good psychologist, historian, and genealogist of morals—is a matter of fundamental importance for Nietzsche.

The postmodernists ignore the fact that the radical nature of Nietzsche's epistemological reflections is motivated *by his fundamental commitment to naturalism and empiricism.* Nietzsche is interested in denuding naturalism of its secret antinaturalist elements, not replacing naturalism with aesthetic or playful interpretations of the world. Nietzsche's goal can be accomplished only by providing an account of our judgments that does not presume an antinaturalistic conception of the self and by offering a theory of nature that does justice to what is provided to us by the senses. Unfortunately, these attempts to create a purified naturalism suffer from incoherence and self-contradiction. It is this problem that is the dominant theme of Nietzsche's epistemology and the organizing principle of this essay.

3. Outline of My Argument

Chapter 1: The Problem of Nietzsche's "Error Theory"

Nietzsche repeatedly argues that all of our judgments are false. A reading of Nietzsche's epistemology that fails to do justice to this aspect of his thought cannot be adequate. But the difficulties with providing a plausible interpretation of the error theory are formidable. In the first chapter, I outline these problems.

Nietzsche's arguments for the error theory take two forms. The first type of argument, which is particularly prominent in his early, posthumously published essay "On Truth and Lies in a Nonmoral Sense," is that our *sensations* are responsible for error. But because such arguments suffer from intractable problems, past interpreters of Nietzsche's epistemology, who tend to consider only arguments of the first type, have deemphasized Nietzsche's error theory in general.

The second type of argument is that our *concepts,* not our sensations, are responsible for error. Our concepts err because they categorize or schematize the flux and becoming that is provided by sensations. I believe that these are the primary and most enduring arguments for the error theory in Nietzsche's thought.

But unless one looks to the transcendental tradition motivating Nietzsche's epistemologies, making sense of this second type of argument is also difficult. How can it be that our concepts *always* falsify what our sensations tell us? Even if the world changes far more than our current scientific theories suggest, true conceptualization of the world seems *possible.* The fact that objects are not stable does not mean that we cannot in principle describe the properties that they have *at a particular instant.*

Furthermore, to justify his claims that the world is substantially different from the way we think it is, it appears that Nietzsche must have knowledge of the world as it really is. If the world is really flux and becoming, then the description of the world as flux and becoming must, it seems, be true. Rather than arguing that all our beliefs are false, Nietzsche appears to be merely offering an alterative, and wildly implausible, quasi-scientific theory about the world.

Small wonder then that some analytic interpreters of Nietzsche hope to separate his error theory from his considered epistemological views by attributing it to an earlier stage in his development. In the second half of chapter 1 I argue that Nietzsche's error theory is present throughout his period of philosophical activity, both in his Nachlaß and his published works, from the early 1870s to the final works of 1888. This raises the stakes of making sense of the error theory. If the theory is indeed incoherent, as some have argued, then there is little chance of making sense of Nietzsche's epistemology as a whole

Chapter 2: Nietzsche's Neo-Kantian Roots

In chapter 2 I lay the groundwork for a sympathetic interpretation of Nietzsche's error theory and for my general approach to Nietzsche's epistemologies. I begin with Kant's argument that a naturalistic account of human judgments is incompatible with their truth or falsity. According to Kant, a naturalistic account can at most explain how the mind moves blindly from one image to the next according to empirical laws of association. It cannot explain how the mind refers to objects. I then spell out the antinaturalist, transcendental theory of cognition that Kant provides as an alternative. Under this theory, the unifications by means of which judgment is accomplished are necessary and atemporal. It is only in this way that we can judge in a manner that says something about the world.

Kant's argument for an antinaturalist theory of judgment is motivated by the conflict between naturalism and truth that I have claimed stands at the center of Nietzsche's epistemologies. But the Kantian theory of judgment renders problematic the connection between the necessary and atemporal unity of thought, on the one hand, and the plurality, temporality, and becoming of sensation, on the other hand. Kant attempts to bridge this gap between thought and sensation through the transcendental schematism under which the flow of sensations is brought into the unity of thought by means of schematized categories such as substance and causality. Without the schematism, the plurality and becoming of sensation could not be thought.

Kant's schematism is intimately connected to Nietzsche's own epistemological concerns. The missing link between the two is Afrikan Spir, whose book *Denken und Wirklichkeit* exerted a strong influence on Nietzsche's epistemology. Spir argues that Kant's schematism fails and that empirical judgment, by forcing necessary unity and simplicity upon the plurality and change of becoming, always falsifies the world. The necessary falsehood of empirical judgment shows itself in the contradictions that can be drawn out of our everyday idea of an empirical object. Because it is these contradictions that show that our beliefs about the world are false, rather than some comparison between the way we think about the world and the way the world is, Spir's error theory does not suffer from the difficulties I outline in chapter 1.

Spir recognizes that a choice between being and becoming must be made, and he chooses being. The way of being is the way of Parmenides, which preserves thought, but at the cost of making it refer only to a simple, necessary, and unchanging One—an absolutely self-identical substance. Under the way of becoming, which Spir identifies with Heraclitus, the change and multiplicity that show themselves in sensation are affirmed, but at the cost of losing the ability to think.

Nietzsche takes the path of becoming. It is for this reason that we find him vacillating between the error theory and a noncognitivist approach. To the extent that he concentrates on the contradictions in our idea of an empirical object—contradictions that show that such objects partake of both being and becoming—he offers an error theory that has strong parallels with Spir's. To the extent that he concentrates on human judgment itself, which Nietzsche insists must take place within becoming, he denies the possibility of thought.

Chapter 3: Nietzsche's "Error Theory" Explained

Chapter 3 is devoted to describing Nietzsche's and Spir's error theories in greater detail. Parallels with Spir allow me to make sense of passages in Nietzsche that have bedeviled past interpreters, including his arguments that causality is modeled after free will; that nothing moves and nothing happens at a particular rate of time; and that things are not equal to themselves, even at the same moment in time. All of these arguments have strong analogues in Spir and in Kant's antinomies.

The Spirean and Kantian themes in Nietzsche's error theory also help clarify Nietzsche's theory of absolute becoming. I argue that Nietzsche agrees with Spir that absolute becoming (Spir's term as well as Nietzsche's) is a conception of the world based upon the antithesis positions in Kant's antinomies. This allows me to make sense of a number of Nietzsche's seemingly paradoxical claims about becoming.

But Nietzsche's argument for the error theory suffers from a crucial problem as well. Thought can falsify becoming only if thought exists, and Nietzsche, by taking the path of becoming, does not allow for the type of necessary unity and simplicity required for thought. This problem leads him to explore theories of judgment other than his error theory; these theories are the topic of the fourth chapter.

Chapter 4: Antirealism and Noncognitivism

I begin the fourth chapter by returning to the problem that motivated Kant's theory of judgment, the conflict between naturalism and truth. I argue that someone might be inclined to reconcile the two through a form of antirealism under which the content of the concepts employed in our judgments is tied to the naturalistic causes of these judgments. The more the content of our concepts is tied to these causes, the more plausible it is that we are actually employing these concepts when judging.

Two antirealist theories of truth have most often been attributed to Nietzsche: a pragmatic theory and a coherence theory. Under each it is admitted that we have concepts that outstrip and cognitively constrain our natural dispositions to judge, but the content of these concepts is more closely tied to these natural dispositions in order to make it more plausible that we judge in response to this content. I argue that both theories, and the interpretations of Nietzsche that employ them, are inadequate because they fail to overcome the tension between naturalism and truth. If the ability of these concepts to normatively bind our judgments is understood in non-naturalistic terms, then there appears to be no reason to even *begin* limiting the content of our concepts: cognition is fully compatible with naturalism after all. However, if one sticks to one's naturalism, how is it that we have *any* concepts that outstrip our natural dispositions to judge, including those concepts relied upon by the antirealist?

To put the problem in the simplest terms: Concepts are *oughts* that can assess and condemn what *is*. That a judgment is false is a condemnation of what is by what ought to be. The tension between naturalism and truth is the problem of how such oughts are possible, given that all that exists *is*. To the extent that one allows oughts that outstrip what is, one has retreated from naturalism. To the extent that one reduces these oughts to what is, one has rid the oughts of their normative ability to assess and condemn what is.

I end chapter 4 with the argument that Nietzsche, for this reason, finds himself driven to a noncognitivist theory of judgment under which there are no oughts constraining our judgments. Our judgments have no content at all; that is to say, we apply no concepts when we judge. We do not think. This noncognitivist reading of Nietzsche is confirmed, I argue, by Nietzsche's views concerning the principle of noncontradiction; his discussions of consciousness, intention, and desire; and his views concerning the self.

Chapter 5: Nihilism, Hedonism, and the Self-Reference Problem

In chapter 5 I address two fundamental objections to a noncognitivist reading of Nietzsche. The first is that the absence of cognitive constraint upon our judgments gives us no reason to judge one way rather than another. If Nietzsche really were a noncognitivist, he would have no reason to recommend certain views about the world as true and others as false and so would have no reason to engage in his well-known critiques of Christianity, asceticism, and Platonism.

The essence of my response to this objection is that unless one is willing to entertain an antinaturalist account of judgment, all feelings of cognitive constraint must be reducible to one's current empirical makeup. The feeling that judgments can be mistaken and that one ought to work hard to get them right must be expressible naturalistically. All feelings of *ought* must be something that *is*. As a result, feelings of normativity when judging are no reason to assume the existence of anything more than what *is*, and so are no reason to believe that noncognitivism is false.

By the same token, any feeling of a *lack* of cognitive constraint—any feeling that one *cannot* make a mistake in judgment and that "anything goes" in the way of belief—is likewise expressible in terms of an empirical makeup. And there is no reason that the acceptance of noncognitivism should cause one to have such a makeup. Thus there is no reason to think that Nietzsche's acceptance of noncognitivism would lead him to give up his critique of Christianity or put less effort into his attempt to get this critique right.

In his ethics and his epistemology Nietzsche himself provides this argument. The feeling that one should struggle to get judgments right is praised by Nietzsche not because one thereby respects one's cognitive duties but because it indicates a form of healthy self-control. Likewise, the feeling that mistakes are impossible is rejected by Nietzsche not because it is cognitively irresponsible but because it shows a lack of self-discipline. Rather than addressing views about the objectivity of our judgments head-on, Nietzsche naturalizes them and assesses them on the basis of their pragmatic effect on human life.

By the same token, Nietzsche argues that, to the extent that we desire a stronger form of constraint upon our judgments than that provided by our own empirical makeup, we must have an ascetic hatred of our empirical nature. It is for this reason that he sees a relationship between the will to truth and asceticism.

But if epistemological noncognitivism is able to preserve all of our cognitivist attitudes, why isn't this position actually a form of cognitivism that provides a fully naturalized account of what human thought is like? Against this conclusion, I argue that the error theory and noncognitivism are the dominant positions in Nietzsche's writings because Nietzsche found himself convinced by Spirean arguments that cognition has to be understood in antinaturalist terms. He was convinced particularly by Spir's argument that the antinaturalist presuppositions of our descriptions of nature are evident in the antinomies that can be drawn from our idea of an empirical object. As a result, he is compelled to assess our judgments according to this antinaturalist ideal of what cognition is like.

The second problem that I address in chapter 5 is the problem of self-reference, that is to say, the problem of reconciling Nietzsche's ability to articulate his epistemologies with the restrictions on human judgment demanded by those epistemologies. The self-reference problem can be simplified as follows. Each epistemological position that can plausibly be attributed to Nietzsche puts some limitations on our referential capacity. Under noncognitivism the referential scope of our judgments shrinks to an extensionless point; under the error theory our judgments always misrefer; and under antirealism the reference of our judgments is in some way subjectivized. The problem is that *articulating* these limits seems to presume a form of representational capacity beyond that allowed by the theories themselves.

I do not think that the problem can be circumvented. I finish the fifth chapter with the suggestion that the problem should not be overemphasized in interpretations of Nietzsche's epistemology, however. Nietzsche does not seek to condemn our judgments on the basis of these referential limitations. Instead he hopes to describe these limitations to encourage us to affirm our judgments about the world by affirming the drives standing behind these judgments. The epistemological positions that one can find in Nietzsche, including his problematic theory of absolute becoming, are presented by him in part because they provide the proper framework within which the sources of our judgments can be affirmed. If so, the fact that these positions outstrip the limits that they place upon our judgments may not be a serious flaw, provided that it does not stand in the way of Nietzsche's project of epistemological self-affirmation.

Conclusion

In the conclusion, I sum up my interpretation of Nietzsche's epistemologies. First of all, there is no *one* epistemology that can be found in his writings. His epistemology is best seen as a set of responses to the conflict generated by his dual commitment to naturalism and to transcendental theories of cognition. The tension between these two ideas, which was never adequately resolved by him, generates a number of epistemological positions in his writings.

Second, I argue that Nietzsche cannot be seen as arguing for a simple naturalistic theory of cognition under which empirical subjects can make judgments with truth-values. Although I personally am attracted to such a theory, Nietzsche was not. The reason is his continued commitment to the transcendental tradition. As a result, Nietzsche argues that cognition either falsifies the world or is impossible. In either case, the foundations for our descriptions of the world are undermined.

Nevertheless, I argue that the ultimate goal of Nietzsche's epistemology is quite similar to these naturalized theories of cognition. He is not interested in rejecting scientific description and replacing it with playful or aesthetic descriptions of the world. In the end he seeks to affirm the drives standing behind our scientific descriptions of the world. His radical epistemological positions play a role in this self-affirmation because they provide a framework for genuine affirmation of these drives.

4. Some Remarks on Method

Treatments of Nietzsche's epistemology commonly include a discussion of methodological issues—particularly the problem of Nietzsche's Nachlaß and whether it is appropriate to apply to Nietzsche the issues and terminology of other philosophers.

This essay relies heavily on the Nachlaß, although it is unusual in looking not merely to the notebooks of the mid- and late-1880s but also to the rich material in Nietzsche's *early* notebooks, which were not included in *The Will to Power*[10] and have not been translated into English. It is difficult to talk about Nietzsche's epistemology without discussing material in his Nachlaß. Even those who seek to arrive at an interpretation based solely on the published materials (e.g. Clark 1990, 25–27) rely heavily on the essay "On Truth and Lies in a Nonmoral Sense," which Nietzsche never intended to publish. The temptation to look to the Nachlaß is overwhelming because they contain much more material on epistemological topics than the published works. The danger, of course, is that one will attribute to Nietzsche views that were merely experimental.

I don't believe that any categorical rule concerning use of the Nachlaß can be formulated. It is possible that they are a collection of random thought experiments that contain nothing of value to understanding Nietzsche's epistemology. It is also possible that Nietzsche felt that the goal of clearly articulating his epistemological views in his published works should be compromised in the light of broader rhetorical purposes. This could make the published works less useful than the Nachlaß for understanding his epistemology. We can answer these questions only by examining all sources and separating pervasive themes from anomalies.

In the end, I think that there is less to this debate than meets the eye. There is a good deal of uniformity in what Nietzsche says about truth and knowledge as one moves between his notebooks and the published materials and as one moves from the early 1870s to the late 1880s. The interpretative difficulty is not figuring out which source or period one should choose as the real Nietzsche. It is instead making sense of the variety of contradictory comments that can be found within any source or period. I attempt to overcome this difficulty by looking at Nietzsche's epistemology as a set of different responses to the same underlying problem rather than as a coherent system.

The second issue is my reliance, like so many interpreters of Nietzsche before me, on terminology and themes drawn from analytic philosophy. Here too no categorical rule is possible. Whether drawing analogies with other philosophers clarifies or obscures Nietzsche's thought can be answered only by looking at the particular interpretation at issue.

There are some philosophers, however, that I believe not only *may* but *must* be compared with Nietzsche. To understand Nietzsche's epistemology, we must look at him in the light of his philosophical influences—the philoso-

phers that Nietzsche himself read. Given the huge volume of English-language literature on Nietzsche's epistemology, the number of historically sensitive studies is shamefully small. Some important influences on Nietzsche,
such as Schopenhauer, have always been discussed. Lange's influence has been
the topic of a book-length study (Stack 1983; see also Salaquarda 1987), as has
Nietzsche's relationship to the pre-Socratics and Plato (Richardson 1996). But
other writers who may have influenced Nietzsche's thought in profound ways
are still ignored. Because Nietzsche so often fails to provide the arguments
standing behind his conclusions, looking to philosophical influences is more
important for understanding him than it is for understanding other philosophers.

It is a fallacy to think that only famous philosophers influence famous
philosophers, particularly in connection with Nietzsche, who, by virtue of
his lack of professional training, picked up his ideas from unusual and obscure sources. It is easy to succumb to this fallacy, since famous philosophers
are more likely to be translated and more likely be the subject of secondary
works that can guide one's interpretation. But ignoring the influences exerted
on Nietzsche by obscure philosophers is a luxury Nietzsche studies cannot
afford.

This essay will look to Afrikan Spir. As I believe the details show, Spir was
a writer of profound importance for Nietzsche, in addition to being an extremely interesting philosopher in his own right. But there are other influences that need to be examined, such as Teichmüller, and I invite other philosophers who want to get to the bottom of what Nietzsche thought about
truth and knowledge to consider their influence. There are some encourag-
ing signs that such work on Nietzsche has finally begun (e.g. Small 2001;
Brobjer n.d.). It is only after these studies are completed that any responsible assessment of Nietzsche's place in modern philosophy and culture will
be possible.

1. The Problem of Nietzsche's "Error Theory"

EVEN A CASUAL READER of Nietzsche will be struck by his repeated arguments that our beliefs about the world are false: "The world with which we are concerned is false, i.e. it is not a fact but a fable and approximation on the basis of a meager sum of observations; it is 'in flux,' as something in a state of becoming, as a falsehood always changing but never getting near the truth: for—there is no truth" (*WP* 616). Our truths are "merely . . . irrefutable errors" (*GS* 265) "without which a certain species of life could not live" (*WP* 493).[1] Nietzsche's error theory is one of the most unusual positions in the history of epistemology, and making sense of it is an important test of the adequacy of an interpretation of his epistemology.

Some interpreters have accepted this position as Nietzsche's considered epistemological view (Mittelman 1984). But most hope to qualify it or explain it away (e.g. Nehamas 1985, 65–67).[2] The desire to minimize the error theory is overwhelming—despite the frequency with which it can be found in his works—because taking it seriously appears to render Nietzsche hopelessly inconsistent.

I have three goals in this chapter. The first is to outline the seemingly insurmountable philosophical problems with the error theory. The second is to spell out two types of argument that Nietzsche provides for the theory, the most important and enduring of which has been ignored in the literature. The third is to raise the stakes concerning the coherence of the error theory by showing that it is an essential element of Nietzsche's epistemology throughout his period of philosophical activity—from the early 1870s right up to his collapse in 1889. If the error theory does not make sense, then the chances of making sense of Nietzsche's epistemology as a whole are slim.

1. The Problem of the Flexibility of Conceptualization

Let me begin with some general obstacles to making sense of the error theory. The first might be called the problem of the *flexibility of conceptualization:* no matter what the world is like, it appears *possible* for our concepts to accommodate themselves to the world. Consider the position that Willard Mittelman attributes to Nietzsche: "This world of becoming can also be called false, since there is no abiding truth for us to get ahold of. That is, as soon as we declare something to be the case, our statement is refuted by the alteration of the situation which we have described" (1984, 4). Mittelman neglects the fact that even if things changed much more than experience suggests, we can always create predicates of sufficient inclusiveness to allow for generally true judgments. Although my chair might be shifting around more than I thought it was, it is not shifting around so much that it is not within a light year of the earth. Furthermore, we are able to *index* our statements about the world according to time, to avoid falsification by future changes. I don't have to say that Richard Nixon was, is, and always will be president of the United States; I may instead say that he was president from 1969 to 1974. No matter how fast things change, such a strategy will always be open to us (Bittner 1987, 74–75; Richardson 1996, 81–82, 87–88; Stack 1983, 123).

Negation is another means by which our concepts can accommodate themselves to the world. It seems that the error theory can be refuted by two people, each entertaining a proposition that is the negation of the other's. If A believes something is green, and B believes it is not green, doesn't logic (specifically, the law of the excluded middle) require that *one* of them has a true belief?[3]

One might argue that Nietzsche is merely claiming that all *positive* judgments (roughly, judgments that predicate something of the world) are false and that all or some negative judgments (judgments that deny something should be predicated of the world) are true (Mittelman 1984, 6).[4] But it is unlikely that a coherent distinction between positive and negative judgments could be drawn that would protect Nietzsche from inconsistency. The problem is that some negative judgments entail positive judgments. "Not fast," for example, entails "slow or at rest." To claim that negative judgments are true without the positive judgments entailed by them being true would deny the laws of logical implication, and it was precisely to preserve these laws that we limited Nietzsche's error theory to positive judgments. Furthermore, it is not even clear that preserving logic is in keeping with the spirit of Nietzsche's error theory, for he often argues that logic and mathematics themselves falsify reality (*GS* 111; *BGE* 4; *WP* 512, 515–16) because they rely on the presuppositions "that there are identical things, that the same thing is identical at different points in time," and that there is an "exactly straight line" or an "absolute magnitude" (*HA* 11).

But the fact that the error theory also applies to logic and mathematics only highlights its implausibility. It is not easy to get one's mind around what it would mean for logic and mathematics to falsify reality, for they seem to provide frameworks within which a true description of the world *must* be possible. Consider geometry and arithmetic. Anything existing in space is in principle describable geometrically in terms of its shape; all existing things can in principle be enumerated. The fact that the world becomes makes no difference to the possibility of such descriptions—it simply means that the descriptions must keep up with changes.

Logic too opens up a descriptive framework within which true judgments must be possible. Nietzsche criticizes logic because it assumes the existence of timeless self-identical substances that cannot be found within the world of experience. But logic makes no assumptions about the types of objects there are in the world. The laws of noncontradiction and the excluded middle, for example, are just as true of a world of fleeting objects as they are of a world of timeless ones (Poellner 1995, 193–95).

Sometimes Nietzsche's error theory appears to be based on a sort of "nominalism," namely, the view that nothing has sufficient equality with anything else to make appropriate the application of a concept (*TL* p. 83; *HA* 18–19; *WS* 11; *KSA* 12:9[144]; *WP* 501).[5] Concepts falsify the plurality and heterogeneity of experience because they assume *the identity*—the absolute sameness—and not merely the similarity of the things that fall under them: "The dominant tendency . . . to treat as equal what is merely similar—an illogical tendency, for nothing is really equal—is what first created any basis for logic" (*GS* 111). But the idea that concepts demand such identity seems clearly false. When I judge something to be square, I do not judge it to be *exactly* the same as everything else that is square. Rather, I judge it to be similar to these other things only in its *squareness*.

It is for this reason that some interpreters have read these passages as expressing the view that everything is different *in every way* (Grimm 1977, 78–79). From this view it would follow that all our judgments are false because conceptualization requires *some* similarity between things in the world. But how can *everything* be different from *everything else* in *every way,* such that all our judgments turn out to be false? We understand things to be different from one another in terms of the presence or absence of particular qualities (one is square and the other is not) or relations (one is bigger than the other). This commits us to the possibility of a true description of that by virtue of which their difference consists. One cannot argue that everything is different in *every* respect, such that a description of these differences is impossible, without losing the sense of what these differences could possibly consist of.

2. The Problem of Justification

The first problem with the error theory is that it seems to be part of the very nature of conceptualization that a true judgment is *possible*. But the problems with the theory run even deeper. Insofar as Nietzsche hopes to justify the theory he must, it seems, assume that some true judgments exist. One must *know* (and so have true beliefs concerning) a good deal about the world and ourselves to even begin to argue about our cognitive inadequacies. This problem is related to the problem of self-reference, that is, the worry that if the error theory refers to itself then it must be false by its own lights.[6] But the problem is not solved simply by denying that the theory refers to itself, for even if we provide the error theory with some isolated status there is still the question of what reason we have to believe the theory. Given that the beliefs that we use to justify the theory must also be assumed to be true, the set of true beliefs threatens to expand to the point that the error theory can't possibly be right.

Accordingly, even if one assumes the truth of Nietzsche's claims that "appearance is an arranged and simplified world, at which our practical instincts have been at work" (*WP* 568) and that what is arranged and simplified is a world of becoming, chaos, and flux (*GS* 111, 121; *BGE* 4; *WP* 515, 517), it is hard to see how *all* our beliefs about the world can be false. First of all, we presumably have true beliefs about how things appear to us, for arguing that appearance is different from reality presupposes at the very least an adequate grasp of what appearance is like. But Nietzsche is at pains to deny the truth of beliefs about the "inner world" as well (e.g. *WP* 476, 479), which presumably would include beliefs about appearances. "I maintain the phenomenality of the inner world, too: everything of which we become conscious is arranged, simplified, schematized, interpreted through and through. . . . The 'apparent *inner* world' is governed by just the same forms and procedures as the 'outer' world. We never encounter 'facts'" (*WP* 477).

But even if Nietzsche conceded that we can have true beliefs about how the world appears to us, he would still need to have true beliefs about the real world to argue that our beliefs about it are false. If appearance is an arrangement and simplification of the world of flux, then beliefs that the world is actually flux must be true. And if these beliefs are to be more than mere leaps in the dark, they must be justified on the basis of other beliefs that cannot be considered false. If Nietzsche offered an a priori argument for the falsehood of our beliefs, there would be some hope that this set of true beliefs would be fairly small. But what is remarkable about Nietzsche's error theory is that he generally offers empirical arguments in its favor. Such arguments appear to presuppose a large set of true beliefs about the world.

Consider, for example, Nietzsche's argument that "it is from the period of the lower organisms that man has inherited the belief that there are *identical things* (only knowledge educated in the highest scientificality contradicts this proposition)" (*HA* 18). This assumes true beliefs about what the world is really like, namely, "knowledge educated in the highest scientificality." Such an argument cannot possibly show that *all* our beliefs are false (Clark 1998, 75; Stack 1983, 123).

3. Arguments That Sensations Falsify

Despite these serious problems with the error theory, it can be found everywhere in Nietzsche's works. Why? What are his reasons for holding the theory? Nietzsche's arguments appear to be of two general types: arguments that our *sensations* are responsible for error and arguments that our *concepts* are. Let's start with arguments of the first type.

Nietzsche's argument that sensation leads us to falsify the world appears to derive support from modern attitudes toward secondary qualities. Since the early modern period, physicists and natural philosophers have held that the physical world can be fully characterized in terms of primary qualities (such as extension, position, and motion) and that secondary qualities (such as color and taste) should be understood in terms of primary qualities' dispositions to bring about sensory states in human observers under normal conditions. These theories suggest that certain naive views about objects possessing secondary qualities are false.

Of course, modern theories of secondary qualities are part of a broader scientific explanation of the world and man's relationship to it that thoroughly depends upon the truth of our beliefs about objects' *primary* qualities. Could one argue, however, that our beliefs about primary qualities are likewise in error? After all, our sensations of primary qualities must be as qualitatively dissimilar from the objects themselves as are our sensations of secondary qualities. We cannot have sensations of primary qualities that are not also sensations of secondary qualities. Sensations of extension are always sensations of *colored* extension. Nietzsche's error theory could be a critique of the view, which one finds expressed by Locke, that the qualitative nature of our sensations of primary qualities provides us with knowledge of the primary qualities in objects (Locke 1979, §2:8:15).

But even if we do draw a distinction between our sensations of primary qualities and the objects themselves, we still are assuming that we can have some empirical knowledge of objects' real qualities. We are free to argue that a naive Lockean understanding of primary qualities is erroneous, but our argument will rely on knowledge of objects' genuine primary qualities, which bring about in us sensations. Without this assumed knowledge, we lose the perspective from which we can think about our sensations of primary qualities as *different* from what the objects are really like. And so Nietzsche cannot show that *all* our beliefs about objects are false on the basis of the dissimilarity between sensation and object.

Furthermore, even if this argument had succeeded, much of Nietzsche's error theory would still remain unaccounted for. We would still have no argument that judgments about inner experience are false. Nor would we have an argument that logic and mathematics falsify the world.

Sometimes Nietzsche's error theory rests on a *theory of representation* that reduces the content of our beliefs to our sensations. We falsely treat the world as similar to our sensations, not because of a scientific error, but because the very nature of representation compels us to do so:

> This creator [of language] only designates the relations of things to men, and for expressing these relations he lays hold of the boldest metaphors. To begin with, a nerve stimulus is transferred into an image: first metaphor. The image, in turn, is imitated in a sound: second metaphor. And each time there is a complete overleaping of one sphere, right into the middle of an entirely new and different one. . . . It is this way with all of us concerning language: we believe that we know something about the things themselves when we speak of trees, colors, snow, and flowers; and yet we possess nothing but metaphors for things—metaphors which correspond in no way to the original entities. (*TL* pp. 82–83)

From this Nietzsche concludes: "What then is truth? A movable host of metaphors, metonymies, and anthropomorphisms. . . . Truths are illusions which we have forgotten are illusions" (*TL* p. 84).

But this argument is also flawed. For it presumes that we can *represent* a world that is different from our sensations. Without this assumption, Nietzsche cannot articulate how our beliefs about the world are distorting. Accordingly, either the theory that we must always represent the world as similar to our sensations is false or, if it is true, one lacks the representational capacity to present an argument that our representations falsify.[7]

Considerations of this sort have pushed those who hold such theories of representation into phenomenalism. Rather than arguing that our beliefs are about external objects and therefore false, one instead argues that our beliefs are about our actual or possible sensations themselves and are therefore true. Because no content can be provided to beliefs about external objects, one gives up on the idea of them entirely. Nietzsche's denial, particularly in his later works, of the distinction between appearance and reality, or his claims that we have perspectives without there being objects for us to have perspective of, could therefore be understood as a recognition of our inability, given his account of representation, to represent a philosophically significant distinction between perspective and object. Indeed, sometimes Nietzsche makes explicitly phenomenalist claims (Hollingdale 1973, 134–36), for example, that "beings . . . have to be thought of as sensations that are no longer based on something devoid of sensation" (*WP* 562). Because we have "nothing but sensations and representations," we "cannot think of what does not have its source in the contents of representations" (*KSA* 7:26[11]). But because phenomenalism holds that our beliefs about phenomena are *true,* not false, it cannot account for Nietzsche's error theory.

Furthermore, it is questionable whether phenomenalism is an adequate response to the problem of outstripping the limits of representation by articulating those limits. Phenomenalists argue that we can refer only to our sensations and not material objects. The everyday term "material object," in this view, refers to actual or possible sensations. But if this position is articulated in the "first-order" language to which this theory applies, it will be false or contentless according to phenomenalism itself. It is false to say that we cannot refer to material objects if this means that we cannot refer to actual or possible sensations. The only other possibility is that the term "material object" as the phenomenalist is using it is meaningless, in which case the content of the theory is undermined.[8] Of course, it might be claimed that the phenomenalist position is articulated in a language that lacks the representational constraints that it puts upon the first-order language. But if that's so, why doesn't the possibility of this robust second-order language show that phenomenalism is wrong after all?

4. Skepticism Distinguished

The arguments I have presented above should not be taken to mean that the fact that our cognitive access to objects proceeds through sensations or other perspectives has no important epistemological consequences. But these consequences are primarily *skeptical.* Consider the following argument: I believe

I perceive objects by means of causal intermediaries like my sensations. I would usually appeal to the existence of such causal connections to justify why my beliefs about objects are, in general, true. But the existence of my sensations does not *entail* the existence of what I take to be their causes. I cannot exclude the possibility that these sensations have other causes and thus that my perceptions are incorrect. I cannot even exclude the possibility that there are no external objects. If I cannot exclude these possibilities, then my beliefs about external objects are not *justified,* whether they are true or not (for they still may all be true). And from this it follows that I do not have knowledge of such objects. The only way I could have knowledge would be to get direct access to these objects without the intermediary of my sensations. But such access, I have already admitted, I am denied.

It is crucial to distinguish this skepticism, which concerns the *justification* of our judgments, from the denial of their *truth.* It may be, as Nietzsche puts it, that we have "no criterion of correct perception" (*TL* p. 86). This would mean that the judgments we come to as a result of our sensations are not justified. But it is something else to say that correct perception is "a contradictory impossibility" (*TL* p. 86). To say correct perception is impossible is to say that the beliefs I arrive at on the basis of my sensations are false, something about which skepticism is utterly silent.

Nietzsche sometimes seems to present a form of skepticism rather than the error theory in "On Truth and Lies in a Nonmoral Sense." For example, after claiming that the distinction between individual and species "does not originate in the essence of things," he offers the skeptical warning that "we should not presume that this contrast does not correspond to the essence of things; that would be just as undemonstrable as its opposite" (*TL* pp. 83–84).[9] But reading Nietzsche as a skeptic fails to do justice to the many passages in which he says that our beliefs are indeed false, passages that are far too common to chalk up to mere infelicity of expression (Clark 1990, 90–93; Nehamas 1985, 46–47). Although it is possible that Nietzsche expresses skeptical views at times, particularly in his early works, skepticism does little to illuminate his more radical epistemological views.

5. Arguments That Concepts Falsify

In section 3 we looked at arguments that the role of sensations in our beliefs about the world is what makes these beliefs false. But it is much more common for Nietzsche to argue that *conceptualization* is responsible for the falsehood of our beliefs (e.g. *KSA* 7:19[48], 10:24[18]; *WP* 477, 479, 515)[10] because concepts falsify or schematize the evidence of the senses: "The fictitious world of subject, substance, 'reason,' etc., is needed—: there is in us a power to order, simplify, falsify, artificially distinguish. 'Truth' is the will to be master over the multiplicity of sensations:—to classify phenomena into definite categories" (*WP* 517). Rather than being the source of error, sensations provide us with the truth: "It is what we make of [the senses'] evidence that first introduces a lie into it, for example the lie of unity, the lie of materiality, of substance, of duration. . . . 'Reason' is the cause of our falsification of the evidence of the senses" (*TI* 3:2).

How could concepts *necessarily* falsify the evidence of the senses? Consider the concept of a stable material object. It seems at least *possible* that such an object could give rise to a multiplicity of sensations in us. To the extent that applying the concept of a material object helps us understand why our sensations occur, it would seem that it contributes to truth rather than falsity.

But perhaps Nietzsche combines a phenomenalist theory, under which reality consists only of the flux of sensations, with an argument that our concepts falsify because they "schematize" this flux by identifying sensations with material objects. Cognition falsifies because it takes the only thing that has reality—our sensations—to be other than what they are. It takes them to be schematized when they are in fact in chaos. But if this is Nietzsche's argument, one could rightly respond that it is simply the result of not taking the phenomenalist's argument far enough. Assume that the world that we experience is the schematized world—that is to say, the process of schematization affects not merely what we think about experience but the character of our experience itself. If so, then the phenomenalist should say that our judgments are *true* of the schematized world, not that they are false concerning some world of flux of which we have no experience. If Nietzsche allows the content of beliefs to reach out far enough beyond our experience to refer to unschematized sensations, why not give up phenomenalism entirely and allow them to reach all the way out to material objects?

But perhaps we actually experience the sensations as flux. We only believe, falsely, that they are schematized. If this is Nietzsche's argument, one can rightly ask just how what we believe about our sensations is so contrary to the way we experience them that all our beliefs are false. At this moment I am looking at my copies of the *Kritische Studienausgabe* of Nietzsche's works. In doing so I believe myself to be perceiving mustard-yellow rectangles over time. How is my belief concerning this stability or duration of sensation false to my actual experience?

6. A Possible Analogy with Mackie's Error Theory

Because of the role of our interests and needs in our conceptualization, Nietzsche frequently suggests that cognition is, in some sense, an evaluation of the world (e.g. *GS* 114; *WP* 507). "[T]he apparent world" with which we are concerned is "a world viewed according to values; ordered, selected according to values" (*WP* 567). Evaluations are often thought to be false—or at least suspect—interpretations of the world. Can an argument for the error theory be constructed out of this idea?

Consider John L. Mackie's error theory concerning evaluative sentences. Mackie's argument has two parts. The first is a semantic theory of evaluative language, which takes such language to be cognitive or descriptive. The second is an argument that the qualities that evaluative language describes the world as having are so "queer" that no evaluative sentence could possibly be true. As Mackie puts it, "If there were objective values, then they would be entities or qualities or relations of a very strange sort, utterly different from anything else in the universe" (1977, 38). What makes values queer is the necessary relationship between perceiving values and having certain motivating reasons for action, a relationship that shows itself in the (alleged) incoherence of judging something to be good and taking oneself to have no reason to prefer it:[11]

> Plato's Forms give a dramatic picture of what objective values would have to be. The Form of the Good is such that knowledge of it provides the knower with both a direction and an overriding motive; something's being good both tells the person who knows this to pursue it and makes him pursue it. An objective good would be sought by anyone who was acquainted with it, not because of any contingent fact that this person, or every person, is so constituted that he desires this end, but just because the end has to-be-pursuedness somehow built into it. (40)

The real world must be, as John McDowell has put it, "motivationally inert" (1978, 19). One could never truthfully describe the world as having a quality from which a motivation followed.

Although Mackie presents this queerness of value as if it were an empirical discovery (the way magical qualities are considered queer), this is misleading. It is the incoherence of something's character necessarily determining our response to it that makes values queer.[12] Valuations can be rejected as false without any knowledge of what the objects evaluated are really like. Thus if Nietzsche were arguing that all judgments are false because they are evaluative, he would not have to provide us with substantive empirical theories about what the world is really like.

Nietzsche does sometimes suggest that it is contradictory to want true beliefs about a world that is independent of our cognitive interests. This can make him sound similar to Mackie: "Coming to know . . . is always 'placing oneself in a conditional relation to something'—one who seeks to know the unconditioned desires that it should not concern him, and that this same something should be of no concern to anyone. This involves a contradiction . . . between wanting to know and the desire that it not concern us" (*WP* 555).

But the fact that our descriptions depend upon our cognitive interests is materially different from the relationship to our interests that makes evaluations necessarily false under Mackie's error theory. Mackie sees evaluations as false because they describe the world as having qualities that *justify* or *make appropriate* our interests. That is not the case with our descriptive judgments, even if it is assumed that the presence of certain interests is a condition for these judgments' being made.

For example, let us assume that the Inuit identify a type of snow that is very useful for building igloos as *snowgloo*. It is only because of their desire to build igloos that they came up with the term and seek to discover snowgloo in the world. The non-Inuit pass over snowgloo without noticing it. Although judgments about snowgloo are dependent upon the need to build igloos, there is no reason to believe that these judgments are false, because the presence of snowgloo is not taken to justify or make appropriate the desire to build igloos. Thus the fact that our world is "ordered, selected according to values" (*WP* 567) does not mean that our judgments about the world are evaluative—it merely means that the various nonevaluative qualities one looks for in the world are determined by what one is interested in.

Of course, the fact that our practical interests require us to limit our investigation of the world does open up the possibility that our beliefs *could be* false. But this simply means that we should be skeptical about our beliefs, not that we should conclude that they are false. Furthermore, if my cognitive interests lead me to adopt *general* beliefs, they could *increase* the chances that I will judge truthfully. Generalization can help ensure that my beliefs remain true despite the limitations provided by my cognitive interests because, by reducing the content of my beliefs, it reduces the possibility of conflict with what the world is like (cf. Clark 1990, 155–58).[13]

7. Summary of the Problems with the Error Theory

So far, the arguments we have encountered in favor of Nietzsche's error theory have been disappointing. The first problem is that it is part of the nature of conceptualization that true judgment is in principle possible. To deny this would be to reject the logical frameworks within which description occurs. The possibility that Nietzsche does reject these frameworks makes his error theory more interesting, but it also stands in the way of finding a plausible argument in its favor.

The second problem concerns how Nietzsche can justify the error theory without relying on the truth of so many other beliefs that it becomes fatally limited in scope. Someone who claims that all our beliefs about the world are false would be best advised to offer an a priori argument for this thesis. Empirical arguments for the falsehood of our beliefs presume the existence of empirical knowledge about the world as it is independent of those beliefs and so cannot show that most of our beliefs about the world are false. Because Nietzsche's arguments for his error theory tend to be empirical, they appear destined to fail.

These arguments take two forms. The first, which we have found in "On Truth and Lies in a Nonmoral Sense," suggests that our *sensations* are responsible for error. Understood as a straightforward comparison between our sensations and the way the world is, such arguments fail for the obvious reason that they presume knowledge about the way the world is. Understood as more sophisticated arguments that we are unable to represent the world except as similar to our sensations, such arguments fail for the more sophisticated reason that if such a theory of representation were true, Nietzsche would be unable to represent the claimed difference between our sensations and the world upon which his arguments rely. The most that the role of sensation in knowledge can do is introduce skeptical worries about the justification of our beliefs. But it is clear that Nietzsche wants to go well beyond skepticism.

The second form of argument is that *conceptualization,* not sensation, is responsible for error. This argument would explain why not merely beliefs about the outer world but also beliefs about inner experience falsify their objects—a view that Nietzsche seems to hold. It also promises to explain why logic and mathematics falsify. But so far we are in the dark about how the process of conceptualization or schematization could possibly make *every* belief false.

8. Clark's Interpretation of Nietzsche's Development

Should we simply conclude that Nietzsche's epistemology is incoherent? Maudemarie Clark's interpretation of Nietzsche saves him from incoherence by assigning the error theory to an earlier stage of his development. Clark sees the early Nietzsche as arguing for the falsity of our beliefs on the basis of an argument similar to that outlined in section 3. The early Nietzsche holds a theory of representation under which the content of our beliefs is cashed out in terms of perceptual states. As a result, he insists that our beliefs can be true only of these perceptual states themselves. But rather than drawing the phenomenalist consequences from this theory of representation that one would expect, Nietzsche incoherently retains the idea that the thing-in-itself is the true object of cognition. As a result he understands all our beliefs to be false (Clark 1990, 77–93).

It is only when Nietzsche comes to realize that the thing-in-itself can not even be represented that he gives up speaking of our beliefs as errors (Clark 1990, 95–125). According to Clark, this realization occurs between the publications of *Beyond Good and Evil* and *On the Genealogy of Morals* (Clark 1990, 103). After the change, Nietzsche no longer sees a reason to denigrate our beliefs about the world. He begins to praise science and other forms of empirical knowledge (see also Leiter 1994, 335) and attacks only religious and metaphysical beliefs as errors. Although Nietzsche still holds a form of perspectivism even in his "mature" period, this is merely the denial of something "contradictory"—namely, metaphysical truth, understood as knowledge of the thing-in-itself or knowledge "independ[ent] of our cognitive interests" or "our best standards of rational acceptability" (Clark 1990, 49, 134).

In what remains of this chapter I will argue against Clark's reading of Nietzsche's development by showing that Nietzsche holds the error theory throughout his period of philosophical activity—right up until his breakdown in January 1889. This means that if the error theory is incoherent, so is Nietzsche's epistemology as a whole.

The first reason to question Clark's reading is that Nietzsche never once says that his views on truth underwent any change. Since he does not shy away from intellectual autobiography or self-criticism in other areas (*BT* Preface to 2d ed.; *EH*), one would expect him to have identified such an important change in his views, for example in the *Genealogy of Morals* itself or later in *Ecce Homo*. Instead, in the *Genealogy of Morals* Nietzsche makes an effort to stress its *continuity* with earlier works such as *Thus Spoke Zarathustra* (*GM* Preface:8), *Human, All Too Human* (*GM* Preface:4), *The Gay Science* (*GM* 3:24), and *Daybreak* (*GM* 3:24). The title page of the *Genealogy of Morals* is followed by the words "A Sequel to My Last Book, *Beyond Good and Evil*, Which It Is Meant to Supplement and Clarify." This is strong evidence against the idea that Nietzsche's views changed radically between the publications of those two books.

A second reason to question Clark's reading of Nietzsche's development is that the motivation for the change—the recognition that the thing-in-itself is incomprehensible—and the consequence of the change—the praise of empirical methodologies—are both expressed in Nietzsche's works before the spring of 1887, when the change would have had to have occurred.[14] In *Human, All Too Human, The Gay Science,* and *Beyond Good and Evil* Nietzsche speaks of the thing-in-itself as "actually empty, that is to say empty of significance" (*HA* 16) and as a contradiction (*GS* 54; *BGE* 16; *GS*2d 354) and argues in favor of empiricism, stating, for example, that "all credibility, all good conscience, all evidence of truth come only from the senses" (*BGE* 134).[15]

What is more important, Nietzsche continues to express the error theory after the spring of 1887 (e.g. *WP* 517, 539, 544, 569, 584). Consider the following passage from the Nachlaß: "The aberration of philosophy is that, instead of seeing in logic and the categories of reason means toward the adjustment of the world for utilitarian ends (basically, toward an expedient falsification), one believed one possessed in them the criterion of truth and reality. The 'criterion of truth' was in fact merely the biological utility of such a system of systematic falsification" (*WP* 584).

Clark ignores these passages because of her methodological commitment to rely upon Nietzsche's published works alone (1990, 25–26; cf. Leiter 1994, 335). But it is unlikely that Nietzsche had a dramatic realization that cognition does not falsify, which he chose to express in his published works, and yet continued to present the error theory in his notebooks (Poellner 1995, 23).

Furthermore, even if one looks to Nietzsche's published works alone, Clark's argument fails. She claims that "in the six books that follow [*Beyond Good and Evil*] there is no evidence of Nietzsche's earlier denial of truth: no claim that the human world is a falsification, no claim that science, logic, or mathematics falsify reality" (1990, 103). In fact, there are passages in the *Twilight of the Idols* and the *Genealogy of Morals* that are indistinguishable from pre-*Genealogy* expressions of Nietzsche's error theory. I will deal with these passages in a moment. But that there are *few* expressions of the error theory in Nietzsche's published works after *Beyond Good and Evil* shouldn't surprise us. Most of these works aren't concerned with epistemological themes at all. There is nothing for *or against* the error theory in *The Case of Wagner, Nietzsche Contra Wagner,* or *Ecce Homo.* The first two are works of cultural criticism (as is much of *Twilight of the Idols*[16]) and the last is a quasi autobiography. The absence of Nietzsche's error theory from these works is about as relevant as its absence from his laundry lists.

Furthermore, *The Antichrist* and much of the *Genealogy of Morals* and *Twilight of the Idols,* rather than discussing epistemological themes, are critiques of Christianity. Clark is quite right that Nietzsche criticizes the Christian in these books as the enemy of science, experience, and the senses. He claims that the Christian believes in things—such as free will, the soul, and God—that do not exist. But the fact that he does not introduce his error theory in the middle of these critiques is not surprising and does nothing to show that he does not still hold the view that cognition falsifies. For in his pre-*Genealogy* works Nietzsche likewise refrains from introducing his error theory when attacking Christianity on these grounds.

For example, in *The Gay Science,* after having introduced "the greatest recent event—that 'God is dead,' that the belief in the Christian God has become unbelievable," Nietzsche writes that "all the daring of the lover of knowledge is permitted again" (*GS*2d 343). He fails to mention that knowledge is impossible. Likewise, in *Human, All Too Human,* Nietzsche argues that "one cannot believe . . . dogmas of religion and metaphysics if one has in one's heart and head the rigorous methods of acquiring truth" (*HA* 109)—without noting that no method of acquiring truth exists. Clark is right that an interpreter of Nietzsche who attributes to him the error theory should offer an explanation of how Nietzsche can claim that his views are true and the views of his opponents are false. But this philosophical problem cannot decide the exegetical issue of whether and when Nietzsche holds an error theory.

But the most significant problem with Clark's interpretation is that Nietzsche expresses the error theory a number of times in the works he published after *Beyond Good and Evil.* The most important passages are in *Twilight of the Idols:*

> It is what we *make* of [the evidence of the senses] that first introduces a lie into it, for example the lie of unity, the lie of materiality, of substance, of duration. . . . "Reason" is the cause of our falsification of the evidence of the senses. In so far as the senses show becoming, passing away, change, they do not lie. (*TI* 3:2)

> Today . . . we see ourselves as it were entangled in error, *necessitated* to error, to precisely the extent that our prejudice in favor of reason compels us to posit unity, identity, duration, substance, cause, materiality, being; however sure we are on the basis of a strict reckoning, *that* error is to be found there. The situation is the same as with the motions of the sun: in that case error has our eyes, in the present case our *language* as a perpetual advocate. . . . It is *this* which sees everywhere deed and doer; this which believes in will as cause in general; this which believes in the "ego," in the ego as being, in the ego as substance, and which *projects* its belief in the ego-substance on all things—only thus does it *create* the concept "thing." . . . Being is everywhere thought in, *foisted on,* as cause; it is only from the conception "ego" that there follows, derivatively, the concept "being." (*TI* 3:5)

Clark argues that these passages criticize only the possibility of rationalist metaphysics, not empirical knowledge. Nietzsche's rejecting the faculty of reason "is equivalent to rejecting nonnatural interpretations of our reasoning abilities" (1990, 106) or denying the "idea of a soul as an unchanging substrate" (108).[17] Souls or other non-natural epistemological subjects are unnecessary for empirical knowledge. Along the same lines, Clark argues that the metaphysical concepts, such as substance, that Nietzsche thinks are tied to this pure subject of thought are likewise unnecessary for empirical beliefs about the world. This reading, she argues, is supported by Nietzsche's claim (*TI* 3:5) that "everything empirical plainly contradict[s]" these concepts (Clark 1990, 107).

But there is a good deal of evidence in the passages themselves that the errors of which Nietzsche speaks are committed by all of us, not only a priori metaphysicians. His emphasis on their source in our language invites such an interpretation, for example. And Nietzsche explicitly claims that "mechanists and physicists" employ the erroneous concept of substance (*TI* 4:4). In addition, he does not merely criticize the concept of substance but also concepts such as "duration," "materiality," and "cause." Metaphysicians are not the only people who talk about enduring material objects in causal relations.

In the *Genealogy of Morals* too Nietzsche attacks the causal reasoning relied upon by scientists: "A quantum of force is equivalent to a quantum of drive, will, effect—more, it is nothing other than precisely this very driving, willing, effecting, and only owing to the seduction of language (and of the fundamental errors of reason that are petrified in it) which conceives and misconceives all effects as conditioned by something that causes effects, by a 'subject,' can it appear otherwise" (*GM* 1:13). For Nietzsche, "our entire science still lies under the misleading influence of language and has not disposed of that little changeling, the 'subject'" (*GM* 1:13).[18]

A comprehensive argument that Nietzsche considered metaphysical concepts of substance and causality necessary for empirical judgment before and after his alleged transformation in 1887 will have to wait until I discuss Spir's influence on Nietzsche, however.

Consider the following passage from *Human, All Too Human*, where Nietzsche spells out the concept of substance: "*Fundamental Questions of Metaphysics.*—When one day the history of the genesis of thought comes to be written, the following sentence by a distinguished logician will also stand revealed in a new light: 'The primary universal law of the knowing subject consists in the inner necessity of recognizing every object in itself as being in its own essence something identical with itself, thus self-existent and at bottom always the same, in short as substance'" (*HA* 18). Clark recognizes the importance of this passage to understanding what Nietzsche means by "substance" (1990, 108). But the passage is from Afrikan Spir's book *Denken und Wirklichkeit* (1877, 2:177) and cannot be understood without knowing something about both this book and Nietzsche's complicated attitudes toward Spir's thought.

As we shall see in chapters 2 and 3, both Nietzsche and Spir take this concept of substance to be a precondition for the possibility of *thought,* for the application of *any concept.* Furthermore, both think that an atemporal non-natural subject is a precondition for the application of a concept. For Nietzsche, the very possibility of cognition depends upon this pure subject of thought: "Belief in the 'ego' stands or falls with belief in logic . . . if, on the other hand, the ego proves to be something in a state of becoming: then—" (*WP* 519). It is precisely for this reason that he often links together pure subjects of thought and self-identical substances (e.g. *BGE* 17; *WP* 574): "The concept of substance is a consequence of the notion of the subject: not the reverse! If we relinquish the soul, 'the subject,' the precondition for 'substance' in general disappears" (*WP* 485).

Clark is right that in the end Nietzsche denies that pure subjects of thought and unchanging self-identical substances exist. And he does so for the reason that she says he does—because they are contrary to experience. It is because experience suggests change and becoming, while thought and substance must exist outside of time and plurality, that he argues that the "prejudices of reason" falsify the testimony of the senses. As we shall see, Spir takes the opposite approach and argues that sensation falsifies because it is incompatible with the requirements of thought. Although these arguments will be spelled out in detail later, for the moment one can think of Spir as Parmenides to Nietzsche's Heraclitus. Like Parmenides, Spir argues that the only thought that is possible is thought in being and of being. This leads him to reject the evidence of the senses as deceptions. Like Heraclitus, Nietzsche argues that sensations provide us with evidence that reality is becoming. But the cost of the Heraclitean approach is that it threatens the very possibility of thought. Thus Clark radically minimizes what Nietzsche believes are the consequences of exposing the "prejudices of reason." Without these prejudices, we lose the ability to see ourselves as thinking beings at all.

Spir's influence can account for Nietzsche's comprehensive claims about the falsifying role of the concept of a timeless substance and can explain why this concept is so foundational that it plays a role in *every* judgment, including mathematics, logic, and judgments about inner experience.[19] But, so understood, Nietzsche has no reason to give up these views after rejecting a phenomenalist form of the error theory. Even if it is true that sensations do not distort our view of reality, the problem of concepts distorting the evidence of the senses remains. And this is precisely what the exegetical evidence shows. Nietzsche's concerns about conceptualization falsifying are the same throughout his period of philosophical activity. He consistently argues that thinking means presupposing eternal substances, and because experience shows change and becoming, thought must falsify the character of experience.

Because of her emphasis on the first argument for the error theory, under which sensations are responsible for error (Clark 1990, 83–84), Clark argues that any claims by Nietzsche that sensations provide us with the truth must mean that he has abandoned the theory. But from the very beginning Nietzsche predominantly argues that concepts falsify the evidence of the senses, by positing identity where only plurality can be found. This argument can be found in his Nachlaß as early as 1872, when he was exposed to Spir's writings, and it continues to appear through the 1880s:[20] "Every cognition that is useful for us is the *identification of the unequal,* the similar, that is, is essentially unlogical" (*KSA* 7:19[236]). "Concepts arise from the equation of the unequal: i.e. through the deception that there is equality, through the assumption of identity: thus through false conceptions" (*KSA* 7:23[11]). "That there are equal things, equal cases, is as much the foundational fiction behind judgment as it is behind conclusions" (*KSA* 11:35[57]).

9. Conclusion

My purpose in this chapter has been to make explicit the significance of the error theory throughout Nietzsche's period of philosophical productivity and the difficulty of finding a coherent argument in its favor. On the basis of what I have said, an adequate interpretation of Nietzsche's error theory must explain the following:

1. The *comprehensiveness* of Nietzsche's error theory—including its applicability to mathematics, logic, and inner experience;
2. How the error theory can be justified on the basis of the evidence of the senses, in particular the fact that they show change and becoming;
3. How concepts in general, and in particular the categories of substance and causality, generate error;
4. The role of the ego as the source of these erroneous categories.

Clark's emphasis on the phenomenalist form of Nietzsche's error theory makes these aspects of the error theory inexplicable. In chapter 3 I will present a reading of Nietzsche's error theory that, I believe, can explain them. This reading will draw upon the work of Afrikan Spir, a writer who exerted a powerful influence on Nietzsche's epistemology and metaphysics.

I do not want to suggest that the error theory is all that can be found in

Nietzsche's epistemological reflections, however. The interpreter of Nietzsche faces the doubly difficult task of making the error theory look plausible while making sense of the alternative epistemological positions found in Nietzsche. In the next chapter I will spell out what I believe is the core problem motivating all of Nietzsche's epistemologies. In the process, I will lay the groundwork for my explanation of the error theory.

2. Nietzsche's Neo-Kantian Roots

So FAR, I have only gestured toward the tension between naturalism and truth that stands behind Nietzsche's epistemologies. I want to begin to flesh out the heart of my interpretation of Nietzsche's epistemology in this chapter. I will begin by looking in some detail at Kant's argument against naturalistic accounts of cognition and his criticism of Hume's approach to causal judgments in particular. I will then argue that Nietzsche's epistemologies are Kantian in motivation. The key to seeing the Kantian themes in Nietzsche will be the strong analogies between Nietzsche's thought and the Neo-Kantian philosophy of Afrikan Spir.

1. The Conflict between Naturalism and Truth in Kant

For Kant, any adequate account of judgment must provide for what he calls "objective validity" (1965, B140–42[1]). The objective validity of a judgment is what allows it to have a truth-value (Allison 1983, 72–73). Objective validity can be understood by contrasting it with the merely subjectively valid uniting of representations according to psychological laws of association, such as those proposed by Hume. Kant argues that Hume's explanation of causal judgments in terms of the habitual association of ideas is inadequate because such association is powerless to represent the necessity of the causal connections between the events the ideas are about and so can't bring about true or false judgments about those causal connections (1965, B4–5).

Notice that the problem that Kant thinks Hume is unable to solve is not whether we can *know* that every event has a cause, that is, the problem of justifying this synthetic a priori truth. Nor is Kant concerned with whether experiencing the constant conjunction of two events provides justification for the judgment that a causal relation between the two exists and will exist in the future, that is to say, the problem of induction.[2] The problem is rather how I can *represent* a causal relation between two events—even one that does not exist—merely as a result of having experienced the constant conjunction of the two events and being now disposed to associate them. According to Kant, this contingent fact about me—that I am disposed to associate the events—is powerless to represent the *necessity* of the causal connection between the events themselves. To say that the causal relation is necessary is not to say that it had to exist but rather that, given that the causal relation is as it is, the relation between the two events is a necessary one: If the first event happens, then the second event *must happen,* no matter what variations might be made to anything else besides the causal relation and, in particular, even if the person making the judgment no longer had the disposition to associate the two. It is only by representing this necessity that the objective validity of a causal judgment is possible.

Hume would likely agree. His argument is best understood as an account of what we are really doing when we *think* we are making judgments about causal connections. It is for this reason that Hume denies that we have an *idea* of causality (1983, §7). Hume's approach to causal judgment is noncognitivist: We are not representing anything when we make causal judgments and so are not, strictly speaking, *thinking.*

Kant is not only concerned with showing the inadequacies of Hume's account of causal judgments. His target is also a Humean account of more fundamental judgments, in which we treat objects (understood by Kant in the broadest possible terms as the subjects of judgments) as that to which the application of a concept, such as *heavy,* is appropriate. Kant hopes to explain how we can think of objects *as heavy.* The merely psychological association of objects under the concept *heavy* will not do the trick. According to Kant, such an account of conceptualization is inadequate because it fails to represent the unification of concept and objects as *necessary.* Once again, this is not to say that one must represent the objects as necessarily heavy, that is, heavy in all possible worlds. The point is rather that the unification must be seen as necessary *given the objects as they are.* The question is whether our merely contingent association of concept and object can represent that the two, as Kant puts it, "are combined *in the object,* no matter what the state of the subject may be" (1965, B142), even if the subject no longer had any psychological disposition to associate.

The general judgmental form under which one represents a necessary connection between a concept and an object is an example of what Kant calls a *category.* Through the category of substance, which stands behind "categorical" judgments, a predicate is applied to a subject. In the transcendental deduction, Kant is also concerned with showing the objective validity of other categories, for example, the category of causality and dependence. This category stands behind judgments of the form "if A then B," where A and B are categorical judgments. Because Kant thinks that his table of categories exhausts the logical forms of judgment, establishing the objective validity of these categories means establishing *the possibility of thought.*[3]

Kant argues that a judgment can have objective validity only if the unification of representations in the judgment is *necessary* in the sense that, holding what is judged as it is, the conditions for unifying these representations can never change. The problem with the Humean account of judgment is that the conditions for unifying representations would *vary* given changes in the dispositions of the judger.

This notion of objective validity captures something of what we mean when we say that someone judges in a manner that has a truth-value. Imagine that some children call something "square" only when threatened by their parents. We would probably say that they have not yet genuinely judged anything to be square and so are not yet in a state that is a candidate for truth or falsity. This is because the same object can be judged as square or not square depending upon whether they are threatened.

The problem with all naturalistic accounts of judgment, according to Kant, is that our reasons for judging an object will always be something other than the character of the object our judgment is about. Even if the naturalistic causes of our judgments are different from Hume's dispositions—for example firing neurons—the objects of and reasons for our judgments become unhinged.

It appears that the only way our judgments could have objective validity is if our reasons for uniting objects under concepts referred solely to characteristics of the objects themselves. Judgments employing such concepts would then be objectively valid descriptions of the objects as having those characteristics. For example, I can judge something to be square in a manner that has objective validity if my rule for uniting objects under the concept *square* is that they should be so united only if they are square. This captures our feeling that it is only when we become concerned about the *objects of our judgments themselves,* rather than extrinsic factors like threats from our parents, Humean dispositions, or firing neurons, that we can judge truly or falsely.

Let us understand *realism* to be this view that the rules for uniting objects under concepts have to do solely with what the objects are like. One reason that realism is attractive is that it provides our judgments with objective validity. Indeed, it seems that rejecting realism means denying that our judgments have objective validity. By making the conditions for a judgment refer to something other than the character of the objects the judgment is about, the antirealist, it seems, would make it impossible for our reasons to judge to remain the same whenever the objects judged remain the same. Our judgments would be like those of the children threatened by their parents.

But why identify one's *reasons* to judge with naturalistic *explanations* of our judgments? Why not instead use naturalism to explain only why we actually come to make judgments and look to the objects these judgments are about to explain why the judgments *are true*? Why aren't realism and naturalism compatible?

If one adopts such an approach, one will have run afoul of what we can call the *principle of cognitive sensitivity,* that is, the view that the only concepts that we have are those that make a *difference* to what we do, in the sense that we regulate our judgments to satisfy these concepts. If striking and lighting ought to be associated only if striking causes lighting, but we actually associate the two due to a Humean disposition, then we are insensitive to the concept that binds our causal judgments and gives them truth-values. The way we make judgments about causal relations becomes unhinged from their truth. *Skepticism* about whether we have a reason to think causal relations exist merely because we judge that they exist would follow.

The skeptic denies the principle of cognitive sensitivity. And a powerful motivation for the principle is the feeling that the skeptic makes improper demands on our judgments by applying to them criteria of truth that are irrelevant to what we do in the way of judging.

To sum up, Kant's antinaturalist argument is that if *any* judgment is considered naturalistically, it will never be the case that conditions for the application of the concepts employed in that judgment are concerned solely with the objects judged—provided that these conditions are those to which we are cognitively sensitive. This is because there must be something about judgers themselves over and above the character of the object judged that will bring them to judge the object as they do. Naturalism is unable to give our judgments objective validity because it will make the correctness of our judgments about an object change given contingent changes in the subject.

2. Kant's Apperceptive Account of Cognition

Because of his antinaturalism, Kant argues that objectively valid judgments cannot have their source in a self that is an object of empirical knowledge.

For this reason, he insists that thought cannot be *experienced*, whether through psychological introspection or observation of the physical world (Allison 1983, 275–78). For no naturalistic (that is, psychological or physical) account of our judgments is one in which they could be seen as objectively valid and so as *thought*.

But, Kant argues, since I *can* employ concepts, the "I" that does this must not be an empirical self. Conceptualization is a form of "spontaneity" (1965, B75/A51), a term Kant uses for an ability of the will to "begin to act of itself, without requiring to be determined to action by an antecedent cause in accordance with the law of causality" (B561/A533). Such spontaneity cannot be given in experience (A546–47/B574–75).

The spontaneous agent responsible for conceptualization is the apperceptive self, also known as the transcendental subject:

> If I investigate more precisely the relation of the given modes of knowledge in a judgment, and distinguish it, as belonging to the understanding, from the relation according to laws of the reproductive imagination, which has only subjective validity, I find that a judgment is nothing but the manner in which given modes of knowledge are brought to the unity of apperception. This is what is intended by the copula "is." It is employed to distinguish the objective unity of given representations from the subjective. It indicates their relation to original apperception and its *necessary unity.* (B141–42)

Apperception is, briefly put, a unity of the self of which we are not empirically aware. It is qualitatively different from any empirically known and so merely contingent unity to the self (for example, that provided by physical or psychological continuity). We have independent evidence of the apperceptive self through the "I think" that we can reflectively attach to any of our representations. The self indicated by the "I think" is this subject of experience that is never able to be made an object of experience (B131–33). If the unification of representations in judgment took place only in the empirical world—including the mental world that is the subject of empirical psychology—we could have only affective or impulsive rather than rule-bound motivations for our judgments. Indeed, we would not be able to be *aware* of the fact that we associate—we would pass from one thought to another unconsciously. The fact that we are so aware shows that we have a unity to the self that cannot be reduced to empirical regularities.

But how does the apperceptive self represent objects when the empirical self is not able to? Isn't this still a form of antirealism, in which the conditions for the application of concepts to objects take into account something other than the character of the objects of the judgments? Doesn't this mean that, as in the Humean associationist account of causal judgments, one should judge that a causal relation between events exists when the self (now the apperceptive self) has a "disposition" to associate the two events? How is objective validity established?

The nonempirical character of the apperceptive self is part of the solution to this problem. To worry about the transcendental subject changing its dispositions we must, in fact, treat this subject as an object of experience. But this is precisely what the transcendental subject is not. It is for this reason that, although the conditions for the correctness of a judgment refer to the transcendental self, the correctness of a judgment about the same object cannot be thought of as something that could vary due to changes in this transcendental self; any self that one could point to that could change would not be the transcendental self under consideration. The unification of representations provided by the transcendental self is a necessary unification (or, rather, not representable as a contingent unification).

But by arguing that one cannot point to our motivations in judging, hasn't Kant shown only how we can *feel* that our judgments have objective validity? Aren't our judgments objectively valid only if the conditions for judging are in fact necessarily tied to what the object judged is like? So aren't our judgments still without objective validity, since the conditions for judging are still irrelevant to the character of the objects represented?

This problem is answered by Kant's "Copernican Revolution." He takes the character of the object judged to involve the transcendental conditions for our representing it and distinguishes this represented object from the thing-in-itself, which is the same object considered independently of these conditions. In other words, Kant is an antirealist. The conditions for the correctness of our judgments must take us into account. But because his antirealism is *transcendental,* it preserves the objective validity of our judgments: there can be no variability in how an object can be judged, because the transcendental conditions for representation must be fulfilled. Kant's transcendental account of judgment, unlike its naturalistic alternative, makes antirealism and objective validity compatible.

3. The Schematism

In establishing the objective validity of the categories, Kant has explained only the formal character of thought. Insofar as we apply concepts at all, we must do so in a nonempirical and necessary fashion. But an important question that is not answered by this formal account is why we engage in the *particular* conceptualizations that we do. Why is it that one empirical concept is used rather than another? Why is it that *heavy* is necessarily connected to a body and not *light*? Why are the striking of a match and its lighting necessarily connected and not the striking of a match and the appearance of a genie?

If Kant explains the choices of empirical concepts in naturalistic terms, then our empirical judgments once again fail to have objective validity. But if he argues that they follow from the necessary character of apperception, *every characteristic of the world would be necessary.* Heavy objects could not be anything but heavy because the character of apperception would require that they always be represented as heavy.

Kant does argue that certain necessary aspects of the world as experienced—for example, that it consists of enduring substances and causal relations—follow from the necessary character of apperception. But he cannot explain our choice of specific empirical concepts, under which objects may or may not fall, in terms of the character of apperception. He cannot appeal to the *necessary* unity of apperception to explain these *contingent* choices. Conceptualization cannot be solely a matter of the necessity and self-determination of apperception. Sensations—the given character of the world as experienced—must play a role in cognition as well.

In the end, Kant relies upon an empiricist explanation of our employment of particular empirical concepts. The choice to apply one empirical concept rather than another is determined by certain sensory criteria (Allison 1983, 65–68). Such an account is plausible. After all, we can't help thinking that the reason we choose to apply the concept *red* to a tomato has to do with the fact that we have sensations of red in connection with the tomato. But such an account of empirical concepts threatens to be *naturalistic,* in the sense that unifications of objects under concepts is causally determined by the character of sensory content. Such an account opens up causal gaps between judgment and object that threaten the objective validity of empirical judgments. One example is the causal gap between the tomato and the sensation of red that leads us to put the tomato under the concept *red.* The natural response to the existence of the first gap is to argue that the world we judge is constituted by our sensations in phenomenalist fashion. Phenomenalism, by closing the first gap, claims to restore the necessary unity between the conditions for our judgments and what the judgments are about, making the objective validity of our judgments possible. Much of Kant's approach in the *Critique of Pure Reason* has a phenomenalist character.

The phenomenalist elements in Kant and his apperceptive approach are very different and arguably incompatible. And yet they have been so often conflated, perhaps because Kant himself does so, that some time should be spent distinguishing them. Phenomenalism explains the objective validity of empirical judgments about objects by identifying judgment with the passivity of experience. It offers sensory states as the true object of our knowledge because judgments about these states seem necessarily tied to the character of the states themselves. One cannot have a green sensation, it is claimed, and not see that sensation *as green.*

Rather than seeing the objectivity validity of our judgments to be a product of their *passivity*—that is, a unity of concept and object compelled upon us from without—the apperceptive approach treats their objective validity to be a product of our spontaneous activity as judgers. The necessity, and thus the objective validity, of our judgments about the world comes from within us. It is a form of rule-governedness that we require of ourselves in a manner similar to our self-determination as moral agents. In emphasizing the spontaneity of judgment, the apperceptive approach treats our knowledge as comparable to the intellectual intuition possessed by God. God's knowledge lacks a compelled element—for him to make a judgment about an object is equivalent to the object's existing.[4]

The tension between the apperceptive and phenomenalist elements in Kant is a product of his insistence that human cognition has both spontaneous and passive elements. The element of spontaneity shows itself in the fact that a merely empirical uniting of representations is insufficient to create rule-governed association—only the necessary unity of apperception can do that. Because an empirical judgment is a rule-governed association of representations on the basis of certain sensory criteria, however, it cannot be wholly spontaneous.

But there is a second naturalistic gap in phenomenalism that threatens even our ability to make judgments about sensations. Because there is no necessary relationship between sensations and judgments about those sensations, one can be just as worried about empirical judgments' relationship to sensations as one was about their relation to external objects. Although the phenomenalist hopes to identify having a sensation with making a judgment about it, there is clearly a difference between being presented with a green sensation and uniting that sensation with other green sensations. There is an important difference between *seeing* and *seeing as.*

Accordingly, how can one show that what leads the judger to unite sensations under the concept *green* is hooked up to the sensations' greenness? Something more than the presence of a green sensation is needed to bring us to lump that sensation with other green sensations. These facts should be included in the conditions for the application of the concept *green* in order to avoid violating the principle of cognitive sensitivity. But that means that, barring an apperceptive account of empirical conceptualization—that is, an account that makes such conceptualization both radically free and necessary—its objective validity will not be established. Phenomenalism fails to account for the objective validity of empirical judgments precisely because it fails to see such choices as spontaneous.

This tension between Kant's phenomenalism and his apperceptive account of judgments is at its height as he attempts to explain how the categories can apply to sensations. As we have seen, Kant does not want to suggest that sensations—the passive element in knowledge—simply determine how one should judge objects, for that would be to treat empirical conceptualization as a merely blind Humean association of sensory particulars. Neither does he want to deny the passive element in knowledge and claim that the known world must have its entire source in the spontaneity of thought.

Kant's unhappy solution to this problem is through the deus ex machina of the transcendental synthesis of the imagination, which is supposed to function as a bridge between the passive and the spontaneous elements in cognition. It is the imagination that unites representations together so that they can be taken up by the spontaneity of the understanding (Kant 1965, A77–78/B102–3). It is therefore crucial to the formation of empirical concepts. Furthermore, by synthesizing the pure intuitions of space and time so that they can be represented within one consciousness, the imagination provides the "sensible conditions under which alone pure concepts of the understanding can be employed" (A136/B175). In other words, the synthesis of the imagination makes the formal categories relevant to intuition by creating sensory conditions or markers for their application. It is by means of the requirements for the schematization of space and time that Kant explains the existence of the synthetic a priori truths that every event has a cause and that the world consists of enduring substances.

The schematism is widely acknowledged to be the weak link in Kant's transcendental deduction (Allison 1983, 160–64). My goal is not to spell out all its infirmities but merely to suggest how it fails to connect the passive and the spontaneous elements that Kant sees in cognition. Let's begin with the creation of empirical concepts. Insofar as Kant claims that all concepts "are based on the spontaneity of thought" (1965, A68/B93), it may sound as if the process of creating and applying empirical concepts is the result of apperceptive spontaneity. But in fact the production and employment of empirical concepts must have a quasi-psychological—even mechanical—character. In contrast to apperception, which can be thought of as the expression of radically free spontaneity, the imagination, which provides the link between empirical concepts and sensory content, is *constrained from without* by the character of sensation. Sensation must determine how the imagination responds to that sensory content, on pain of making our empirical concepts irrelevant to our sensations. But since it seems impossible to think of the manner in which the sensory content determines empirical conceptualization other than *causally,* according to the Kantian antinaturalist argument it would appear that the application of empirical concepts cannot have objective validity. This causal gap between sensory content and empirical concept separates our empirical judgments from what they are about.

The same point is generally true of the manner in which the imagination synthesizes the pure intuitions of space and time in order to allow these intuitions to be represented as a unity. If this process is understood in a causal fashion, it is impossible to see how it can be linked to the spontaneity of thought. If it is an act of spontaneity, however, it is hard to see how it can connect with the determinate character of intuition.

Kant's approach suffers from a dilemma. Either the sensory requirements of the synthesis of the imagination limit the understanding or they do not. If they limit the understanding, then they undermine its spontaneity. If they do not, then the world as represented is unconstrained by sensory content. This problem is not solved simply by Kant's naming the process of schematization "transcendental," as if a mere word could turn passivity into spontaneity.

The argument above is, of course, the heart of Hegel's famous critique of Kant. For Hegel, the spontaneous unity of apperception as Kant understood it must, in the end, be purely formal, and thus "the dialectical movement of consciousness in it is not construed as its own activity, but as in itself; that is, for the I, this movement is construed as a change in the object of consciousness" (1981, 11). In other words, the role that Kant assigns to the passive element in knowledge means that the self is seen as *an object* subject to causal laws of change.

It is in large part Kant's inability to introduce a passive element to knowledge without betraying the spontaneity that is required for objective validity that generated German Idealism, in which Kant's apperceptive account of the objective validity of judgments completely overwhelms his phenomenalist account, and all judgments become, in effect, synthetic a priori truths about the necessary character of the world. The passive element in knowledge is rejected, and all the characteristics of objects judged become derivable from the apperceptive self (Pippin 1989, 9). The denial of the cognitive determinateness of any element passively given to cognition can be found in later idealists as well, for example, F. H. Bradley and T. H. Green, and in twentieth-century Anglo-American analytic philosophers, such as Wilfred Sellars, who deny the existence of noninferential awareness of sense data (Williams 1999, chap. 2).

4. Afrikan Spir and the Reality of Becoming

Are these Kantian issues related to what Nietzsche has to say about truth and knowledge? I will argue that they are. The key is Afrikan Spir.[5]

Afrikan Alexandrovich Spir was born in 1837 in Elisabethgrad (now Kirovohrad), in the part of the Russian Empire that is now Ukraine (Schlechta and Anders 1962, 159). After a period as an officer in the Russian navy, he retired on a private income in 1857 and left Russia permanently for Germany in 1867. In 1867 he audited courses at the University of Leipzig at the same time that Nietzsche was there, although it does not appear that they ever met (119–20). In 1869 he moved to Tübingen and in 1871 to Stuttgart. He moved to Switzerland in 1883 and died in Geneva in 1890 without ever having held a university appointment.

Spir's most important works are *Forschung nach der Gewissheit in der Erkenntniss der Wirklichkeit* (Inquiry into certainty in the perception of reality; 1869) and the two-volume *Denken und Wirklichkeit: Versuch einer Erneuerung der kritischen Philosophie* (Thought and reality: An attempt at a renewal of critical philosophy; 1st ed., 1873; 2d ed., 1877). Nietzsche had obtained a copy of *Forschung* by the winter of 1872, which he sold in 1875 (Schlechta and Anders 1962, 119, 166). He borrowed the first edition of *Denken und Wirklichkeit* from the Basel University Library on five different occasions between February 1873 and November 1874, more than any other book during that period (Crescenzi 1994), and bought his own copy of the second edition when it was first published in 1877 (Schlechta and Anders 1962, 118–19, 122). All the evidence points to the book's great importance to Nietzsche. We know, for example, that he read and made notes on *Denken und Wirklichkeit* in 1873–74, early 1877, 1880–82, and 1885, and that his copy shows signs of having been read very carefully (Schlecta and Anders 1962, 122).[6]

Nietzsche quotes Spir in *Philosophy in the Tragic Age of the Greeks* (15) and in *Human, All-Too-Human* (18).[7] Spir is also undoubtedly the "rigorous logician" referred to in *Human, All Too Human* (16). Spir or his works are also mentioned in Nietzsche's notebooks nine times.[8] As a means of comparison, Friedrich Albert Lange, who has rightly been held to be an important influence on Nietzsche's epistemology (Stack 1983), is never mentioned in Nietzsche's published works and is mentioned or quoted in his Nachlaß only three times.[9] But it is when one looks beyond Nietzsche's explicit references to Spir and considers the similarities between the two thinkers that Spir's significance becomes particularly clear.

Kant's argument against the naturalization of thought is a cornerstone of Spir's account of judgment. Like Kant, Spir is concerned with the problem of whether "the association of reproduced content alone . . . can bring about judgments and inferences" (1877, 1:77). Like Kant, Spir argues that "the relation of the contents to objects is . . . alone the source of the possibility of judgments and inferences. But for that reason this relationship could never arise from association" (1:78). To judge something about the world is to represent its necessity—for example the necessity of causal relations between events or the necessary unity of qualities in an object. But this representation of necessity is not possible through merely contingent associations of ideas (1:9). It can occur only through the inner necessity of a nonempirical representing subject (1:76; D'Iorio 1993, 288).

One way of thinking of the inability of psychological associations to bring about thought is that such associations merely concern the temporal *flow* of representations in empirical consciousness. They explain, for example, why my thoughts move from the striking of a match to its lighting or from a beer keg to a gold bar to a dumbbell. But for me to *think* that the striking of a match causes its lighting or that a beer keg is heavy is for me to unify representations in a manner that stands above this temporal flow. It is only in this way that these ideas can be unified in the *same mind* rather than simply blindly following one another: "The actual representing, comparing, judging and inferring is therefore necessarily a unity, which embraces a manifold of content and executes all the operations that we find in the understanding. This unity one calls the perceiving and knowing *subject*" (Spir 1877, 1:73). For Spir, the distinguishing characteristics of the Kantian transcendental unity of apperception, which is required for thought, are its *timelessness* and *unity*.

But there is the problem, which we have already encountered in our discussion of Kant, of how this timeless unity of apperception *connects* with the temporal flow of sensations. This is the gap that Kant tries unsuccessfully to bridge through the transcendental schematism. In connection with Kant, I characterized this problem as one of connecting the passivity of sensation with the spontaneity of apperception. Spir generally speaks of the problem as one of connecting the temporality and particularity of sensation with the timelessness and simplicity of apperception. Spir takes this gap so seriously that he denies that it can be bridged at all. Insofar as we *think,* we must be thinking of a world *without any time or particularity*—an atemporal Parmenidean One. The nature of representation is always the same—it is the necessary unity standing outside the temporal flow of consciousness: "It therefore follows that individual representations do not actually exist at all, rather only *individual content,* and that the representations differ from each other only in this content and receive the semblance of individuality" (1:73). That there are *particular* representations, for example, of a tomato as red or of a causal relationship between striking a match and its lighting, is only the "semblance of individuality" created by the existence of a sensory manifold. Thought itself is independent of such particularity.

Spir's account of objectively valid judgment is like that of the German Idealists, in which the sensory element is rejected entirely and all objectively valid judgment becomes a form of self-determination—a unity of knower and known analogous to God's intellectual intuition of objects. But unlike the German Idealists, Spir does not allow for any means by which particularity or temporality can enter into objective valid judgment. As a result, the only objectively valid judgment that is possible is about an atemporal and absolutely simple unity.

For Spir, thought exists in inescapable tension with the world of experience; cognition of experience is contradictory because it is an attempt to force the image of necessary unity onto the temporal flow of sensations. We are thinking about the world only to the extent that we apply the image of unity, and yet in so doing we conceive of a world that contradicts particularity and the flow of time. The idea of the empirical world contains within itself this contradiction between particularity and unity, between time and timelessness. The bulk of *Denken und Wirklichkeit* is devoted to spelling out this contradiction as it manifests itself in various areas of empirical knowledge, and much of what Nietzsche says about the falsity of our judgments—their incompatibility with change and becoming—has strong parallels in Spir's thought.

Thus we should not be surprised to find Spir criticizing Kant precisely where he attempts to link the sensory manifold to the unity of consciousness—in the transcendental schematism (1:13–19). For Kant, the temporal flow of sensations can be *thought*—that is, perceived as a succession rather than simply being a succession of perceptions—only if it is brought into the unity of apperception. The function of bringing the temporal flow within the unity of one consciousness is, according to Kant, the job of the transcendental synthesis of the imagination, and the requirements of this synthesis justify the synthetic a priori truths that every event has a cause and that there are enduring substances in the world. The creation of causal connections and enduring substances is the means by which the temporal manifold becomes a conscious unity.

I have already noted the difficulty of understanding how the spontaneity of apperception can connect with the passivity of sensation. Spir generally emphasizes the related difficulty of how a temporal flow can be related to an atemporal consciousness. His treatment of this problem was of such importance to Nietzsche that a substantial portion of *Philosophy in the Tragic Age of the Greeks* is devoted to the topic.

The problem can be put in the following fashion: Is time objectively real, in the sense that it exists independently of its being represented within a timeless consciousness? If so, then there will be a problem connecting time to the unity of apperception. Perhaps the strongest reason to think that time is objectively real is that our thoughts themselves appear to us as a succession that is only subsequently (if ever) taken up into apperceptive consciousness. As Nietzsche puts it in *Philosophy in the Tragic Age of the Greeks:* "If thinking in concepts, on the part of reason, is real, then the many and motion must partake of reality also, for reasoned thinking is mobile" (13).

According to Spir, Kant nevertheless endeavors to deny the objective reality of time. Kant insists that time exists only insofar as it is represented to a timeless consciousness. Kant offers this response in the *Critique of Pure Reason* when he argues that the succession of thoughts in the mind are merely thoughts *as represented* in the inner sense (1965, B54/A37). Nietzsche provides his own gloss on the passage: "What has to be distinguished here is pure thinking, which is timeless like the one being of Parmenides, and our consciousness of this thinking. The latter comes already translated into the forms of semblance, i.e., into succession, multiplicity and motion" (*PTG* 15). Or as Spir puts it, "The succession of representations can in no way be differentiated from the representation of succession" (1877, 1:209). In other words, the experience of a temporal flow of thoughts is always already an experience of these thoughts *as represented to a timeless consciousness.* For this reason the objective validity of my thoughts is not undermined by the fact that my thoughts appear to flow in time.

But, in a long passage quoted by Nietzsche in *Philosophy in the Tragic Age of the Greeks* (15), Spir argues that Kant's approach fails and that time *must* be thought of as objectively real:

> The main question is this: how can the beginning and the end of conscious life itself, together with all its inward and outward senses, exist only in the interpretation of the inward sense? The actual fact is that one absolutely cannot deny the reality of change. If you throw it out the window it will slip back in through the keyhole. One can say "it merely seems to me that ideas and conditions change," but this semblance itself is something objectively given. Within it, succession indubitably has objective reality; within it something actually follows upon something else. . . . Besides, it is necessary to note that the entire

critique of reason can have its foundation and justification only in the presupposition that our *ideas* appear to us as they are. For if they appeared to us as other than they really are, one could not make any valid assertions about them, hence produce no epistemology and no "transcendental" examination of objective validity. And it is beyond all doubt that our ideas appear to us as successive. (1873, 1:264–65)[10]

Although one can quibble with some of the details of Spir's interpretation of Kant, the essential point is a penetrating one: It is impossible to think of the flow of time solely as something represented to a timeless consciousness, for the very fact that ideas *appear* to be occurring over time requires that something happens over time. Even if one argues that the temporal flow of consciousness exists only as representation, these representations themselves must occur in time. If you throw becoming out the window, it will come back through the keyhole.

Indeed, Kant *must* assume that this temporal flow is something real that is given to us prior to its being represented in a unified consciousness. Otherwise there is nothing that needs to be *brought into* the unity of consciousness, and so no transcendental synthesis of the imagination and no synthetic a priori truths. And because what the transcendental synthesis works upon is *in time,* one cannot imagine it as anything but a *temporal process,* something happening in time. But, so understood, it is impossible to see how this process can be hooked up to something, like the apperceptive self, that stands outside time.[11]

5. Spir and Nietzsche

In Spir's thought there is an intimate connection between the epistemological problem of the possibility of objectively valid judgment and the metaphysical problem of the reality of becoming—a connection that was well known to Nietzsche. Becoming—the occurrence of events in time—is incompatible with the truth or falsity of our judgments. This might lead one to deny that becoming is objectively real, but Spir insists that the reality of time cannot be denied. The final inescapable argument for the existence of time is the succession of our own thoughts and sensations—the fact that our mental life itself becomes. For this reason, Spir argues that human knowledge has within itself a "fundamental antinomy" (1877, 1:377). It has elements of being and becoming, but the two cannot be bridged.

Spir's discussion of the problem of becoming allowed Nietzsche to link the two philosophical traditions with which he was most familiar: Neo-Kantianism and the pre-Socratics. According to Nietzsche, the Eleatics, such as Parmenides and Democritus, were motivated by a Kantian antinaturalist conception of judgment: "The Eleatics, in order to ascribe to themselves the position of possessing the truth, rather than natural errors . . . had to attribute to themselves, fictitiously, impersonality and changeless duration, they had to misapprehend the nature of the knower; they had to deny the role of impulses in knowledge; and quite generally they had to conceive of reason as a completely free and spontaneous activity" (*GS* 110). As a result, they were compelled to deny the reality of becoming. As Nietzsche, spelling out Parmenides's philosophy, puts it: "In thought there is no movement: a motionless perception of being. To the extent that thought moves and comes to pass out of other things, it is no longer being, but appearance" (*KSA* 7:23[12]).

Against this Parmenidean "identity of thinking and being" (*PTG* 12), Nietzsche offers an ontology of becoming. For Nietzsche, as for Spir, the final inescapable argument in favor of the reality of becoming is the fact that thoughts themselves become: "Reasoned thinking is mobile. It moves from concept to concept. . . . Against this, no objection can be made; it is quite impossible to designate thinking as a rigid persistence, as an eternally unmoved thinking-in-and-on-itself on the part of a unity" (*PTG* 13). One cannot think of becoming as existing only *as thought* by a timeless being, for this thinking of becoming would still have to be in time.

This argument does not only occur in Nietzsche's early thought. He often returns to the fact that thought moves to argue for the reality of becoming (*HA* 2; *KSA* 7:23[12 and 39], 9:11[292]; *WP* 1062).[12] When Nietzsche argues that the sensations provide us with evidence of change and becoming, he is making the same argument. Consider the following passage from *Twilight of the Idols,* which I discussed in the previous chapter: "It is what we *make* of [the evidence of the senses] that first introduces a lie into it, for example the lie of unity, the lie of materiality, of substance, of duration. . . . 'Reason' is the cause of our falsification of the evidence of the senses. In so far as the senses show becoming, passing away, change, they do not lie" (*TI* 3:2). In reading Nietzsche's praise of the senses and becoming as the expression of an unproblematic empiricism that merely seeks to deny the possibility of a priori metaphysics, Maudemarie Clark and Brian Leiter radically underestimate what Nietzsche believes are the costs of claiming that the world is becoming. Nietzsche's appeal to sensation to show that becoming exists is part of a sophisticated argument against the *possibility of objectively valid judgment.*

Thus Nietzsche's rejection of a real world of "being" in favor of a contingent world of "becoming" is less a claim about what the world is like than a claim about our cognitive relation to the world.[13] It means questioning our ability to make objectively valid judgments about the world at all, despite Nietzsche's tendency to put the point in ways that suggest that it is itself an objectively valid judgment that the world becomes:

> [Philosophers] will not learn that man has become, that the faculty of cognition has become. . . . The philosopher here sees "instincts" in man as he now is and assumes that these belong to the unalterable facts of mankind and to that extent could provide a key to the understanding of the world in general: the whole teleology is constructed by speaking of the man of the last four millennia as of an *eternal* man towards whom all things in the world have had a natural relationship from the time he began. But everything has become: there are *no eternal facts,* just as there are no absolute truths. (*HA* 2)

Nietzsche's denial of "eternal facts" or "absolute truths" suggests that his main point is the rather trivial one that nothing in the world is permanent, as if he could make objectively valid judgments about change. But his real point is that the reasons we come to our judgments are not permanent. Since they are merely contingent, our judgments lose their objective validity and so their ability to be true: "Knowledge is possible only on the basis of belief in being" (*WP* 518). In contrast, "a world in a state of becoming could not, in a strict sense, be 'comprehended' or 'known'" (*WP* 520).

Despite Nietzsche's radically naturalistic approach to human judgment, he nevertheless accepts Kantian and Spirean antinaturalism by arguing that cognition presupposes *being,* that is to say, timeless objects and timeless subjects of knowledge (*WP* 517–19). The argument that the presupposed beings are modeled after pure subjects of knowledge can be found everywhere in Nietzsche: "It is [reason] . . . which believes in the 'ego,' in the ego as being, in the ego as substance, and which *projects* its belief in the ego-substance on to all things—only thus does it *create* the concept 'thing'" (*TI* 3:5). "Must all philosophy not ultimately bring to light the precondition upon which the process of reason depends?—our belief in the 'ego' as substance, as the sole reality from which we ascribe reality to things in general? . . . Here we come to a limit: our thinking itself involves this belief; . . . to let it go means: being no longer able to think" (*WP* 487).

Spir was an attractive figure for Nietzsche because Spir provided him with a clear articulation of what he was for and what he was against. In denying any possible connection between the world of becoming and the world of being, Spir provided Nietzsche with some of his best arguments in favor of the reality of becoming. In insisting on the existence of timeless subjects of knowledge, however, Spir provided Nietzsche with a Kantian/Parmenidean vision of cognition that Nietzsche claims could never be realized.

6. Nietzsche's Critique of Platonism

Because he is well aware of Kant's argument that naturalism threatens the possibility of objectively valid judgment and that Kant's solution is to reject naturalistic accounts of human cognition, Nietzsche tends to lump Kant with Plato, despite the significant differences between these two thinkers (*WP* 412, 428). For Plato, like Kant, argues against naturalistic accounts of thought.

An example of Plato's antinaturalism is his famous argument for recollection (1961, *Meno* 80d–86c).[14] One way of reading Plato's argument is that we must recollect true judgments rather than be taught them because we cannot *teach* someone to apply a concept in an objectively valid fashion. If we are *taught* to judge that two and two are four, such teaching must involve giving us reasons to make the judgment other than the fact that two and two are four. For if our reason were solely that two and two are four, one should have had this reason before one was taught, for two and two equaled four before one was taught. Teaching is an event *in time* and so can provide only new dispositions to judge. The satisfaction of these dispositions must be the reason those taught judge as they do. But the satisfaction of contingent dispositions is not thought. Thought cannot occur in becoming: "If all things are in change, any answer that can be given to any question is equally right; you may say it is so and it is not" (*Theaet.* 183a). As Plato puts it in the *Cratylus:*

> We cannot reasonably say . . . that there is knowledge at all, if everything is in a state of transition and there is nothing abiding. For knowledge too cannot continue to be knowledge unless continuing always to abide and exist. But if the very nature of knowledge changes, at the time when the change occurs there will be no knowledge, and if the transition is always going on, there will always be no knowledge, and, according to this view [that reality is becoming], there will be no one to know and nothing to be known. (440a–b)

Plato solves this problem through his doctrine of recollection. Because we have an eternal soul that has always made true judgments and needs only to recollect them, we do not have to explain why we judge through an appeal to the satisfaction of our contingent dispositions.

Kantian antinaturalism is also the reason that the relationship between our thoughts and their objects must be nonsensory intellectual intuition for Plato. If our thought of something is brought about through causal relations between it and us via the senses, then what brings us to judge something will always involve more than the way it is. For the way it is would never be sufficient to get us to think of it. Objectively valid judgments about the world cannot proceed through contingent causal chains, since such contingency will always unhook thought from object (see *Tim.* 27d–28a). But, having emphasized that our faculty of judgment cannot occur in the contingent world and that the relationship between our judgment and its object cannot be contingent, Plato concludes that what we judge cannot be contingent as well. For uncontingent judgments could never be necessarily related to something contingent. All truths must be necessary truths.

That Nietzsche reads Plato in a Kantian and Spirean fashion is evident in his notebooks as well (e.g. *KSA* 7:6[14], 7:7[156]). "Plato: first a Heraclitean, consequently a skeptic, everything, including thought, is Flux. Through Socrates he is brought to the eternity of the good, beautiful. These are taken as being" (*KSA* 7:23[27]). Nietzsche lumps Plato and Kant together because both deny naturalistic accounts of human judgment. So it is understandable why Nietzsche should often make Kant sound as if he, like Plato, thinks that the only truths are necessary truths (*WP* 530). Kant is taken by Nietzsche to hold the view that objectively valid judgments must involve the exercise of a non-natural faculty to arrive at necessary truths about a non-sensible "real world" of "being."

7. Reason and Desire

Nietzsche accepts the Kantian antinaturalist theory of cognition but refuses to reject naturalism. As a result he argues against the objective validity of our judgments. Our judgments cannot have objective validity because when we arrive at them we are always sensitive to something other than the apparent objects of the judgments. Nietzsche often argues that we are sensitive to pragmatic considerations when judging (*WP* 423, 474). But he offers other naturalistic explanations of human judgment as well (e.g. *KSA* 11:26[114], 12:5[19]). "*What is truth?*—Inertia; that hypothesis which gives rise to contentment; the smallest expenditure of spiritual force, etc." (*WP* 537). "'True' from the standpoint of feeling—: that which excites the feeling most strongly ('ego'); from the standpoint of thought—: that which gives thought the greatest feeling of strength; from the standpoint of touch, seeing, hearing—: that which calls for the greatest resistance" (*WP* 534).

We have already seen that Nietzsche frequently argues that judgments are evaluative (*WP* 507) and that "all experiences are moral experiences, even in the realm of sense perception" (*GS* 114). These passages can likewise be made sense of in terms of his naturalization of judgment. As we saw in chapter 1, section 6, the fact that human judgment is affectively motivated—in the sense that we choose, on the basis of our practical interests, where to direct our inquiry—could not generate any interesting epistemological conclusions. That we know only what we need to know does not undermine the idea that we nevertheless *know.* But if the very act of uniting objects under a concept were understood as affective—if such uniting were simply the satisfaction of a desire or tendency to associate, the way Hume sees causal judgments as the satisfaction of desires or dispositions—then it makes sense that Nietzsche thinks that the affectivity of cognition has radical epistemological consequences. For the affectivity of judgment in *this* sense undermines its objective validity.

Because Nietzsche identifies conceptualization with the satisfaction of dispositions to associate, it also makes sense that he would identify reason with desire (*GS* 333). Reason is merely desire that is ordered and structured in a certain fashion, "a system of relations between various passions and desires" (*WP* 387).

8. Naturalism and the Law of Noncontradiction

Nietzsche's comments concerning logic provide further support for a Neo-Kantian reading of his epistemologies. As we have already seen in chapter 1, Nietzsche's comments concerning logic pose one of the most serious obstacles to making sense of the error theory. One problem, which we shall discuss in the next chapter, is why Nietzsche thinks that logic requires the existence of self-identical substances. At this point I will be concerned with another aspect of Nietzsche's discussion of logic, namely his questioning the validity of the law of noncontradiction.

Nietzsche's views on logic have not been much explored in the literature.[15] The fact that he questions the validity of logic has generally been discussed only by those who argue that his philosophy itself must be understood independently of logic (e.g. Haar 1977, 6–7). But this approach ignores the fact that Nietzsche praises logical form in reasoning (*HA* 265) and that he provides, or at least attempts to provide, logically consistent, if extremely compressed, arguments for his conclusions. To argue from Nietzsche's critique of logic to the position that his philosophical arguments themselves are logically unconstrained is to take a controversial stand concerning what I have called "the self-reference problem"—the status of Nietzsche's epistemological pronouncements within the context of his epistemology itself. We shall deal with this problem later. For the time being, if an interpretation of Nietzsche's critique of logic can be framed within logic, it should be, since Nietzsche's arguments themselves invite such a formulation.

Nietzsche does not argue that the principle of noncontradiction should be abandoned. He does, however, argue that an acceptance of the principle is not demanded by the nature of the world. It is instead a consequence of a merely psychological disinclination to contradict (e.g. *KSA* 7:7[110]; *WP* 535). "The subjective compulsion not to contradict here is a biological compulsion: the instinct for the utility of inferring as we do infer is part of us, we almost *are* this instinct—But what naiveté to extract from this a proof that we are therewith in possession of a 'truth in itself'!—Not being able to contradict is proof of an incapacity, not of 'truth'" (*WP* 515). "We are unable to affirm and deny one and the same thing: this is a subjective empirical law, not the expression of any 'necessity' but only of an inability" (*WP* 516).

But isn't the principle of noncontradiction demanded by the world? Isn't it *impossible* for something in the world to be both square and not square?

Our attachment to the principle of noncontradiction is intimately tied to a belief in our ability to form concepts. And once this assumption is rejected, a denial of the principle is far less disturbing. Consider a meaningless word, such as "frob," around which one has developed certain associative tendencies. Because one's use of "frob" is not rule-governed, there is no reason not to say that something is both frob and not-frob *except* one's psychological disinclination to do so. If one were to ignore this disinclination and say that something is both frob and not-frob, one will have done no injustice either to reality or to one's concepts.

Because Nietzsche denies the objective validity of all judgments, he denies that anything but our subjective dispositions stands in the way of contradiction. The law of noncontradiction can be demanded by the world only if we are able to form concepts:[16] "The conceptual ban on contradiction proceeds from the belief that we are able to form concepts" (*WP* 516). It is only because we believe that our judgments have objective validity that we think that the nature of things themselves demands that we not contradict (see *KSA* 9:6[124]; *WP* 516).

Nietzsche's views concerning the principle of noncontradiction are worth emphasizing because they are incompatible with most interpretations of his epistemology by philosophers in the analytic tradition. The majority of these commentators believe that Nietzsche is not so radical a thinker as to have rejected our ability to conceptualize. Nietzsche does not reject thought, but only metaphysical or transcendent knowledge of things-in-themselves. Consider Maudemarie Clark, who takes Nietzsche to hold that our judgments can be true or false not with respect to things-in-themselves but according to our "best standards of rational acceptability" (1990, 50), which our current theories about the world can fail to meet. Nietzsche's critique of the principle of noncontradiction does not make sense under such an interpretation, for if there is anything that violates our best standards of rational acceptability, it is contradictions.

Another example is Brian Leiter's discussion of Nietzsche's "perspectivism." Leiter accepts that Nietzsche abandons metaphysical realism (1994, 343–51), but he rejects what he calls the "Received View" of Nietzsche's epistemology, under which "no perspective can enjoy an *epistemic* privilege over any other" (334): "The *epistemic* merits of a view are those bearing on its claim to count as knowledge; at a bare minimum, then, an epistemically privileged view must be capable of being true or false. Truth carries an implicit requirement of objectivity: what counts as being the case (as true) must be independent of our predilections" (336). If this is Nietzsche's considered view, then he should reject contradictions. He doesn't.

9. Conclusion

My goal in this chapter has been to make clear that the Kantian argument that conceptualization is incompatible with naturalism is an important theme running through Nietzsche's epistemological reflections. Given his commitment to naturalism, one would think that he would conclude that thought is impossible. I will argue in chapter 4 that he does indeed come to this conclusion at times. Nevertheless, he often argues instead that cognition falsifies the world. It is this idea that we will address in the next chapter.

3. Nietzsche's "Error Theory" Explained

1. The Interpretive Problem

WHAT WE KNOW about the error theory so far is the following: It is a comprehensive attack on the very idea of conceptualization, applicable not merely to judgments about external objects but also to mathematics, logic, and judgments about inner experience. It claims that all these judgments falsify because they apply erroneous concepts such as substance and cause, concepts that are in some way dependent upon the model of the ego. Finally, the fact that the world is becoming, which is evident from the testimony of the senses, is important to showing that these concepts falsify.

How far have we come in explaining the theory? We know that Nietzsche thinks that objectively valid judgment is incompatible with the becoming and change that present themselves through the senses. But we would then expect him to claim that we fail to cognize at all. As we shall see in chapter 4, sometimes he does. But why does he also say that cognition *falsifies*? To the extent that our judgments can be false, they must have objective validity. But if they have objective validity, it seems, thought is not incompatible with becoming after all.

I believe that Nietzsche's error theory can be reconciled with his noncognitivism. Let me begin with an analogy in the realm of meta-ethics. We have already been exposed to John L. Mackie's error theory of ethical language.[1] Under this theory, ethical language is cognitive, in the sense that it describes states of affairs in the world, but false, because these states of affairs cannot exist. Mackie does not have to argue that ethical sentences are false by showing that the ethical qualities in things are always different from the way our evaluative sentences describe them. Instead he argues that ethical qualities are *inherently contradictory* because they are independently existing qualities that somehow necessitate or make appropriate affective states in those who perceive them.

Let us imagine a philosopher who alternates between the view that ethical judgments lack a truth-value and the view that they are false—that is, someone who vacillates between noncognitivism and an error theory. Although such a philosopher might be seen as lacking philosophical precision, these positions need not be fundamentally contradictory. It need not be an essential element of the error theory that ethical judgments have a truth-value. It *might* be that the philosopher is driven to an error theory because of a commitment to the existence of ethical cognition. But the error theory might instead be motivated simply by a recognition of the contradictory nature of ethical qualities. When concentrating on the nature of these qualities, the philosopher is motivated to be an error theorist. When concentrating on ethical judgments themselves, the philosopher tends toward noncognitivism.

Nietzsche's error theory is similar to Mackie's because Nietzsche is motivated to say that our judgments about the world are false because of the *contradictory* nature of empirical objects. He does not have to argue that our beliefs are false by demonstrating an inadequacy between our thoughts about objects and the objects themselves. (It will be remembered from chapter 1 that any attempt at such a demonstration would undermine the error theory's comprehensiveness.) For this reason, Nietzsche's error theory can complement his fundamental critique of the possibility of thought.

But *why* are empirical objects contradictory? Once again, Afrikan Spir's influence on Nietzsche's thought provides us with an answer. Spir relies a great deal on Kant's antinomies of pure reason (Kant 1965, A405–567/B432–595) to argue that empirical objects contain irreconcilable elements of both being and becoming. The lesson that Kant himself draws from the antinomies is that the empirical world is transcendentally ideal. The antinomies are generated by the assumption that we have knowledge of things-in-themselves. For Spir, empirical knowledge cannot be saved by Kantian transcendental idealism because, as we have seen from chapter 2, Kant fails to explain how we can arrive at objectively valid judgment through the senses. Kant cannot connect the multiplicity and temporal flow of sensations to the unity and timelessness of thought. Because becoming and being cannot be reconciled, objects within space and time, which are themselves a union of being and becoming, are internally contradictory. The only knowledge that is possible is of being—that is, an absolute unconditional Parmenidean One.

This chapter is devoted to making sense of Nietzsche's error theory by outlining its strong analogies with Spir's thought. Nietzsche, like Spir, claims that concepts of being—including the idea of a self-identical object—are both necessary for cognition and incompatible with the becoming that is evident through our sensations. For this reason, Nietzsche argues that the objects of empirical knowledge are contradictory.

Spir's solution to the antinomies is to concede that empirical knowledge is inherently false and to argue that the only true knowledge is of a timeless world of being, knowledge that consists solely of the pure logical principles of self-identity and noncontradiction. Nietzsche accepts the first but not the second part of Spir's approach. Empirical knowledge is false, but we have no alternative knowledge of being. To the extent that we think at all, what we think must be false: "Parmenides said, 'One cannot think of what is not';—we are at the other end of the extreme, and say, 'What can be thought must certainly be a fiction'" (*WP* 539).

2. Diachronic and Synchronic Self-Identity

As we have seen, an important unifying thread in Nietzsche's error theory is the idea that thought distorts the world by assuming that it consists of *self-identical* objects. Although Nietzsche presents this idea repeatedly—both in his published works (*HA* 11, 18–19; *BGE* 4; *TI* 3:5) and in his Nachlaß (*KSA* 9:11[329–30]; *WP* 516, 521, 552, 574)—it has not been given much attention by commentators. To the extent that the idea has been addressed, it has generally been assumed that Nietzsche rejects *diachronically* self-identical objects, that is, objects that are identical to themselves over time, as opposed to *synchronically* self-identical objects, that is, objects that are self-identical at the very same moment in time.[2] An example is Maudemarie Clark, who reads Nietzsche as rejecting a metaphysical world of *eternal* substances only (1990, 104–9). For Clark, Nietzsche's denial that reality is self-identical is compatible with standard empirical and scientific knowledge.

One motivation for Clark's interpretation is undoubtedly the difficulty of getting one's mind around what it would be like for reality to fail to be synchronically self-identical. To claim that something is not the same as itself at the same moment in time means rejecting not merely the law of self-identity but the law of noncontradiction, and, as we have seen, commentators have preferred to read away any evidence that Nietzsche questions the law of noncontradiction.

The first piece of evidence that Nietzsche's main target is synchronic self-identity is that he links his rejection of self-identical substances with a rejection of the logical principle of self-identity (*KSA* 8:9[1, p. 136], 12:7[4, p. 266]; *WP* 520). To read Nietzsche as rejecting merely diachronic self-identity is to conclude that he is confused about one of the simplest and most rudimentary logical principles, for the logical principle of self-identity concerns synchronic self-identity only. It says nothing about whether an object is the same thing over time. Nor can one argue that Nietzsche means something else by "law of self-identity," for he makes it clear that his target is one of "the basic laws of logic" (*WP* 530).

The second piece of evidence is Nietzsche's frequent claims that reality is *contradictory* (e.g. *PTG* 15; *KSA* 7:19[239], 9:21[3.53]).[3] "The character of the world in a state of becoming as incapable of formulation, as 'false,' as 'self contradictory.' Knowledge and becoming exclude one another" (*WP* 517). Once again, the idea that reality is contradictory must be a claim about a lack of synchronic self-identity. For nothing about an object changing *over time* is incompatible with the law of noncontradiction.

3. Spir on Self-Identity

Why then does Nietzsche deny that reality is self-identical? Once again, Spir can provide the answer. The influence of Spir on Nietzsche in this area is evident not merely in striking similarities in language and philosophical theme. When Nietzsche spells out the self-identical objects whose existence he is rejecting (*HA* 18), he quotes Spir (1877, 2:177).

Contrary to the philosophical tradition, the principle that everything is identical with itself is, for Spir, a *synthetic* rather than an analytic proposition. "The concept of the real or the actual and that of the selfsame [*Sichselbstgleichen*] or the self-identical [*Mitsichidentischen*] are . . . not one and the same, but instead two different concepts" (1:164). Analogously, the principle of noncontradiction is synthetic for Spir; it is something that reality could fail to satisfy (1:168–70). To say that something cannot be both square and not square is to make a substantive claim about the world.

But what would it mean for the world not to have self-identical things? Spir characterizes a world that would violate the law of self-identity, in language virtually identical to Nietzsche's,[4] as a world of "unending flux or change" [*unaufhörlichen Fluss oder Wechsel*] (1:164). This suggests that what is at issue is whether things change over time, not whether things are different from themselves at the same point in time. But Spir leaves no doubt that he means a lack of self-identity at the same moment in time. If experience were to "completely conform" to the law of self-identity, then "the entire content of experience could be and would have to be described only in identical and not in synthetic sentences. The only thing that one could say of an object would be this: 'A is A' and 'A is not B,' but never 'A is B'" (1:166). But the character of experienced objects at any moment in time is that they cannot be fully described in such identical sentences. As Spir puts it in a passage that Nietzsche paraphrases in his Nachlaß:

> Now we definitely encounter many things whose essence cannot be described through the sentence "A is A." For example, what representation would someone have of the essence of a pencil if one said to him: A pencil is a pencil? Obviously none. In order to describe a pencil, one must say something like— A pencil is an extended thing, long, thin, cylindrical, colored, hard, heavy, etc. Thus here we see in a unity (in the pencil) an entire collection of qualities encompassed or embraced that are different from one another. The unity of the different is generally called *synthesis*. . . . The general formula of synthetic sentences, the general expression of a synthesis is the sentence: "A is B." (1869, 13)[5]

Experience of objects does not, therefore, fully conform to the law of self-identity. This is because experience shows that things possess plurality, and "the absence of inner differences in a thing is another way of putting *identity* of this thing *with itself*" (1877, 1:190; see also 1869, 10). The objects of experience show themselves to be *contradictory* in the sense that they are unconditioned and immediate unities of different qualities (1877, 1:174–75, 179, 190). To claim that hardness and cylindricality are both qualities of the pencil, Spir argues, is to claim that hardness and cylindricality are one and the same, which is a contradiction (1:179). For Spir, every synthetic judgment is in conflict with the laws of self-identity and noncontradiction (1:166).[6]

At this point, Spir's argument might sound implausible. What could possibly be wrong with judgments like "the pencil is hard and cylindrical at the same time"? One way of seeing why such synthetic judgments are problematic is to consider how they could be accomplished, given the Spirean theory of judgment. As we have seen in chapter 2, the necessary unity through which thought is possible cannot bring together the temporal flow of representations. But judging a pencil to be both hard and cylindrical involves unifying this temporal flow, insofar as it involves bringing the representations of hardness and cylindricality together in the same mind. Anytime we make a synthetic judgment, we must bring a multiplicity together into the same consciousness (1:106–7).[7] The laws of self-identity and noncontradiction ("A is A" and "A is not B") are of such importance for Spir because they express the purity and lack of particularity in thought itself. They designate the "concept of the true unconditioned essence of a thing" (1:153).

Thus, for Spir, thinking of an empirical object involves the equation of the unequal in violation of the laws of noncontradiction and self-identity. Insofar as an empirical object is *thought* it is a simple unconditional unity. Insofar as it is *sensed* it has plurality. To think of the plural as simple is to treat differences as if they were the same: "If we conceive of an unconditioned object *A,* whose essence consists of two qualities *a* and *b,* then *A* is just as much *a* as *b.* . . . But because *a* and *b* are different from one another, so it would follow that the object *A,* insofar as it is the quality *a,* is different from itself, insofar as it is the quality *b*" (1:190).

Spir, like Nietzsche, also describes the unconditioned essence of a thing as *diachronically* self-identical. But this should not be surprising. The only synchronically self-identical object is one that has no particularity. But such a simple substance has no possibility for change and therefore will also be diachronically self-identical. Nevertheless, the heart of both Spir's and Nietzsche's argument is that experience violates synchronic self-identity.

4. The "Fundamental Antinomy"

So far, we have only an argument that the multiplicity in a substance cannot be *thought.* Synthetic judgments must be accomplished through the aid of empirical associations, which, as we have seen, are not thought (Spir 1877, 1:83). But what reason is there to believe that we *err?* Shouldn't Spir have said instead that we can think only about simple, unconditioned unity, but that when we do so our thoughts are true?

Spir admits that "if the function of thought were determined only though logical laws, falsehood in cognition could not occur" (1:107). He recognizes that it is a significant problem for his theory that error is possible (1:81–89). But he argues that error occurs because thought about multiplicity, rather than being only empirical association, "stands under the influence of two sorts of laws"—the empirical laws of association *and* logical laws (1:107). Thus, rather than failing to be thought, our beliefs about multiplicity are false.

Spir's argument is not persuasive. The question remains how these contingent laws of association *connect* with the pure being of thought. Spir appears to assume precisely the connection between thought and sensation that he argues Kant fails to establish in the transcendental schematism.

The difficulty Spir finds in explaining error is remarkably similar to Kant's difficulty explaining the possibility of evil. It seems to follow from Kant's ethics that one behaves freely and so is morally responsible for one's actions to the extent that one acts on the basis of the moral law. For it is precisely in acting so as to conform to the moral law that one's actions can be conceived of as standing outside of the causal nexus and so as free. Thus if we diverge from the moral law, it would appear that this is the result of causal influences upon us, which would make us not responsible for our actions. Responsible agency that violates the moral law—that is to say, evil—appears to be impossible.[8] By analogy, one can argue that, for Spir, we are thinking only to the extent that our thoughts are of an unconditioned unity. If we deviate from this unconditioned unity and admit plurality, we do not err—we simply fail to think.

Is there any other argument in Spir for our ability to think about plurality? In the end, his most important evidence is the fact that we can draw out of the *empirical objects themselves* the contradiction that results from their partaking of both being and becoming, thought and sensation. I will argue that it is this contradictory nature of empirical objects that motivates Nietzsche to present an error theory as well.

But why are empirical objects contradictory? The short answer is that, for Spir, empirical objects are both conditional and unconditional unities at the same time. The short answer needs to be expanded, however, because it remains unclear why a substance must be a unity of qualities that is unconditional. Spir himself recognizes that there is no contradiction in the idea of a merely conditional unity of different qualities (e.g. 1:179–80). "A *conditional* unity of different qualities in an object is not a difference of this object from itself, i.e. not the contradictory antithesis of the principle of identity" (1:191).

So why is it that we must think of objects as unconditional unities? We do not appear to think of a pencil as *necessarily* hard. The pencil, it seems, *could* have been soft. It is hard for a conditional reason, that is, for a reason that could have failed to be the case.

Spir's argument that objects must be unconditional unities derives in large measure from arguments in Kant's antinomies of pure reason. Under the first antinomy, for example, sound arguments are presented in favor of time and space being substances within which the world occurs (the Newtonian or thesis position) and in favor of their being exhausted by the relations between objects (the Leibnizean or antithesis position) (Kant 1965, A426–34/B454–62). One way of putting the argument for the thesis position is that if time and space were not independent substances, there would be no sense to the question of *where* or *when* the world—understood as the totality of relations between things—occurs. But there must be an answer to these questions. Empirical objects demand an answer—they always demand a metric with respect to which their spatial and temporal dimensions may be determined. For example, my height is determinable by reference to a ruler, which is itself determinable with respect to the standard meter bar in Paris, and so on. But these spatial determinations would be completely *indeterminate* without the *totality* of relations also having a metric in unconditioned space, that is, in a space that has its character absolutely rather than merely in relation to other things.

Analogous arguments can be drawn up concerning substances. Everything about a substance appears conditioned. Consider Spir's example of a pencil. It is conditioned causally in the sense that it has these qualities due to its manufacturer. It is conditioned by virtue of its being constituted by parts. It is conditioned by virtue of its underlying molecular structure. With respect to each condition, a further condition for that condition must exist. If one claims that the hardness and cylindricality of the pencil are a unity because the pencil was made that way by a machine, one can ask why the *machine* made the pencil that way. If one answers that the manufacturers who made the machine are responsible, one can ask why the manufacturers are such that they made the machine that way, and so on. Analogously, if one claims that the pencil is both hard and cylindrical by virtue of its molecular structure, one can ask why the molecular structure is that way, which means appealing to atomic and then subatomic structure.

So what's wrong with simply accepting that the world is *infinitely* conditioned in this fashion, which would mean adopting the antithesis position as the correct description of reality? One way of putting the problem is that if one characterizes the world as infinitely conditioned, then there are an infinite number of possible collections of substances. Consider someone who treats the hardness of the Eiffel Tower and the shape of a pencil as one object and the hardness of a pencil and the shape of the Eiffel Tower as another object. Both objects could themselves be conditionally supported by two separate sets of Eiffel Tower/pencil molecule amalgamations, which in turn could be supported by Eiffel Tower/pencil atom amalgamations, and so on down the line of conditions. If the possibility of finding a condition is all that is required for a substance, then our two Eiffel Tower/pencil gerrymandered substances are as respectable as the Eiffel Tower and a pencil. The only way of excluding potentially arbitrary unification of qualities as substances is to assume that an unconditional unification can be found, that is, by adopting the thesis position. This unconditional unification is a substance.

Spir argues that empirical objects, by their very nature, refer to unconditioned substances such as atoms or a Spinozistic God (1877, 1:281, 295). Without these substances there would be no objective connections between qualities in the world. The concept of such unconditional unities is latent within the nature of the empirical world, in the fact that every object demands a condition for why its qualities are united (2:75). This tendency of objects to refer to the unconditioned is the objective correlate of the fact that our thoughts about objects must be unconditioned unities.

I will not spend time in this essay examining whether the arguments for the thesis (or the antithesis) position in the antinomies are, in fact, sound.

But it should be noted that the most forceful critiques of the thesis position emphasize that it is insufficiently *ontological* in nature because it appears to rely upon the impossibility of *thinking* of the world as an infinite chain of conditions rather than the impossibility of the existence of such an infinite chain. As Norman Kemp Smith puts it, "From the subjective impossibility of apprehension [Kant] infers an objective impossibility of existence" (1962, 485). If Spir's argument for the thesis position reduces to the argument that multiplicity cannot be *thought,* then his error theory would be weakened. Rather than saying that empirical objects contain contradictions such that our empirical judgments are always false, he would be able to say only that empirical objects cannot be thought, which would push him toward a non-cognitivist position.

Although Spir argues that empirical objects demand to be conditioned by the unconditioned, he also argues that this demand can never be satisfied. Empirical objects are a multiplicity, and no unconditional unification of multiplicity is possible. A multiplicity will always require something standing outside of itself to determine why it inheres in an object. The only unconditional unity possible is that of something with no particularity at all—an absolute simplicity that Spir associates with things-in-themselves (1877, 1:161, 188). But absolutely simple and unconditioned substances cannot intersect with the multiplicity of the world that they are meant to explain. The unconditioned can never condition the conditioned.

Consider, once again, the Newtonian position concerning absolute space. Absolute space was supposed to determine how big and where things are over and above the size and position of things in relationships to other things. It was supposed to be the measurer of all things that does not itself get measured. But how does absolute space perform this act of determination? The totality of relations are compatible with *any* relationship with absolute space. They could be within a vast expanse or within the head of a pin. They could be slightly to the left in absolute space or slightly to the right. But that means that there is no content to the connection between absolute space and the totality of relations that will determine how big or where the totality is.

The same point can be made concerning the simple substances, or atoms, out of which the thesis position claims the world is constituted.[9] Any unconditioned substance would be absolutely simple and thus could not account for the unity of multiplicity that needs explaining. What explains why multiple qualities inhere in an object is never an unconditioned substance—it is instead always another set of qualities inhering in *another* object. The states of a thing "are not conditioned by the essence of the given thing itself, but rather through the states of other things" (1:285). When we explain why a multiplicity inheres in an object, we do so only by reference to another multiplicity, for example, a multiple object is explained by a multiple part, which is explained by yet another multiple subpart, and so on down the line. This argument that only the conditioned can condition the conditioned is, of course, the argument for the *antithesis* position in Kant's antinomies.

Thus the fact that the empirical world consists of substances that possess multiplicity shows that this world is contradictory. The tension between the conditioned and the unconditioned in empirical objects is the objective correlate of the tension between sensation and thought in the mind.

For Spir, there is a "fundamental antinomy" ["*fundamentale Antinomie*"] in nature (1:377). To the extent that we explain anything, it must be in terms of the unconditioned, but that which we want to explain—multiplicity—is foreign to the unconditioned:

> Here one can grasp the antinomy lying in the essence of the conditioned world with both hands. Thesis and antithesis have within them the same common source. Because the conditioned given character of reality is foreign to its original essence, it must have an external condition. But precisely because it is entirely foreign to reality in itself, it cannot have an external or any other form of condition, because there is nothing outside of reality. Thus the very thing that makes an explanation of the world necessary shows that an explanation is not possible. (1:379–80)

Our thought of objects is inherently contradictory: "We cannot rid ourselves of the illogical character of our knowledge of objects" (2:73).

Spir concludes that, since all knowledge of becoming is contradictory, the only genuine knowledge we have is of the thing-in-itself, which we know through the logical laws of self-identity and noncontradiction: "This fundamental law of thought, which conditions our knowledge of objects and which finds its expression in the principle of identity, is a concept of the true unconditioned essence of a thing. . . . With this law of thought the data of experience clearly fails to correspond—since experience never offers us anything unconditioned—but precisely through this lack of correspondence this law manifests its objective validity" (1:30–31).

In a revealing passage in his notebooks, Nietzsche paraphrases much of Spir's discussion of the fundamental antinomy (Spir 1877, 1:379–80) and then offers his *own* solution (see D'Iorio 1993, 277–83), under which *only* error, and not true knowledge of the self-identical, exists:

> The *antinomy:* "the elements in given reality that are *foreign* to the true essence of the thing cannot be derived from this true essence, and thus *must* have been added to it—but from where? there is nothing outside the true essence of

things—therefore an explanation of the world is just as much necessary as impossible." I untie the knot in this way: the true essence of the world is a *fabrication* of the representing being, without which it would be unable to represent. Those elements in the given reality that are foreign to this fabricated "true essence" . . . are *not* added. But also the representing being, whose existence is tied to the *erroneous* beliefs, must be itself *created* . . . representing *and* the belief in the self-identical and enduring must be created *at the same time*.—My view then is that *everything organic* presupposes representation. (*KSA* 9:11[329])

Nietzsche agrees with Spir that all empirical knowledge is contradictory and therefore false. But he disagrees with Spir about the true nature of reality. Instead of claiming that reality is in its essence simple and unitary, as Spir does, Nietzsche argues that reality is becoming. *This amounts to adopting the antithetic positions in Kant's antinomies as the correct description of reality.* But Nietzsche nevertheless accepts that thinking requires the application of the *thetic* position to the world. Therefore the true nature of reality cannot be correctly described.

To the extent that Nietzsche relies upon antinomial arguments to claim that cognition always falsifies, his error theory does not suffer from the more obvious problems that I spelled out in chapter 1: Nietzsche's argument is sufficiently comprehensive, insofar as it applies to *any* form of conceptualization, and does not rely upon a direct comparison between what we think about reality and the way it really is. The problem with such a comparison, it will be remembered, is that it presupposes an adequate conceptualization of the nature of reality, which undermines the error theory itself. But Nietzsche does not need to compare antithetic reality and our thetic conception of it. Instead he can merely point to the *contradictions* within the very idea of an empirical object to show that cognition falsifies.

Nevertheless, as we shall see, Nietzsche is sometimes motivated to present more detailed accounts of becoming. But if his error theory is correct, such descriptions of becoming, insofar as they involve thought, must employ concepts of being and so must be contradictory.

5. How Is Error *Possible*?

By taking the position that only becoming is real, Nietzsche encounters a problem explaining error that is curiously the complement of Spir's. As we have seen, Spir devotes some energy trying to solve the puzzle of how error is possible (1877, 1:81). Spir's problem is not explaining the possibility of thought but explaining why thought is not always about being. This is analogous to Kant's problem of the possibility of evil—that is, the problem of why responsible action is not always moral action. In a suggestive passage, Nietzsche links the two problems: "If . . . the conditioned world is causally conditioned by the unconditioned world, then freedom to err and incur guilt must also be conditioned by it: and . . . one asks, what for?—The world of appearance, becoming, contradiction, suffering, is therefore willed: what for?" (*WP* 579). Error and guilt are deviations from being. The question for believers in being, such as Kant and Spir, is: How is it that something that is in its essence being wills its own deviation from being? How is that possible?

Nietzsche's proposed solution to this problem is, once again, to reject being and to explain its source in becoming: "The unconditioned is only logically derived out of the conditioned, the way nothingness is derivable from being.—As—'unconditioning' [*unbedingend*]—" (*KSA* 10:7[143]). "Error must be derivable out of the 'actual true essence' of things. . . . The belief in the unconditioned must be derivable from the essence of reality [*Wesen des esse*], out of the general contingency!" (*KSA* 9:11[321]). But because Nietzsche does not accept the existence of a pure timeless subject of thought, *his* problem is explaining how *thought* is possible at all in the world of becoming. Just as Spir has the problem of explaining how becoming can arise out of a world that is in its essence being, so Nietzsche has the problem of explaining how being—both self-identical objects and the subject of knowledge that thinks them—can arise out of a world that is in its essence becoming.

Nietzsche suggests at times that such an explanation is possible:

> For a *subject* to exist at all, something enduring must exist and likewise there must exist a great deal of equality and similarity. . . . Without something enduring there would be no mirror to which a next to and after one another [Neben- und Nacheinander] could present itself: the mirror always presumes something enduring.—But I believe: the subject could arise at the same time that the error of equality arises. (*KSA* 9:11[268])

> In order to think and infer it is necessary to assume beings: logic handles only formulas for what remains the same. That is why this assumption would not be proof of reality: "beings" are part of our perspective. The "ego" as a being (—not affected by becoming and development). . . . The character of the world in a state of becoming as incapable of formulation, as "false," as "self contradictory." Knowledge and becoming exclude one another. Consequently, "knowledge" must be something else: there must first of all be a will to make knowable, a kind of becoming must itself create the deception of beings. (*WP* 517)

But it is unclear how becoming can "create the deception of beings." If the subject is merely something relatively enduring, and not timeless, then how, given Nietzsche's Kantian account of the requirements for thought, is it capable of even these *erroneous* thoughts of being? Of course, if Nietzsche were to give up his commitment to the Kantian argument that thought requires a non-natural subject, then such a self would be capable of erroneous thoughts. But if so, then Nietzsche would have also lost the heart of his argument that cognition must falsify. Cognition must falsify because it takes up the multiplicity and change of becoming into the timeless simplicity of thought. But if thought can occur in becoming, then there is no reason to think that cognition must be timeless.

Thus Nietzsche's error theory remains inconsistent. It appears to be predicated upon an antinaturalist theory of cognition, which, given Nietzsche's rigorous naturalism, will not allow cognition to exist at all—even erroneous cognition. Two solutions to this problem seem possible. The first is to bite the bullet and deny that cognition occurs. This is the noncognitivist approach that I believe has been ignored by past interpreters of Nietzsche's thought. The second is to allow that thought within becoming is possible.

If one adopts either approach, then Nietzsche has lost his argument that thought falsifies. The first approach will view the error theory as a sort of reductio ad absurdum of the idea that we think. If we assume that we think, everything that we think of is in error, thus we do not in fact think. The noncognitivist will see the error theory as simply making concrete the impossibility of the unconditional unification of particularity that is required for thought. The second approach, in contrast, will see the error theory as applying only to those who improperly apply concepts of being to the world. The application of concepts of being is not *necessary* for thought, however. Truthful thought within becoming is possible.

If the error theory is contradictory, why then does Nietzsche so often argue in favor of it? I believe that he is compelled to the error theory for the same reason that Spir is: the problem of the antinomies, that is, the fact that the very idea of an empirical object contradictorily refers both to the conditioned and the unconditioned. *Whenever* we begin to speak about anything, what we speak about contains this contradiction of being and becoming. Nietzsche could find no account of the world that does not suffer from the antinomies. For this reason he believes that thought *must* falsify.

It is this tendency of our idea of an empirical object to generate the antinomies that, I will argue, explains Nietzsche's vacillation between the error theory and noncognitivism. When he concentrates on the antinomial character of our idea of an empirical object, he is motivated to present an error theory. But because Nietzsche is unwilling to accept the existence of both being and becoming, he must think of the false ideas of being that we apply to the world as having their source in becoming. But the minute that judgments are considered to occur within the world of becoming, they cease to be able to be true or false. To the extent that Nietzsche concentrates upon our judgments themselves, rather than their objects, his position lapses into noncognitivism.

But noncognitivism is itself unstable. If one entirely denies the existence of truth and falsity but allows that the sources of our judgments in becoming give us reasons to continue judging as we did before, the question then arises why these reasons are not sufficient to formulate a naturalized theory of *truthful* cognition. But such a position, by reintroducing the possibility of the description of an empirical object, generates the antinomies and the error theory once again. Nietzsche's tendency to move between these epistemological theories will be discussed in greater detail in chapter 5.

6. Nietzsche's Antithetic Theory of Substance

I have argued that the becoming that Nietzsche thinks is the true character of reality corresponds to the *antithetic* positions in the Kantian antinomies. Sometimes Nietzsche clearly puts the antithetic position in terms of a chain of conditions that extend out infinitely without ever encountering the unconditioned: "'Knowledge' is a referring back: in its essence a regressus in infinitum. That which comes to a standstill (at a supposed causa prima, at something unconditioned, etc.) is laziness, weariness" (*WP* 575). But Nietzsche often *telescopes* the antithetic arguments. Whereas Spir argues that we explain the fact that a set of qualities inhere in an object in terms of a set of qualities of another object, creating an infinite chain, Nietzsche sometimes argues that there simply is no condition for the unification of qualities in an object. The attempt to explain why certain qualities are unified in terms of an underlying object would simply refer to *that same* collection of qualities: "The 'thing' in which we believe was only invented as a foundation for the various attributes. If the thing 'effects,' that means: we conceive all the other properties which are present and momentarily latent, as the cause of the emergence of one single property; i.e., we take the sum of its properties—'x'—as cause of the property 'x': which is utterly stupid and mad!" (*WP* 561).

This telescoping of the antithetic position is not a product of philosophical confusion—indeed, it shows a deep philosophical understanding of the comprehensiveness of these antithetic arguments. To claim that certain qualities are united in an object by reference to the qualities of *another* object is no more philosophically satisfying than claiming that those qualities are united by reference to *themselves*. Both positions show that, in the end, there is no reason why certain qualities should be united rather than others. The idea that substance is a necessary unity breaks down entirely.

That Nietzsche's approach to reality is antithetic is evident in his repeated denials that the unconditioned could ever enter into a relationship with the conditioned (e.g. *KSA* 9:6[441]; *WP* 555). Nietzsche clearly alludes to Spir when spelling out this view:

> Philosophers . . . draw a conclusion . . . as to the nature of the thing-in-itself, which it is customary to regard as the sufficient reason for the existence of the world of appearance. As against this, more rigorous logicians, having clearly identified the concept of the metaphysical as that of the unconditioned, consequently also the unconditioning, have disputed any connection between the unconditioned (the metaphysical world) and the world we know: so that what appears in appearance is precisely *not* the thing in itself, and no conclusion can be drawn from the former as to the nature of the latter. (*HA* 16)

Once one recognizes the origins of Nietzsche's views concerning substances in the antithetic positions in Kant's antinomies, they start making a good deal of sense. Consider Nietzsche's famous claim that a thing is constituted by its relationships with other things (e.g. *WP* 558, 560, 583). "A thing, completely isolated, would not exist at all—it would have no relations" (*KSA* 9:12[17]). "The properties of a thing are effects on other 'things': if one removes other 'things,' then a thing has no properties, i.e., there is no thing without other things, i.e., there is no 'thing-in-itself'" (*WP* 557). At first glance, the idea that a thing is its relationship to other things is nonsense. There cannot be relations without relata—without *things* being related. But if objects are understood as unending *chains* of conditions, without anything unconditioned being met, then it makes sense to say all there is to objects are relations (for example, causal relations, relations of parts to whole, relations of structure to form) without there being any nonrelational relata.[10]

That we nevertheless rebel at such a notion and demand relata for these relations simply shows the antinomial nature of the argument—the fact that to think at all means seeing the world as being. Our dissatisfaction with the conception of a thing as a system of relations is analogous to our feeling that the Leibnizean conception of time and space, under which placement in space or time is exhausted by relationships, leaves it uncertain just *where* and *when* we are. This dissatisfaction is one that Nietzsche is well aware of: "We are somewhere in the middle—between the vastness of the world and the smallness of the inexhaustible world. . . . Is the world nothing for us but the collection of relations according to a measuring rod? As soon as this arbitrary measure disappears, our world dissolves into nothing!" (*KSA* 9:11[36]).

That we cannot help but see becoming from the perspective of being is why Spir argues that the physicist Hermann von Helmholtz's theory that things are their effects upon other things is incoherent: "Relations are naturally not able to be conceived without the objects between which they exist. . . . A substance that consists of relations is a *contradictio in adjecto*. Thus the illogical irrational character of our experience of bodies manifests itself despite all theoretical attempts to overcome it" (1877, 2:92–93). Given that Nietzsche himself recognizes the antinomial nature of his arguments concerning becoming, we should expect that he would agree with Spir that his theory of substances as relations is also contradictory.

7. Nietzsche's Antithetic Theories of Space and Time

Nietzsche's views concerning space and time are worth investigating in some detail because they offer further confirmation of the strong relationship between his theory of becoming and the antithetic positions in the antinomies. Consider again the antinomies concerning space. The thetic or Newtonian argument is that absolute space is necessary to make sense of what *size* anything is. The Newtonian position is usually understood as the view that space is a single unconditioned substance, in reference to which empirical objects are of a determinate size. But it is equally possible to argue that space consists of numerous indivisible space-atoms. The size of something would be unconditionally determined by reference to the number of space-atoms out of which the object is constituted. So understood, the antithetic counterargument is obvious: space is infinitely divisible. If space is infinitely divisible, then there cannot be a *unit* of space in reference to which things have an unconditioned size. To claim that space-atoms can be infinitely divided is to claim that the totality of spatial relations could be infinite in size or exist on the head of a pin, which is, once again, to say that there is no unconditional answer to the question of what size anything is.[11]

Under the antithetic position it is not merely impossible to say what size anything is but also whether anything moves. We can know that A moves in relation to B, but if B itself is moving, then A may in fact be standing still. Without measurement with respect to absolute space, all that exists is an indefinite becoming—a generalized movement that cannot be attributed to any thing. Since Nietzsche takes the antithetic position and denies that absolute space exists, we shouldn't be surprised to discover that he rejects the idea of nonrelational movement (*WP* 562). Nevertheless he argues that to *think* of things as moving we must falsify this antithetic reality and assume the existence of unconditional movement—movement with respect to being: "We speak as if there were *beings* [*seiende Dinge*] and our science speaks only about these things. But a being exists only according to *human optics:* we cannot escape it. Something becoming, a movement in itself is completely inconceivable. We *move only beings*. . . . If we think things away, we also think away movement" (*KSA* 9:6[433]).

Analogously, the infinite divisibility of time supports an antithetic position under which time is exhausted by the relationship between processes. The argument against this antithetic position is that it leaves it unclear how *fast* anything is happening—all that can be said is that things are happening faster or slower with respect to a metric, such as our heartbeat. We need an absolute time to determine how fast anything is really happening. Nietzsche entertains the idea of absolute time in his Nachlaß: "To the actual passage of things an *actual* time must correspond, irrespective of the feelings of longer or shorter spaces of time, as perceiving beings have them. Probably the actual time is unutterably much slower than we humans perceive time. . . . [T]he circulation of our blood [*Blutumlauf*] could in truth have the duration of a day and a year [*Erd- und Sonnenlaufs*]" (*KSA* 9:11[184]). But he almost always expresses the antithetic positions concerning time and space (*D* 117; *KSA* 7:19[140 and 153], 9:6[439]; *WP* 487, 545, 563). Nietzsche explicitly rejects the theory that time consists of absolute time-atoms, making use of an argument drawn from Spir (*KSA* 9:11[281]).[12]

In keeping with the antinomial nature of his arguments, however, Nietzsche claims that we must employ the falsehood of unconditioned time in order to think of processes as happening at a certain rate. The positing of determinate time-atoms or fixed points in the flux of becoming is required for us to perceive time at all: "First the after-on-another [*Nacheinander*] produces the representation of time. If we were to perceive . . . a continuum, we would not believe in time. For the movement of becoming does *not* consist of *motionless* points [*ruhenden Punkten*], of uniform still expanses [*gleichen Ruhestrecken*]" (*KSA* 9:11[281]).

Thus Nietzsche argues that the infinite divisibility of space and time show their *contradictory* nature—the fact that they both demand and will not accept simple unconditional atomic units out of which they are constituted: "Our sensations of space and time are false, for tested consistently they lead to logical contradictions. The establishment of conclusions in science always unavoidably involves us in calculating with certain false magnitudes . . . the conclusions of science acquire a complete rigorousness and certainty in their coherence with one another; one can build on them—up to that final stage at which our erroneous basic assumptions, those constant errors, come to be incompatible with our conclusions, for example in the theory of atoms" (*HA* 19).

8. Spir on Causality

Nietzsche's views about causality have proven intractable for commentators. Given his naturalism, Nietzsche is obviously well disposed toward causal explanations. Indeed, it is precisely his commitment to causal explanations of human judgment that leads him to deny the existence of cognition. Furthermore, Nietzsche's works often contain cautions concerning the correct use of causal reasoning—for example, that one should not confuse effect with cause (*HA* 608; *TI* 6:1). These passages appear to presuppose the general respectability of causal reasoning.

Nevertheless Nietzsche also engages in one of the most radical critiques of the concept of causation in the history of philosophy. The main theme in this critique is that cause and effect are somehow improperly separated from the flow of events (*BGE* 21; *KSA* 9:6[412 and 433]; *WP* 624, 633). Causality is the product of applying a concept of being to the flow of becoming:

> Cause and effect: such a duality probably never exists; in truth we are confronted by a continuum out of which we isolate a couple of pieces, just as we perceive motion only as isolated points and then infer it without actually seeing it. The suddenness with which many effects stand out misleads us; actually, it is sudden only for us. In this moment of suddenness, there is an infinite number of processes that elude us. An intellect that could see cause and effect as a continuum and a flux and not, as we do, in terms of an arbitrary dismemberment, would repudiate the concept of cause and effect and deny all conditionality. (*GS* 112)

> At length we grasp that things—consequently atoms, too—effect nothing: because they do not exist at all—that the concept of causality is completely useless.—A necessary sequence of states does not imply a causal relationship between them (—that would mean making their effective capacity leap from 1 to 2, to 3, to 4, to 5). There are neither causes nor effects. Linguistically we do not know how to rid ourselves of them. But that does not matter. If I think of the muscle apart from its "effects," I negate it—In summa: an event is neither effected nor does it effect. *Causa* is a capacity to produce effects that has been super-added to the events—. (*WP* 551)

These fictitious isolated causes, Nietzsche argues, are modeled after human agents (e.g. *GS* 127; *GM* 1:13; *KSA* 9:12[63]; *WP* 550, 552, 547). "The interpretation of an event as either an act or the suffering of an act (—thus every act a becoming other, presupposes an author and someone upon whom 'change' is effected)" (*WP* 546).

What we need is a reading that can make sense of these critiques *and* Nietzsche's philosophical sympathy to causal explanations. Once again, Spir's fundamental antinomy can provide the answer. Spir argues that the concept of

causality, like that of substance, is the result of the application of "the original a priori concept of the original essence of things, which finds its expression in the principle of identity" upon "the fact of change, which can only
be perceived in experience" (1877, 1:247–48). In other words, for Spir, as for
Nietzsche, causality is the result of the application of being to becoming.

For Spir, change is indicative of "a lack of identity or lack of agreement of
the changing thing with itself" (1:255). Because we rebel at the idea that something that is an object—that is, an unconditioned unity—could have within
it plurality or change, we are forced to seek the origin of change in something
outside of the object. But change will likewise be incompatible with *that*
object, so we look even earlier, creating a chain of conditions that continues
infinitely into the past:

> Change is the unification of difference. For example, if a red object becomes
> green, it would unite two different qualities. . . . But the negative formulation
> of our highest principle of thought, the principle of non-contradiction, de-
> mands completely, as we know, the following: An unconditioned unity of dif-
> ference is not possible. Thus it is *a priori* certain, that no change can happen
> unconditionally, that is, without a cause. . . . In order for a change to enter, there
> must have occurred an earlier change, that caused it, and so on backwards into
> infinity. (1:256–57)

The change is, so to speak, *pushed out* of the object and into the change of
an earlier object, which itself must have its change pushed out of it into the
change of an earlier object, and so on. The ultimate image of the world that
the principle of causality produces is that of absolutely simple atoms whose
changes are introduced to them from the outside, for example, due to impact from other atoms, which themselves received their change from still
earlier collisions with other atoms. Such an image naturally both invites and
forbids the introduction of a first cause that explains why this chain of causation exists at all.

It is important to recognize that if the causal laws under which changes
are related to one another themselves changed, change would not be successfully removed from objects. Therefore the relation between cause and effect
must proceed according to *necessary* causal laws (1:268–69). By requiring that
the principles of causation follow necessary laws, we are attempting to see
nature as a whole as one unchanging unit, as a self-identical substance. If the
totality of conditions were known, the world could be seen as a single unconditioned thing: "Accordingly, what does the principle of causality signify in its true meaning? Just this: That nature, despite all changes in its particulars, nevertheless in the aggregate (i.e. in its relationships, in the lawlike

connections of the particulars) *remains the same as itself.* It is in this way that the principle of identity manifests itself in the principle of causality" (1:271). The totality of events considered as a whole would be one *without change,* for this totality would have nothing within it by virtue of which it deviated from itself.

Because causality means viewing nature as one self-identical substance, Spir argues that causal reasoning assumes the existence of *identical cases* (1:102)—each event becomes an aspect of the same self-identical thing: "What the *a priori* concept [of causality] achieves for us here is that it places us in the position to believe with primitive certainty that in the multiplicity of reality [*in der Mannigfaltigkeit des Gegebenen*] there are a number of *completely identical* cases [streng identischer *Fälle*]" (1:260). The validity of induction rests upon the belief in the essential identity of the world with itself (1:271). To see the world as becoming, however, is to reject inductive reasoning and to see each event as an uncaused arbitrary happening (2:134).

But the principle of causality's attempt to force the image of being and self-identical unity onto becoming and plurality fails. For the unconditioned can never intersect with the changes or alterations in the world (1:327, 2:130–31). Any "first cause" would have to itself be caused. Any general law of nature will not be necessary but will always require an explanation of why it is the way it is rather than some way else (1:329–30). It is just as impossible to see the totality of the world as a self-identical substance as it is any other plurality. The only way that the world could be seen as a necessary and self-identical unity is if it had no multiplicity or change. But if so, then there would be nothing for the principle of causality to explain.

That, instead of being a necessary substance, the world is an unending chain of contingency is, of course, the antithetic position concerning causality. Under this position, in the end no alteration or change is ever *explained* (1:373–74). As Spir puts it, adopting what can be called the *telescoped* antithetic position concerning causality: "That something happens *at all,* that alterations occur at all, that change exists, that cannot have a condition or cause" (2:131). In the end, change simply happens without a cause: "Thus we must view change in general simply as a given state of reality, which is maintained through its own impulse, and not ask about its original source" (2:132). Our feeling that this is intolerable is simply our desire to apply the concept of being to becoming.

Thus why anything happens at all is left out of causal explanations, which merely push the radically contingent nature of change out of sight. Spir sees in the everyday (as opposed to the scientific) conception of causality an attempt to overcome this inadequacy of causal explanation. Under the scientific understanding of causality, only a change can be the cause of a change. Science merely speaks of the relationship between changes, not why change itself happens. In contrast, the everyday notion of causality, in the attempt to *explain* change, looks to *substances* as causes, as if causation were the injuring [*Leiden*] of something at the hands of an agent (1:261–67). So in common parlance, *the sun,* rather than the *warming* of the sun, is said to be the cause of the melting of ice (1:261–62). The everyday notion of causality treats substances as if they were free agents that could draw change from within themselves (1:264). In effect, it inserts into the present the first cause to which one is inclined to appeal to explain why change occurs.

Such an explanation of change is inadequate, of course, because it ignores the fact that the only thing that can condition the conditioned is the conditioned. A substance can generate change only through its *changes,* which must themselves be caused by other changes. Any alleged first cause must itself be caused.

An alternative attempt to explain change without relying upon substance-agents is the idea of force (1:266–67, 360; 2:92–93, 102), which is something like bare effectuation itself: "By force [*Kraft*] one means the actual driving effectuating principle of becoming. This makes it sound as if force is the cause of change. Only this view is indefensible. The driving principle is not something itself different from or separate from the change itself, but rather, so to speak, simply the power of constancy [*Beharrungsvermögen*] of the general change, its inner impulse to continue moving forward" (2:132). Force cannot be thought of as the *cause* of change, because that would mean conceiving of force either as a substance (in the manner of the everyday notion of causality) or as a mere relation between changes that fails to explain why change happens (in the manner of the scientific concept of cause). The idea of force is instead an attempt to get *behind* causal relations and to explain what really is the necessitating that brings about change. To explain *in terms of force* why billiard ball A's impact with billiard ball B leads B to move is to get at what is provided to B when A hits B. Force is the stuff that, considered *all by itself*—without having to think of any relation to A's impact—is sufficient to bring about B's movement.

But, in the end, the concept of force fails to explain change. It is instead either a scientific connection *between* changes or the admission that change is unexplainable. If one uses force to explain why a particular change *had* to happen the way it did, one is actually conceiving of force as a relation *between changes.* Explaining why billiard ball B had to move the way it did must involve looking at the relationship between that change and another change (the movement of billiard ball A) under a covering law (2:135). If force is instead thought of not as a form of necessitation but as a way of capturing the antithetical position concerning causality, then, rather than being an explanation of change, it is a recognition of an inability to explain why any change happens at all. Force becomes an "inexhaustible source of always new changes" (2:134), a sort of radical generator of arbitrariness in the world.

Spir makes it clear that we do not experience necessitation in our own acts of agency. The fact that there is any relationship between feelings of willing and subsequent actions is something that is learned, like any other causal relationship, through induction: "But because this feeling constantly accompanies the exertion of the muscles, the association of the two in consciousness leads one to the belief that the aforementioned feeling is itself the exertion and an inner force of the will has manifested itself immediately. That is actually false. We can conclude that there is a causality to our wills only on the basis of the fact that the desired movements of our limbs follow invariably after our wishes" (2:136). Thus "our inner states show cause and effect in exactly the same sense as the states of inanimate things" (2:138).

Spir's discussion of the concept of force is significant because he connects it with an idea that is of importance to Nietzsche, namely "absolute becoming" [*ein absolutes Werden*] (1:214). As we have seen, the principle of causality attempts to conceive of becoming in the image of being by making change the result of necessitation by other changes according to a covering law. If, *per impossibile*, this chain of necessitation were completed, change would be nothing but an aspect of one changeless substance. But although change must be viewed according to the image of being, it resists this imposition. The question arises, then, whether one can think of the world without applying the image of being to it—whether one can consider it as becoming alone. This is the idea of absolute becoming.

Spir's characterization of absolute becoming is revealing:

> What will one actually say, if one asserts that change, succession, alteration are the actual unconditioned character of things or of reality? Above all clearly this: That things arise, not simply as appearance, but really, that is, out of nothing, and that they really disappear, that is, fade into nothing. Thus they also have no relationship among one another. . . . Generally considered, absolute becoming or change [*ein absolutes Werden oder Geschehen*] is nothing more or less than a *change without a cause.* (1:213)

Thus, according to Spir, an ontology of becoming involves a plurality of forces that do not interact, each coming out of nothing. If an "object" turns from red to green to blue, the turning from red to green must be understood in terms of a green force arising out of nothing, and the turning from green to blue must be understood in terms of a blue force arising from nothing. The two color changes have no dependence upon one another.

But, in an argument similar to Kant's Second Analogy (Kant 1965, A189–211/B232–56), Spir argues that if changes had no relationship to one another then they could not even be thought by us, since thinking means uniting in our consciousness under a rule (1877, 1:215–16). To think of succession, it is necessary to unify these representations in one consciousness. Causality plays this role by seeing the succession as part of one unified self-identical substance. Thus Spir argues that the thought of absolute becoming is unsustainable. For it is impossible to *think* of a force as something individual—when one thinks of a force, one is always thinking of a *relationship* between changes according to necessary laws, that is, a causal relationship (1:266–67). And when we think of such causal relationships, change is seen as external to reality and brought to it from without.[13]

Thus Spir argues that although someone who attempts to articulate an ontology of absolute becoming would be inclined to understand becoming in terms of Boscovichean or Helmholtzean centers of force (2:92–94, 112–13; 1873, 2:81–82, 97–98, 111–12; 1869, 165–67), such a theory must, in the end, collapse into one in which becoming is seen from the perspective of being.[14]

9. Nietzsche's Spirean Account of Causality

One cannot read Spir's views on causality without noticing striking analogies with Nietzsche's own views. Let's begin with Nietzsche's argument that making a causal judgment means falsely *isolating* something out of a continuum (e.g. WS 11; WP 520). Consider, once again, the following passage from *The Gay Science:*

> Cause and effect: such a duality probably never exists; in truth we are confronted by a continuum out of which we isolate a couple of pieces, just as we perceive motion only as isolated points and then infer it without actually seeing it. The suddenness with which many effects stand out misleads us; actually, it is sudden only for us. In this moment of suddenness, there is an infinite number of processes that elude us. An intellect that could see cause and effect as a continuum and a flux and not, as we do, in terms of an arbitrary dismemberment, would repudiate the concept of cause and effect and deny all conditionality. (112)

The analogy with motion is revealing. As we have seen, Nietzsche argues that to think of motion as occurring, we must posit absolute space—an unconditional metric with respect to which an indeterminate change is seen as movement or standing still. We must, falsely, take points as fixed, or there will be no movement, only undifferentiated becoming.

An analogous argument concerning causality can be constructed. Thinking of alteration A as *necessitating* alteration B—that is, explaining why B had to happen—means taking A as fixed and ignoring its conditional nature, ignoring the fact that A's existence itself can be seen as having to be only in relation to a prior change. It is only by suppressing this conditionality and thinking of A as if it were a *first cause*—an unconditionally necessary event in itself—that any claims about necessitation of change can be made. We must posit, falsely, one change as a fixed point—a first cause—or there will be no causality, only undifferentiated becoming.

Nietzsche's curious comments concerning the apparent suddenness of effects are in keeping with this reading. Suddenness is a claim about the speed of a temporal flow. But, under the antithetic position, there is no such thing as a slow or a fast process in itself. Instead the speed of a process is relative to the speed of the process measuring it (Small 2001, 6–7). Nevertheless, to think about a temporal flow rather than experiencing it as undifferentiated becoming means falsely positing fixed points within the flow to use as a metric. In an argument similar to Kant's Second Analogy, Nietzsche argues that, without isolating unconditioned points in this flow, neither time nor change could be thought of at all:

> The one-after-another [*das Nacheinander*] first creates the representation of time. If we were to perceive not cause and effect, but a continuum, we would not believe in time. For the movement of becoming does *not* consist of *motionless* points [*ruhenden Punkten*], of uniform still expanses [*gleichen Ruhestrecken*]. . . . A continuum of force is *without after-one-another* [*Nacheinander*] and *without next-to-one-another* [*Nebeneinander*] (these too presuppose human intellect and gaps between things). (*KSA* 9:11[281])

> Continual transition forbids us to speak of "individuals," etc.; the "number" of beings is itself in flux. We would know nothing of time and motion if we did not, in a coarse fashion, believe we see what is at "rest" beside what is in motion. The same applies to cause and effect, and without the erroneous conception of "empty space" we should certainly not have acquired the conception of space. The principle of identity has behind it the "apparent fact" of things that are the same. A world in a state of becoming could not, in a strict sense, be "comprehended" or "known." (*WP* 520)

But, like Spir, Nietzsche believes that Kant is wrong to think that experience actually conforms to these categories of being. What experience shows us is a continuum of change. But to think of this change we must falsify it and treat it as consisting of beings.

Explaining causation in terms of the positing of an unconditioned first cause is analogous to Spir's "everyday" notion of causality, where causation is seen as a form of suffering at the hands of an agent (1877, 1:261–62). Nietzsche even uses Spir's word, "suffering" [*Leiden*], to spell out this notion of causation (e.g. *WP* 589): "The interpretation of an occurrence [*eines Geschehens*] as *either* an act [*Thun*] *or* the suffering of an act [*Leiden*] (—thus for every act a suffering) says: every change, every becoming-other, presupposes an author [*Urheber*] and someone *upon whom* 'change' is effected" (*WP* 546). The paradigm of human agency is deeply attractive to someone seeking to explain change because human agency appears to provide a cause of change that does not itself depend upon a prior change. When a human agent acts, the *self*, understood as an independent substance, is presumed to have generated the change. It is for this reason that the agent can be held *responsible* for his or her actions. In contrast, if the origin of the act was itself dependent upon prior changes, then, rather than there being human agency, change would have merely flowed through the human agent from the outside.

Because of the need to explain change, all causal necessitation is viewed as a form of agency: "In every judgment there resides the entire, full, profound belief in subject and attribute, or in cause and effect (that is, as the assertion that every effect is an activity and that every activity presupposes an agent); and this latter belief is only a special case of the former, so there remains as the fundamental belief the belief that there are subjects, that everything that happens is related attributively to some subject" (*WP* 550).

That the category of causality falsifies is shown by the impossibility of connecting this thetic image of causal necessitation with antithetic experience of change and multiplicity. Nowhere in experience can necessitation by a substance be found. In particular, our internal experience of our actions provides us with no such experience of agency (e.g. *GM* 1:13; *TI* 3:5, 6:3; *WP* 550–52, 671):

> Critique of the concept "cause." We have absolutely no experience of a cause; psychologically considered, we derive the entire concept from the subjective conviction that we are causes, namely, that the arm moves—But that is an error. We separate ourselves, the doers, from the deed, and we make use of this pattern everywhere—we seek a doer for every event. What is it we have done? We have misunderstood the feeling of strength, tension, resistance, a muscular feeling that is already the beginning of the act, as the cause, or we have taken the will to do this or that for a cause because the action follows upon it—. (*WP* 551)

It is only after the model of the subject that we have invented the reality of things and projected them into the medley of sensations. If we no longer believe in the effective subject, then belief also disappears in effective things, in reciprocation, cause and effect between those phenomena that we call things. There also disappears, of course, the world of effective atoms: the assumption of which always depended on the supposition that one needed subjects. (*WP* 552)

10. Causality and Absolute Becoming

As we have already seen with respect to space, time, and substance, absolute becoming has been characterized as the *antithetic* position concerning these concepts. This position has at least two forms, the chain version and the telescoped version. For example, with respect to time, the chain version would say that there is duration, but only relationally—one process is indeed fast or slow, but only with respect to another process. The telescoped version would simply say that there is no such thing as duration at all—experience shows there to be happening, but it has no temporal length. Analogously, with respect to substance, the chain version is that qualities do inhere in substances but only *relationally*—that is, with respect to other substances (for example, parts) that are themselves only relationally substances. Under the telescoped version, there is no inherence in a substance at all—there are only arbitrary collections of qualities.

Nietzsche's position concerning causation is analogous. Occasionally, and particularly in his early notebooks (e.g. *KSA* 7:19[237], 7:29[8.8]; but see also *GS*2d 357), Nietzsche puts his antithetic position in its chain or relational form and argues that all causal necessitation and causal laws are relational: "'Natural laws.' Nothing but relations to one another and to men" (*KSA* 7:29[8.7]). "We define natural laws as *relations* to an xyz, from which each again is known *only as relations* to another xyz" (*KSA* 7:19[235]). Under the chain version causal necessitation exists, but only *relationally.* Alterations are indeed causally necessitated but only with respect to *other* alterations that are themselves necessitated by *other* alterations. There is no nonrelational necessity—no first cause—to explain why any alteration has to occur.

But Nietzsche famously also puts his theory of becoming in a telescoped version as a theory of Boscovichean *centers of force* (*BGE* 12). This is, of course, exactly how Spir predicts a theory of absolute becoming would be formulated. The complicated details of Nietzsche's theory of force and of the will to power[15] are a topic for a book-length work on their own and thus are beyond the scope of this essay.[16] But it should be noted that any interpretation of Nietzsche's theory of the will to power, *understood as a theory of absolute becoming* (and not in the more narrow psychological form in which it is sometimes presented by Nietzsche [see Clark 1990, 227–34]), needs to take into account the fact that, by its own lights, it should appear contradictory. The theory is an attempt to do justice to what experience is like independent of the application of categories of being such as causality. But being is *inescapable*—it will show itself in the doctrine of force itself.

Force can, of course, simply be another name for a causal relationship *between changes*. If so, the two changes are actually seen not as changes at all but as aspects of one unchanging self-identical substance. But that means that if force is to function as a theory of absolute becoming it must be thought of differently. It must be an uncaused generator of change—an "inexhaustible source of always new alterations" (Spir 1877, 2:134)—which means that every change would be *radically separated* from every other change. It is probably impossible to even think of such radical separation. Instead the forces out of which the world is supposed to be constructed will naturally be thought of as influencing one another and as connected over time. But that means seeing the world from the perspective of being, not absolute becoming. It is for this reason that Spir criticizes Boscovich's and Helmholtz's conceptions of centers of force [*Kraftcentra*] as the unsuccessful attempt to make do without the categories of being (2:92–94, 112–13). Given Nietzsche's familiarity with Spir, it is unlikely that his theory of the will to power was not written with a strong sense of its potential incoherence.

If reality is absolute becoming, earlier stages of the world are not causally connected with subsequent stages. It is as if the world flashed into a new arrangement at each moment. Furthermore, each element within that stage of world history would be radically separated from every other. Although Nietzsche sometimes embraces this view that reality is "eternally self-creating and self-destroying" (*WP* 1067), he appears unwilling to forego some connection between forces, some accommodation or struggle between them:

> Two successive states, the one "cause," the other "effect": this is false. The first has nothing to effect, the second has been effected by nothing. It is a question of a struggle between two elements of unequal power: a new arrangement of forces is achieved according to the measure of power of each of them. The second condition is something fundamentally different from the first (not its effect): the essential thing is that the factions in struggle emerge with different quanta of power. (*WP* 633)

It is not a goal of this essay to explore whether Nietzsche succeeds in outlining a noncausal theory of continuity between states of force, but it is difficult to see how these rearrangements can be anything other than causally determined.

11. The Contradiction in Nietzsche's Attitude toward Causality

With these points in mind, we can begin to make sense of why Nietzsche's attitude toward causality is so contradictory, why he tends both to praise and criticize causal reasoning.

This apparent contradiction is a result of the *two* seemingly incompatible antithetic pictures of reality that can be drawn from Nietzsche's critique of causal reasoning. The first antithetic picture, it will be remembered, is a *chain* version, under which causal connections exist but are purely relational, in the sense that every cause must itself be caused. The second is a *telescoped* version—a theory of absolute becoming under which each alteration is a radically contingent happening that cannot be explained in terms of any underlying source. The second view is a repudiation of causality entirely, while the first creates an infinite chain of causal dependence.

Although these images of reality are different, both view change as radically contingent in the sense that there is no genuine explanation of why change occurs. The only difference is that, while the infinite chain version pushes this radical contingency further and further back in the past, the telescoped theory embraces this radical contingency at every moment. Accordingly, the fact that Nietzsche criticizes the concept of causality and argues that events are causally dissociated from one another is not really incompatible with a naturalistic demand that every event have a cause, for the demand that every event have a cause shares with the theory of absolute becoming the rejection of thetic first causes. Nietzsche never wavers in his attack on the idea that substance-agents are the source of change. And he often makes this point not by rejecting the concept of causality entirely but by *applying* the concept to the substance-agents that are claimed to draw change from within themselves. In both approaches, Nietzsche is trying to present a form of naturalism that is strictly empirical in its foundations and does not rely upon thetic first causes or Spinozan world-substances.

12. The Equation of the Unequal

In the first chapter we saw how Nietzsche's error theory depends upon the idea that human judgment involves the equation of the unequal. Such comments are everywhere in Nietzsche, from the early 1870s until the end of 1888: "Every cognition that is useful for us is the *identification of the unequal,* the similar, that is, is essentially unlogical" (*KSA* 7:19[236]). "Concepts arise from

the equation of the unequal: i.e. through the deception that there is equality, through the assumption of identity: thus through false conceptions" (*KSA*
7:23[11]). "That there are equal things, equal cases, is as much the foundational fiction behind judgment as it is behind conclusions" (*KSA* 11:35[57]).
"[E]rror as the precondition even of thought. Before there is 'thought' there
must have been 'invention'; the construction of identical cases, of the appearance of sameness, is more primitive than the knowledge of sameness" (*WP*
544).[17]

Can the Spirean elements in Nietzsche's thought help us make sense of
these passages? We have already seen how Nietzsche, like Spir, argues that
thought about the empirical world requires misapplying the idea of unconditioned self-identical being to the plurality and becoming of sensation. Thus
we should expect Nietzsche, like Spir, to argue that thinking of an empirical
substance means equating the unequal. Insofar as it is a substance that is
thought, it must be absolutely simple, that is to say, everything about it must
be identical to everything else. But insofar as this substance is known through
the senses, it has plurality and change, that is to say, aspects of it are not identical to other aspects. Thus in the idea of an empirical object, the unequal
are equated.

But, as some of the quotations above show, what Nietzsche thinks are falsely equated are not always the differing *qualities* of one substance but the different *objects* that fall under the extension of a concept. These arguments are
essentially related, however. The self-identity of an object is required to make
sense of how one could judge with objective validity that qualities inhere in
it. Without self-identical objects one's judgments become merely subjectively
valid associations of representations. But an analogous identity is required
for the objectively valid thought that two objects share the same quality. The
unification of the objects under a concept must concern the objects themselves and not our subjective tendency to associate them. But that means that
it cannot be created through psychological associations (Spir 1877, 1:77–79).
The conceptual unity must instead be immediate: "In order that things can
be similar, there must be at least two in existence, since similarity is an agreement in character of more than one thing. . . . Contrary to the above, whatever perceives the similarity of two or more things must necessarily be one"
(1:52). Thus to perceive with objective validity that two different things have
the same quality, they must be brought into an absolutely simple unity, which
means claiming that they are identical. To apply a concept is to equate the
unequal.

Nietzsche sometimes puts the idea that conceptualization equates the
unequal as if it were the simple argument that it ignores the differences be-

tween objects. But there is no reason that the concept *square* is inadequate simply because it ignores the nonsquare aspects of the objects that fall under it. Nietzsche's real point is that one must deny the very particularity of the objects that fall under the concept *square*. The true referent of the concept must be a simple unity, but that is not possible if what is conceptualized is known through the senses.

Another way that human cognition equates the unequal is through causal reasoning. As we have seen, Spir argues that causal laws depend upon the thetic assumption that each temporal state of the world is simply an aspect of a single self-identical substance. The concept of causality, by seeing the world as a single substance, falsely treats the events in the world as "*completely identical* cases" (1:260). Inductive reasoning rests upon the belief in the essential identity of the world with itself (1:271). Given the strong similarities between Spir's and Nietzsche's concepts of causality, it is not surprising that Nietzsche too argues that natural laws depend upon the presumption of identical cases: "One should not understand this compulsion to construct concepts, species, forms, purposes, laws ('a world of identical cases') as if they enabled us to fix the *real world;* but as a compulsion to arrange a world for ourselves in which our existence is made possible:—we thereby create a world which is calculable, simplified, comprehensible, etc., for us" (*WP* 521).

13. Logic and Mathematics

What is to be made of Nietzsche's repeated claims that logic and mathematics falsify, which, as we saw in chapter 1, pose a serious obstacle to making sense of his epistemology? Let's begin with logic. We know that Nietzsche repeatedly claims that logic falsifies the world (e.g. *GS* 111; *WP* 512, 515, 516). "[W]ithout accepting the fictions of logic, without measuring reality against the purely invented world of the unconditional and the self-identical, without a constant falsification of the world by means of numbers, man could not live" (*BGE* 4).

As many commentators on Nietzsche have noted, the idea that logic makes ontological assumptions about the stability of entities in the world seems clearly false (Hales and Welshon 2000, 53). Peter Poellner's *Nietzsche and Metaphysics* is an example:

> If this is indeed Nietzsche's train of thought . . . then it clearly rests on a fallacy. . . . The applicability of the axioms and rules of inference of logic does *not* presuppose the existence of even relatively enduring particulars. The law of non-contradiction asserts that "no statement is both true and false." . . . This

would hold even in a world of rapidly changing and chaotic constellations of qualities (Nietzsche's world of "becoming," or of the "chaos of sensations"). (1995, 93)

But once one looks at Nietzsche's comments on logic in the light of Spir—whom, it should be remembered, Nietzsche calls a "distinguished logician" (*HA* 18)—they start making sense. For Spir, as we have seen, judgment means positing self-identical substances. Furthermore, knowledge of these substances is intimately tied to formal logic because such knowledge is exhausted by the logical laws of self-identity and noncontradiction. But since self-identity, which is to say, absolute simplicity, is incompatible with the multiplicity and change that we find in experience, judgment and therefore logic falsify experience. These Spirean elements in Nietzsche's criticisms of logic are obvious in the following passage in his Nachlaß:

> Supposing there were no self-identical "A", such as is presupposed by every proposition of logic . . . and the "A" were already mere appearance, then logic would have a merely apparent world as its condition. . . . The "thing"—that is the real substratum of "A"; *our belief in things* is the precondition of our belief in logic. The "A" of logic is, like the atom, a reconstruction of the thing—If we do not grasp this, but make of logic a criterion of true being, we are on the way to positing as realities all those hypostases: substance, attribute, object, subject, action, etc.; that is, to conceiving a metaphysical world, that is, a "real world." (*WP* 516)

Consider next Nietzsche's criticisms of mathematics: "Mathematics . . . would certainly not have come into existence if one had known from the beginning that there was in nature no exactly straight line, no real circle, no absolute magnitude" (*HA* 11). At first glance, this criticism seems childishly misguided. The idealized nature of mathematical entities—the fact that mathematical lines are perfectly straight unlike the crooked lines we encounter in experience—does not mean that mathematics falsifies. One can simply treat these entities as approximations of reality.

But the heart of Nietzsche's criticism of mathematics is not that the objects it deals with are idealized but that "absolute magnitude" does not exist (*KSA* 9:11[151]). Absolute space, within which anything with a definite shape must exist, is unconditional, and only conditional space exists: "We place a *mathematical average line* [*Durchschnittslinie*] on absolute becoming, moreover we bring all lines and planes to it, on the basis of the intellect, which is error" (*KSA* 9:11[293]). A mathematics of absolute becoming is impossible because it would have to deal with objects of *no* determinate shape and size.

Of course, if mathematics is not applied to the world at all—if it is considered to be a discipline that simply models what absolute space would be like if it did exist—then it might be considered to be true a priori. Thus, we should not be surprised by Nietzsche's remarks in *Twilight of the Idols,* where he appears to suggest that mathematics and logic are true by convention (3:3). Nietzsche speaks of "logic and that applied logic, mathematics," as "science[s] of formulae, sign systems," and argues that in them "reality does not appear at all, not even as a problem" (cf. *TL* p. 81). This attitude toward mathematics is compatible with a continued rejection of the view that mathematical laws apply to the world.

Analogously, Nietzsche's hostility to logic is compatible with his more positive comments in *Twilight of the Idols* (3:3) and "On Truth and Lies in a Nonmoral Sense" (p. 81). Logic falsifies if it is applied to the world, that is to say, if one takes one's judgments to be about the world. But considered in an unapplied fashion, logic can be true as a "sign system." Consider, for example, the law of noncontradiction. One can accept the law -(A & -A) as following from the definition of the logical operators "-" and "&." But one cannot say about something in the world that it cannot be both square and not square. For such a claim would assume that squareness can be predicated of objects, and according to Nietzsche, such predication is possible only assuming the existence of self-identical objects, objects that are incompatible with the plurality and change that show themselves in experience. To put this point in the language of contemporary logic, one can say that the uninterpreted formulas of logic are true, albeit by convention, but that we are unable to provide a semantic interpretation of these formulas without error (Hales and Welshon 2000, 43–44).[18]

14. Conclusion

In chapter 1, Nietzsche's error theory seemed impossibly incoherent. A primary difficulty with the error theory was its empirical nature—the fact that Nietzsche argues for it on the basis of the testimony of the senses. As we saw in chapter 1, this argument presents serious logical difficulties. How could *all* our judgments be falsified by experience? Doesn't that argument presume a *comparison* between our false beliefs about the world and other *true* beliefs about the world that are based on this experience?

The key to understanding Nietzsche's error theory is its dependence upon the idea that empirical objects are *contradictory,* that is, that they have within them both the becoming that is derived from the senses and the being that is required for anything to be thought. Nietzsche does not have to *compare* our beliefs about the world with a correct description of what the world is like—which is not to say that he does not sometimes try to make such comparisons. Instead, the contradictory nature of empirical objects compels the view that our judgments about the world are false. Empirical objects demand the existence of unconditional entities, but these unconditional entities fail to intersect with the conditional world of plurality and change for which they were to provide a foundation. Being and becoming in empirical objects separate upon reflection, even as they demand that they be connected:

> In order that any amount of consciousness can exist in the world, an unreal world of error must arise: substance [*Wesen*] with the belief in the enduring in individuals etc. Only after an imaginary other world [*Gegenwelt*] in contrast to absolute flux has arisen can something be known on this foundation—of course in the end the foundational error can be observed in connection with everything (because, when thought through, they create contradictions [*weil sich Gegensätze denken lassen*])—however this error can only be ended when life ends: the final truth of the flux of things will not allow itself to be *incorporated*. (*KSA* 9:11[162])

What are these errors? They are "unity, identity, duration, substance, cause, materiality, being" (*TI* 3:5). These words were not chosen by Nietzsche at random—sophisticated arguments stand behind each of them. To posit duration means demanding that there is an answer to the question of how fast or slow any process occurs. To posit substance means demanding that there is an answer to the question of what qualities inhere in an object. To posit cause means demanding that there is a reason why change happens. But these demands we make of the world lead inexorably to unconditional entities—absolute time, simple self-identical substances, first causes—that fail to connect with the empirical world. Some of the most impenetrable mysteries of Nietzsche's error theory actually point to philosophically plausible requirements for conceiving of a world at all, requirements that are nonetheless in tension with the plurality and change that we experience through sensation.

For the same reason, Nietzsche's comments concerning our *schematizing* sensations can be made sense of in the light of Spir's influence on his thought. In chapter 1, we saw that Nietzsche repeatedly argues that our judgments about the world are false because the flux or chaos of sensations are schematized: "The fictitious world of subject, substance, 'reason,' etc., is needed—: there is in us a power to order, simplify, falsify, artificially distinguish. 'Truth' is the will to be master over the multiplicity of sensations—to classify phenomena into definite categories" (*WP* 517). "[T]he antithesis of this phenomenal world is not 'the true world,' but the formless unformulable world of the chaos of sensations—; another kind of phenomenal world, a kind 'unknowable' for us" (*WP* 569). Nietzsche's comments about schematization seemed frustratingly unclear about just how our sensations are schematized and why their schematization would make all our judgments false.

We now are in a better position to answer these questions. What does it mean to say that a process has taken place over a definite period of time? Some sensation of duration, for example, one's heartbeat, has to be taken as the metric, as the absolute time by virtue of which all other temporal processes are assessed. If one continually allowed every sensation of duration to be considered fast or slow with respect to another sensation of duration, one would never be in a position to say how fast or how slow any process occurs. A world without such ordering would indeed be a "chaos of sensations" (*WP* 569) that could not be described by us as having any definite temporal character.

Consider as well the schematization that occurs by means of the concept of a substance. If Nietzsche's and Spir's arguments are correct, then giving up the concept of substance in order to allow for the multiplicity that one experiences through sensation would mean giving up the possibility of attributing qualities to anything at all. This would indeed amount to a thoughtless awareness of plurality and change.

The *comprehensiveness* of Nietzsche's error theory also makes sense now. It should be clear why Nietzsche's error theory applies to every *empirical* judgment, for every empirical judgment involves the application of categories of being to the change and multiplicity that can be found in sensation. Although a more comprehensive discussion of Nietzsche's views concerning consciousness will have to wait until the next chapter, Nietzsche's error theory should apply just as much to *inner* experience as to the objects of outer experience, insofar as inner experience too presents us with change. Furthermore, both logic and mathematics can be seen as falsifying experience because their application to the world requires the postulation of self-identical substances and unconditional space and time.

Another mystery associated with Nietzsche's error theory is why the error of positing self-identical substances is so closely related with a conception of the self as a substance (e.g. *TI* 3:5). We are now able to make sense of this idea as well. To believe that the self is a substance is to believe that there is a unity to the self that is present through *thought.* This unity requires a complete simplicity and atemporality. Absolute time, self-identical substances, first causes—the entire realm of "being"—are *the objective correlates of this unity of the subject.*

But why shouldn't we, like Spir and the Eleatics, choose being over becoming? Why not choose the "real world" of unconditional and self-identical substances over the "apparent world" of the senses? For isn't being at least amenable *to thought*, whereas becoming is unthinkable? Indeed, isn't being inescapable—doesn't "every word, every sentence we utter" speak in favor of being (*TI* 3:5)? Why accept instead a world of absolute becoming—a world in which processes occur at no particular rate of speed, in which there is no answer to the question of what qualities inhere in an object, in which change arises from nothing?

The reason is that the real world of being is never able to enter into or explain the world of becoming. Absolute time can never intersect with real succession; self-identical substances can never unite a plurality of qualities; first causes can never bring about change. Thus, if the real world were the actual world, we would never be able to explain how the apparent world is possible. We cannot think of plurality and change as something that occurs only *to* a simple and timeless subject, for if that were true, there would be plurality and change within the simple and the timeless. We must take the other horn of the dilemma and derive being *from becoming*. "The 'real world' has been constructed out of the contradiction to the actual world" (*TI* 3:6). "The 'apparent' world is the only one: the 'real' world has only been *lyingly added*" (*TI* 3:2).

Because Nietzsche's error theory has so often been dismissed by commentators as incoherent, I have spent most of this chapter spelling out how it is philosophically plausible. But it would be wrong to suggest that Nietzsche's error theory is without any internal inconsistencies.

The first problem is Nietzsche's persistent desire to articulate an ontology of absolute becoming. It is an important fact that Nietzsche's error theory can be argued for *without* saying what absolute becoming is like. The error theory need only point to the contradictions that are inherent in empirical objects to show that all our judgments are false. Nevertheless, Nietzsche cannot help but offer us an idea of what absolute becoming is like. In contrast to the comprehensible, if somewhat vacant and sterile, ontology of being, Nietzsche's ontology of becoming teeters on the brink of incoherence. It is almost impossible not to think of his centers of force as *things* that exist in causal relations with one another. Spir is probably right when he argues that those attempting to explain change in the world have the choice "between logical contradictions, that is, mental suicide, on the one hand, and the acceptance of the incomprehensibility of the world on the other" (1877, 1:292). Spir argues that Hegel takes the first option, and he might have said the same thing about Nietzsche.

Of course, Nietzsche himself recognizes that "the doctrine of being, of things, of all sorts of fixed unities is a hundred times easier than the doctrine of becoming, of development" (*WP* 538). He is conscious of the difficulties of describing absolute becoming. Indeed, he sometimes recognizes that if his error theory is true and we cannot think of something except under the guise of being, then a truthful description of the world as becoming is impossible (e.g. *WP* 543). "If the character of existence should be false—which would be possible—what would truth, all our truth, be then?—An unconscionable falsification of the false? The false raised to a higher power?—" (*WP* 542). Although I will not argue the point here, I believe that the doctrine of the eternal recurrence is an attempt on Nietzsche's part to present absolute becoming in a conceivable manner.[19] The fact that Nietzsche finds it necessary to present his theory of becoming within the form of being shows the difficulty he finds in conceiving of absolute becoming in an unadulterated form.

Another, perhaps even more fundamental difficulty is that, by arguing that only becoming exists, Nietzsche makes it difficult to see how error can exist at all. As we have seen, Spir and Nietzsche have different but related difficulties in explaining the existence of error. It is a mystery for Spir how error is possible not because we cannot think, but because the only thing that we seem able to think about is being. If we can think only of being, all of our judgments should be *true,* albeit only about a simple unconditional Parmenidean One. In contrast, it is a mystery for Nietzsche how error is possible because it is a mystery how we think at all. Nietzsche's arguments that only becoming exists appear to make it impossible for thought to arise, which makes error just as impossible as truth. To affirm a world of becoming, it seems, should mean reducing thought to merely aimless happenings. So understood, thoughts should be neither true nor false but simply another part of the world of becoming.

But much of the time Nietzsche does not choose to see human thought in this fashion. Rather, he argues that becoming is in some sense responsible for the error of being arising. Plurality and change somehow create the deception of the unconditional unity of thought. But how does becoming perform this feat? Couldn't one argue that, just as the reduction of becoming to being is not possible because even the appearance of becoming is a form of becoming, so the reduction of being to becoming is not possible because even the appearance of being is a form of being? If everything is in the flow of becoming, isn't even the semblance of being impossible (cf. Small 2001, 11)?

Why does Nietzsche hold onto the error theory? I believe his reason is the same as Spir's—the applicability of the antinomies to empirical objects. Because the antinomies can be drawn out of the objects of our empirical judgments, it appears that our thoughts of these objects must partake of both being and becoming, even when, for Spir, thought should have been entirely being and, for Nietzsche, it should have been entirely becoming. Once it appears that our thoughts of objects have elements of both being and becoming and thus are necessarily erroneous, some account of error needs to be given. Spir's is to assume, incoherently, that the psychological association of particulars could somehow infect the unconditional and simple unity of judgment. Nietzsche's is to argue, perhaps also incoherently, that becoming could somehow create the deception of beings.

I would question whether Nietzsche is right that our everyday concepts of objects generate the antinomies. The antinomies appear to be generated by particular *philosophical* demands that we make upon our explanations of the world, and it is unlikely that natural cognition ever developed means, erroneous or otherwise, of responding to these demands. Consider the fact that one length must be used as the metric with respect to which every other space is measured. In what sense is this limiting aspect the manifestation of the belief in absolute space? Isn't absolute space the product of metaphysical demands that are made only quite late in the game?

This more charitable approach to naturalized cognition motivates theories under which our judgments are not always in error but are instead able to be true in a manner that is compatible with their naturalization. It also motivates theories under which our judgments are neither true nor false. We shall explore these theories, which can also be found in Nietzsche's thought, in the next chapter.

4. Antirealism and Noncognitivism

My goal in this chapter is to outline what I believe are the two major alternatives to the error theory that can be found in Nietzsche's epistemologies: antirealism and noncognitivism. Antirealist interpretations have dominated the literature on Nietzsche's epistemology. I will argue that the antirealist elements in Nietzsche's thought have been overemphasized and that much of what Nietzsche says reflects a noncognitivist approach. These two interpretations can be distinguished by their answer to the question of whether Nietzsche considers thought to be possible. As I've suggested in the previous two chapters, Nietzsche is committed to the Kantian argument that thought is incompatible with a naturalistic account of the self. We have already seen this in his error theory. I will argue in this chapter that it is evident in other areas of his epistemology and that it drives him toward the view that we do not possess concepts.

1. Cognitive Compatibilism and Skepticism

To understand why someone might be motivated to present an antirealist or noncognitivist epistemology, let's return to the fundamental conflict that stands behind Nietzsche's epistemological reflections. This is the conflict between a naturalistic account of human judgment and an account under which human judgment is constrained by concepts. The problem with a naturalistic account of human judgment, it will be remembered, is that it makes the causes of a judgment insensitive to the judgment's apparent object. This makes it unlikely that the content of the concept employed in the judgment is determined by the character of this object. Once again, Hume's account of causal judgment is the paradigm. If what brings us to make a causal judgment is a disposition to associate events that have been constantly conjoined in the past, then it is difficult to see how we have a concept of causal necessitation, since our causal judgments are insensitive to whether causal necessity exists.

As we have seen, this difficulty with explaining cognition naturalistically motivates Kant's transcendental idealist approach and Spir's error theory. Kant's and Spir's accounts of judgment are responses to the inability of empirical laws of association to explain how we can attribute qualities *to an object* and so judge with objective validity. Kant and Spir argue that the only way an objectively valid judgment about an object is possible is if the qualities attributed to the object are *unconditionally* united in the mind, that is, united in an atemporal and necessary manner.

Although Nietzsche rejects Kant's and Spir's view that human judgment actually succeeds in bringing about unconditional unities, he fundamentally agrees with them concerning the requirements for objectively valid thought. It is for this reason that Nietzsche argues that we must take ourselves to be pure timeless substances in order to consider ourselves as capable of thought.

Thus, although Kant, Spir, and Nietzsche each have importantly different views about the existence and nature of empirical judgment, they agree that a truthful judgment is one in which there is a necessary connection between thought and its object. The minute that there is a slippage between what brings us to make a judgment and what the judgment is about, the judgment can no longer be a thought about *that* object. And such slippage is inevitable when human judgment is naturalized.

But why this resistance to naturalism? Just as there are those who think that human freedom is compatible with a naturalization of the sources of human action, why can't one adopt the view that truth is compatible with the naturalization of the sources of human judgment? Why not be a *cognitive compatibilist*?

The cognitive compatibilist accepts naturalistic descriptions of our judgments about squareness, for example, those in which our training as a child or biological tendencies play a role in why we come to the judgments about squareness that we do, but denies that the truth or falsity of such judgments have to do with our training or biological tendencies. Whether such judgments are true has instead to do with whether what we judge is square or not. According to this view, there is no need for philosophers to suffer from the "Egyptianism" (*TI* 3:1) or distrust of the historical contingency of their judgments (*HA* 2) that Nietzsche argues their commitment to objective validity requires of them. That our judgments are caused is perfectly compatible with their truth. To the extent that cognitive compatibilism is not answered, Nietzsche's entire epistemology will appear to be a dead end.

The motivation for Nietzsche's rejection of cognitive compatibilism is that it conflicts with the principle of cognitive sensitivity, that is, the view that the concepts employed in our judgments must *guide* or *influence* us in arriving at our judgments. Concepts that do not satisfy the principle are irrelevant to what we do in the way of judging. If our judgments' truth-values are nevertheless determined by such concepts, we have no reason to believe that the judgments we make are at all likely to be true. In other words, our judgments are not *justified.* Cognitive compatibilism leads to *skepticism.*[1]

2. Antirealism

Like Kant and Spir, Nietzsche accepts the principle of cognitive sensitivity. He insists that what we are thinking about—the content of our concepts—must make a difference to how we think. This approach helps explain Nietzsche's general resistance to skepticism.[2] But the only conceptual content to which a naturalized judgment could be sensitive would concern not its apparent object but its subjective causes. This position, which I will call *antirealism,* is the one most commonly attributed to Nietzsche in the literature.

In chapter 2, I defined "realism" as the view that the rules for uniting objects under concepts have to do solely with what the objects united are like. For example, the realist would see the appropriateness of the application of the concept *green* to grass as depending solely upon what grass is like (namely, that it is green). In contrast, the antirealist denies that the conditions for applying concepts to objects can refer solely to the objects; such conditions must take *us* into account. It is for this reason that the truth-values of our judgments about the world depend upon us.

Consider, for example, an antirealist approach to the concept *taboo.* This would mean asserting that the judgment that dead chickens are taboo is about dead chickens (and not about, say, the attitude of the tribe toward dead chickens) but that the conditions for *taboo* being attributable to dead chickens takes more into account than the dead chickens themselves. What is taken into account is the attitude of the tribe toward dead chickens.

It is often difficult to distinguish antirealism from a position that simply changes the objects of our judgments such that our judgments are realistically true of these objects. An example would be the view that the judgment that dead chickens are taboo is really about the tribe's attitude toward dead chickens rather than dead chickens themselves. Another example is phenomenalism. Although phenomenalists claim that it is our sensations to which we are sensitive when making judgments about material objects, they argue that such judgments can be true because the objects of judgments using material-object concepts are our actual or possible sensations. The manner in which such judgments are true is understood by phenomenalists realistically. The judgment that there is a chair, which is really about one's chair-like sensations, is true if and only if one's sensations are indeed chair-like, that is, not having to do with something other than the object of the judgment.

Thus it is not always easy to tell whether Nietzsche is arguing for antirealism or instead shifting the objects of our judgments to something subjective, in a manner analogous to phenomenalism. Consider, for example, his claim that "the essence of a thing is only an opinion about the 'thing.' Or rather: 'it is considered' is the real 'it is,' the sole 'this is'" (*WP* 556). It seems reasonably clear that this passage is incompatible with Nietzsche's error theory because it does not argue that our opinions falsify the essence of things. But it could be read as a claim that we are realistically describing our opinions rather than independent objects *or* as the claim that the rules for applying our concepts to objects refer not to the objects but to the subjective processes that bring us to have the opinions about them that we do.

In the end, however, there is no reason to draw a sharp distinction between these two epistemological positions. In both cases, Nietzsche sharply departs from the view that the conventional realist would take concerning our judgments and argues that the content of our judgments concerns something other than external objects. Both positions are motivated by the principle of cognitive sensitivity—the demand that we be sensitive to the content of our judgments.

Many passages in Nietzsche suggest an antirealist interpretation. Sometimes he argues that our application of the categories of being creates a world that is true for us (*WP* 514). This suggests that what is primarily responsible for world-making is our application of categories such as absolute space and time, self-identical substance, and causality to the chaos of sensations. Such a view closely resembles Kant's transcendental idealism except that the application of these categories of being occurs within becoming rather than through a transcendental self.

But Nietzsche also sometimes suggests a more free-ranging approach under which our contributions to the world are not obviously tied to categories of being (e.g. *WP* 495, 552, 560, 567, 606). "Insofar as the word 'knowledge' has any meaning, the world is knowable; but it is interpretable otherwise, it has no meaning behind it, but countless meanings—'perspectivism'"

(*WP* 481). "It is enough to create new names and estimations and probabilities in order to create in the long run new 'things'" (*GS* 58). Instead of appealing to categories of being, Nietzsche speaks of the world as depending upon our interpretations, perspectives, or representations: "Against positivism, which halts at phenomena—'There are only facts'—I would say: No, facts is precisely what there is not, only interpretations. We cannot establish any fact 'in itself': perhaps it is folly to want to do such a thing" (*WP* 481).

3. Noncognitivism

The antirealist rejects realism because it is an inadequate (or incoherent) conception of truth and replaces it with another. Nietzsche's *noncognitivism,* in contrast, is the view that our judgments are neither true nor false.

In denying that our judgments have truth-values, the noncognitivist denies that we have the ability to think. We have already seen why Nietzsche might be tempted to deny the existence of thought as a result of his naturalism. I will argue in this chapter that, at times, he succumbs to this temptation: "There exists neither 'spirit,' nor reason, nor thinking, nor consciousness, nor soul, nor will, nor truth: all are fictions that are of no use" (*WP* 480).

Philosophers currently use the terms "cognitivism" and "noncognitivism" primarily to refer to the *semantic* status of a region of *language,* particularly *evaluative* language. The cognitivist holds that terms in that region have referential content and thus their meaning can be understood in terms of their contribution to sentences' truth-value. A noncognitivist interpretation of a region of language holds that terms in that region fail to have referential content.

But the terms "cognitivism" and "noncognitivism" have *psychological,* as opposed to semantic, connotations as well. Kant, for example, is routinely labeled a cognitivist in ethics because he holds that evaluative judgments are the product of reason rather than emotion. For the same reason, Hume is treated as a noncognitivist because he treats evaluative judgment as the expression of sentiments or dispositions of the will. Analogously, Hume's account of causal judgments can be labeled noncognitivist because he denies that we *think* when we make judgments about causal connections. We have no concept of causality but instead simply connect ideas of events according to habits. Such associations of events do not count as thinking because they are governed not by rules but by mere empirical regularities. If I fail to associate constantly conjoined events in the future, I will not have done anything wrong. I will instead merely have done something different from what I did in the past.

Nietzsche worked within the psychological tradition of Hume and Kant, not the semantic tradition common in twentieth-century philosophy. Some discussions of semantic issues *can* be found in Nietzsche, most notably in "On Truth and Lies in a Nonmoral Sense" (e.g. p. 81). These discussions have been the focus of a great deal of attention in the literature, undoubtedly because of the contemporary philosophical focus on semantic issues. But they are rudimentary and pale in comparison with the substantial philosophical discussions of human *judgment* that can be found in Nietzsche's works, discussions that we have already explored in the previous three chapters.

Thus, when I claim that Nietzsche is a noncognitivist, I do not mean by this that he holds any particular semantic view. Rather, I mean that he denies the existence of thought. And I characterize antirealist readings of Nietzsche that are common in the English-language literature on his epistemology as cognitivist because, under them, Nietzsche accepts the existence of thought.

Despite the fact that the noncognitivism I attribute to Nietzsche is not a semantic position, I find it useful to draw a number of analogies between it and twentieth-century noncognitivist positions concerning evaluative language, particularly emotivism. I want to spend some time justifying this approach by arguing that emotivism often has an important psychological component. In other words, emotivists typically hold not merely that evaluative sentences do not have truth-values but also that we are not *thinking* when we judge something to be good. (Those untroubled by the analogies I draw between Nietzsche and the emotivists may skip the remainder of this section.)

Emotivists argue that the sentence "x is good," instead of describing states of affairs, performs the role of expressing our desires or dispositions of the will concerning x.[3] In arguing that the term "good" plays an expressive role, emotivists deny that the term has conditions or rules for correct application. One might think that if the function of the word "good" is to express a positive desire toward that said to be good, then the word "good" *has* conditions for correct application: the application of "good" to something is appropriate if and only if one has a positive desire toward that thing. But emotivists generally reject this account because it would make the evaluative sentence "This is good" semantically equivalent to the descriptive sentence "This is approved by me." If there were such a semantic equivalence, then it would follow that "a speaker typically makes a value judgment in the course of expressing belief. The belief is *about* an attitude, to be sure . . . but it is nevertheless a belief. And the expression of a belief is precisely what the non-cognitive theory is rejecting. It holds that a speaker typically makes a value judgment in the course of expressing his *attitude*—his judgment and his attitude being related directly, without the mediation of a belief" (Stevenson 1963, 80).

This expressive relation between word and attitude is a product of the "emotive meaning" of a term, that is, a term's tendency to cause or be caused by a certain range of emotions: "The emotive meaning of a word is the power the word acquires, on account of its history in emotional situations, to evoke or directly express attitudes, as distinct from designating them" (Stevenson 1944, 33). It is for this reason that evaluative terms have no conditions for their correct or incorrect application. If we were to use "good" in connection with an aversion to something, we would not have used the term improperly, although we would have gone against how we are normally disposed to use the term. Not surprisingly, emotivism has been criticized because it denies that evaluative terms have rules for their application. Rather than being a semantics of evaluative sentences, it appears to be an abrogation of semantics entirely (Kerner 1966, 40–52).

The fact that evaluative terms have no conditions for their correct or incorrect application is important for Stevenson. The minute that evaluative terms are seen as having rules for their application that refer to our emotional states, evaluations turn from being the expression of these emotions to a description of them. If they are understood as descriptions, not only would they have truth-values but people who have different views about whether something is good would no longer be disagreeing with one another—each would merely be describing his or her own subjective attitude toward that thing. The view that evaluative terms are not rule-governed, paradoxically, makes evaluative debate possible.

Thus Stevenson associates a particular psychological account of evaluative judgment with his semantic position. The association of objects connected with my use of the term "good" is not *conceptual*. I associate things as good because I desire them, but this associating does not occur through the application of the concept "desired by me." For Stevenson, associating things together as good is the product of *feeling* rather than thinking. The relationship between the judgment that x is good and one's approval of x is, as Stevenson puts it, "immediate."

I will argue below that Nietzsche provides an account of human judgment that is remarkably similar to the emotivist's account of evaluative judgment. But before I do so, let me outline the two most prevalent forms of antirealism attributed to Nietzsche: the pragmatic and the coherence theories of truth.

4. The Pragmatic Theory of Truth

As we have seen, Nietzsche, in keeping with his commitment to the principle of cognitive sensitivity, attempts to tie the content of our judgments to their naturalistic causes. Because he finds a wide variety of naturalistic causes, he presents a wide variety of theories of truth (*KSA* 11:26[114], 12:5[19]; *WP* 533, 534, 537). But because he tends to emphasize our pragmatic reasons for arriving at the judgments we do, he most commonly suggests a connection between truth and utility (e.g. *WP* 423, 474). Some interpreters have used such passages to argue that Nietzsche advocates a pragmatic theory of truth, under which "*p* is true and *q* is false if *p* works and *q* does not" (Danto 1980, 72).

That Nietzsche holds a pragmatic theory of truth appears to be disconfirmed, however, by passages in which he draws a distinction between truth and utility (e.g. *BGE* 4; *WP* 487, 515):[4] "We have arranged for ourselves a world in which we can live—by positing bodies, lines, planes, causes and effects, motion and rest, form and content; without these articles of faith nobody now could endure life. But that does not prove them. Life is no argument. The conditions of life might include error" (*GS* 121). "[Synthetic a priori] judgments must be *believed* to be true, for the sake of the preservation of creatures like ourselves; though they might, of course, be *false* judgments for all that!" (*BGE* 11).

But it is important to note that some of these passages in which Nietzsche draws a distinction between truth and utility are cases in which he presents his *error theory*. It is undoubtedly true that Nietzsche does not accept the pragmatic theory of truth when he's presenting his error theory. But neither does he accept any other antirealist theory. Under the error theory, true judgment is *impossible*—not subjectivized. Accordingly, such passages cannot be used to argue that some antirealist conception of truth other than the pragmatic theory is Nietzsche's considered view.

But not all of the passages where Nietzsche distinguishes between truth and utility are expressions of his error theory. It is common, for example, for Nietzsche to argue that the feelings of pleasure or power that accompany the acceptance of religious beliefs is no argument for the truth of these beliefs:[5] "*The proof from pleasure*—The pleasant conviction is assumed to be true: this is the proof from pleasure (or, as the church says, the proof from strength), of which all religions are so proud, while they should be ashamed of it" (*HA* 120). "Would blessedness—more technically, *pleasure*—ever be a proof of truth? So little that it provides almost the counter-proof, at any rate the strongest suspicion against 'truth,' when feelings of pleasure enter into the answer to the question 'what is true?'" (*AC* 50). The distinction between truth and utility that Nietzsche draws in such passages appears to tell against Danto's interpretation.

Maudemarie Clark argues further that if Danto's interpretation of Nietzsche were correct, Nietzsche's theory of truth would violate Tarski's famous "adequacy conditions" (Tarski 1944) for any definition of truth:

> "Snow is white" is true in English [if and only if] snow is white. . . . Equivalences of this form seem trivially true for anyone who knows the language(s) involved, and it is difficult to see how one can reject them and still claim to share our concept of truth. . . . Therefore, if, in accord with Danto, Nietzsche equates truth with what satisfies our practical interests, this does not give us a new theory of truth, a new account of what we are doing when we pick out certain beliefs as true. . . . Instead, it discards the very concept of truth, that is, proposes that we use "true" or "*wahr*" in a different way than do speakers of standard English or German. (Clark 1990, 32–33)

One way of putting Clark's point is that if a pragmatic theory of truth were correct, then certain phrases to which speakers of English clearly ascribe different meanings—for example, "useful to believe" and "true"—are in fact semantically equivalent. That Nietzsche denies such semantic equivalence and thus rejects a pragmatic theory of truth is shown in those passages in which he draws a distinction between what is true and what is useful to believe.

The pragmatic antirealist can respond to Clark's criticism, but doing so requires saying more about Tarski's adequacy conditions. It is important to recognize that Tarski's T-schema—which generates sentences of the following form:

"Snow is white" is true in English if and only if snow is white.

"Grass is green" is true in English if and only if grass is green.

Etc.

—is *not* a definition of truth. It is a *material adequacy* condition: a theory of truth must entail all the sentences generated by the T-schema to be adequate. Under Tarski's theory, the truth of sentences in a language is instead a function of the *satisfaction relation* between open sentences (which can roughly be understood as predicates) and objects. For example, the open sentence "x is white" is satisfied by snow, and the open sentence "x is to the north of y" is satisfied by the ordered pair <Portland, Sacramento>. It is for these reasons that "Snow is white" and "Portland is to the north of Sacramento" are true. The employment of the satisfaction relation allows Tarski to show how the truth-values of complex sentences (for example, "Snow is white, and Portland is to the north of Sacramento") are functions of their parts. Because there are an infinite number of sentences, some explanation of the truth of a sentence in terms of its parts is needed to give a *complete* theory of truth for a language.

Because of the role that the satisfaction relation plays in Tarski's definition of truth, some philosophers, such as Donald Davidson, take it to be a form of the correspondence theory of truth: "The semantic conception of truth as developed by Tarski deserves to be called a correspondence theory because of the part played by the concept of satisfaction; for clearly what has been done is that the property of being true has been explained, and non-trivially, in terms of a relationship between language and something else" (1985, 48). Whether or not this is true, it is clear that it is the *satisfaction relation,* not the T-sentences, that captures whatever connection there might be between the truth of a sentence and what the world is like.

Given that the pragmatic theory of truth appears to be a rejection of the correspondence theory, let us reformulate the pragmatic theory as a theory about the satisfaction relation. This would be the view that snow falls under the predicate *white* if and only if it is useful to predicate snow in this fashion. I have already intimated that Nietzsche thinks that it is our desires or interests that lead us to unite objects under concepts. One might understand this theory of conceptualization as a pragmatic theory of satisfaction.

So understood, the pragmatic theory can generate the T-sentences just as easily as Tarski's theory (cf. Haack 1978, 100–102). If I hold the pragmatic theory I can arrive at the biconditional "'Snow is white' is true if and only if snow is white" by surveying all possible worlds and concluding that those worlds about which I would say that snow is white (because it is useful to do so) are the same worlds about which I would say that the sentence "snow is white" is true. *How* I determine that snow is white—whether on the basis of realist or pragmatic conditions for concept application—doesn't appear to make a difference to my ability to accept the biconditional. This is because the biconditional rests not upon any particular theory of correct predication but upon a relationship between assenting to a sentence and applying the truth predicate to that sentence.

Clark makes use of this same relationship to argue that the T-sentences follow from her brand of antirealism:

> Consider the important connection that obtains between our concepts of truth and rational acceptability. We call a belief "true" precisely when we believe it meets our standards for rational acceptability. "'S' is true" is assertable (rationally acceptable), therefore, if "S" is rationally acceptable. If this does not make

the two concepts identical, it certainly makes it imperative for those who deny this identity (e.g., metaphysical realists) to say how truth differs from acceptability. If they cannot explain the difference—that is, explain what it means to say that a belief is false though fully acceptable—we can hardly consider the concept of truth to be so clear. (1990, 43)

But this argument is just as available to the pragmatic antirealist. Clark's argument is not a direct demonstration of some essential connection between our predicating "true" of a belief and its being rationally acceptable. It instead relies upon there being an intimate connection between our predicating "true" of a belief and our *accepting* that belief. It is only on the basis of this premise, in combination with the observation that we accept beliefs when we think that they meet our standards of rational acceptability, that she is able to draw a connection between truth and rational acceptability. Clark's argument is, in essence, the following:

> Premise 1: We call a belief "true" when we accept that belief.
> Premise 2: We accept beliefs when we think that they satisfy our standards of rational acceptability.
> Conclusion: Therefore a belief is true when it satisfies our standards of rational acceptability.

But the pragmatic antirealist can use the same argument, replacing premise 2 with:

> Premise 2_1: We accept beliefs when it is useful for us to do so.

And the conclusion with:

> Conclusion$_1$: Therefore a belief is true when it is useful for us to accept it.

Indeed, once it is spelled out in this fashion, Clark's argument, but not the pragmatist's, reveals itself to be a non sequitur. Premise 2 states that we accept a belief when we *think* it meets our standards for rational acceptability. But the Conclusion is that a belief is true when it *is* rationally acceptable, not when we *think* it to be so. It should be clear why Clark is motivated to waffle here. Premise 2 cannot be that *actually* satisfying standards of rational acceptability is what leads us to accept beliefs, because if that were true then, given her brand of antirealism, we could never make an error. But the Conclusion cannot be that a belief is true if it we think it has satisfied our standards of rational acceptability, or truth will have been reduced to belief in rational acceptability—and "believed to be rationally acceptable" is no more semantically connected to "true" than "useful" is.

So a pragmatist can accept that "Snow is white" is true if and only if snow is white. But wouldn't a pragmatist also say that "Snow is white" is true if and only if it is useful to say that snow is white? And wouldn't *that* be incompatible with our feeling that there is a lack of semantic equivalence between "true" and "useful"?

The two would be semantically equivalent only if one must say "It is useful to say that snow is white" when and only when it is in fact useful to say that snow is white. But to accept this would be to be a *realist*, not a pragmatist, with respect to sentences using the word "useful." It may be useful to say "Snow is white" and at the same time be useful to say "It is not useful to say 'Snow is white.'" If so, then one could say that "Snow is white" is true but deny that it is useful to say so. Thus the pragmatist can retain all of the semantic separation between truth and utility that occurs in our language.

The argument in the previous paragraph might be criticized on the grounds that it assumes that the sentences by means of which the pragmatic theory is articulated are not members of the object language to which the pragmatic theory applies. Consider the following sentence from the argument above: "It may be *useful* to say 'Snow is white' and at the same time be *useful* to say 'It is not *useful* to say "Snow is white."'" The first and second uses of the word "useful" must mean something different from the third. The first and second uses must be referring to something like actual realist usefulness, while the third concerns what it is useful to call "useful."

Is this a substantial objection to the pragmatic theory? No, for, as I will argue in the next chapter, *all competing antirealist theories suffer from the same problem*, including Clark's own theory. We have already alluded to this problem in connection with phenomenalism. The phenomenalist argues that we can refer only to our sensations and not material objects. The everyday term "material object," in this view, refers to actual or possible sensations. But if the phenomenalist position is articulated in the language to which the theory applies, it will be false or contentless. If, by saying that we cannot refer to material objects, phenomenalists are saying that we cannot refer to actual or possible sensations, then they are saying something false. The only other possibility is that the term "material object" as they are using it is meaningless, in which case the content of the theory is undermined. To make sense of phenomenalism, we must assume that it is being articulated in a realist language that, unlike the language that is its object, is able to refer to material objects, if only to deny our ability to speak of them. Otherwise phenomenalists would be unable to contentfully deny the ability of our first-order judgments to refer to material objects.

5. The Collapse of the Pragmatic Theory

Although Danto's pragmatic theory of truth survives Clark's attack, it is not stable in the end. The motivation for the pragmatic theory is the principle of cognitive sensitivity. Pragmatic conditions for correct predication are attractive because they appear to be more closely connected with how we actually go about judging. But the principle of cognitive sensitivity in the end drives the antirealist into a radical form under which the only condition for the truth of one's judgment is the fact that one has made it, and error is impossible. For only such a condition will ensure that there is no slippage between what leads us to come to the judgment and what makes the judgment true. And such a radical antirealism is, in the end, equivalent to noncognitivism: The truth of our judgments is trivially satisfied and so loses its significance as a constraint upon our judgments.

We have already seen the increasingly subjectivizing tendency of the principle of cognitive sensitivity in connection with phenomenalism. Phenomenalists think that they have adequately responded to the principle by reducing judgments about material objects to judgments about sensations. Judgments about sensations satisfy the principle because having a sensation of green is the same thing as seeing it as green. We do not have to worry about misjudging sensations because the sensations themselves are the judgments or, perhaps, because sensations always unambiguously tell us how they should be judged. But, in fact, there is no such necessary connection between having a sensation of green and judging the sensation to be green (see Rorty 1979, 139–48). This is shown by the fact that, when pressed to justify our immediate judgments about our sensations, we do so not on the basis of some necessary unity between sensation and judgment but upon epistemic beliefs concerning our reliability as judgers of our sensations—a reliability that could fail to obtain (Williams 1999, chap. 3).

But this lack of a necessary connection means that there is *something more* bringing about my judgment that a sensation is green than the greenness of the sensation. Any conditions for the application of the concept *green* that would satisfy the principle of cognitive sensitivity would have to refer to whatever this *something more* is. Thus the subjective elements taken into account by the antirealist get pushed further and further back into the subject, behind sensations themselves. Such an approach suggests a more extreme form of antirealism, such as that found in German Idealists such as Fichte, in which even the apparently sensory elements of empirical knowledge are dependent upon the thinking subject. The passive element of knowledge is eliminated entirely, and the entire describable world becomes dependent upon the transcendental self.

Danto's pragmatism can likewise be criticized for being insufficiently subjectivist. Under pragmatism, a false judgment still appears possible—namely, when we make a judgment that is not useful.[6] But we cannot understand such an error as possible without seeing ourselves as cognitively sensitive to considerations of usefulness, and this is just as suspect as any form of realism. Let us say that I make judgments that are not useful and I eventually die. How are we to understand my judgments as bound by truth conditions concerning usefulness when I am insensitive to issues of usefulness? If one sets aside the principle of cognitive sensitivity in this case, why not set it aside in all cases and simply become a realist *tout court* (see Poellner 1995, 21)?

Many of the passages in which Nietzsche appears to present a form of pragmatic antirealism can be understood instead as identifying the truth of a judgment with its acceptance. Consider the following passage:

> The categories of reason . . . could have prevailed, after much groping and fumbling, through their relative utility—There came a point when one collected them together, raised them to consciousness as a whole—and when one commanded them, i.e., when they had the effect of a command—From then on, they counted as *a priori*, as beyond experience, as irrefutable. And yet perhaps they represent nothing more than the expediency of a certain race and species—their utility alone is their "truth"—. (*WP* 514)

Pragmatic considerations are introduced by Nietzsche in this passage not to explain why the categories of reason are true but instead to explain why these categories are treated as unassailable (Poellner 1995, 169). They are not questioned by us because they have become ingrained in us through their utility. If this passage presumes any criterion of truth, it is simple acceptance, not utility (cf. *GS* 110–11).

Sometimes Nietzsche suggests a truly radical antirealism, under which our judgments are always true about a world that we create in the very act of judging. The distinguishing feature of such an antirealism is a resistance to identify *any* criterion by virtue of which our judgments could be in error. Consider Nietzsche's claim that "the essence of a thing is only an opinion about the 'thing.' Or rather: 'it is considered' is the real 'it is,' the sole 'this is'" (*WP* 556). This passage suggests that all it takes to get at the essence of a thing is to have an opinion about it. Radical antirealism is also suggested by those passages in which truth is identified as a process of world-creation that has infinite possibilities: "Truth is . . . not something there, that might be found or discovered—but something that must be created" (*WP* 552). "[T]he world has become 'infinite' for us all over again, inasmuch as we cannot reject the possibility that *it may include infinite interpretations*" (GS2d 374).

We should not be surprised if the antirealist tendencies in Nietzsche drove him to a position under which all judgments are true in the making and error is impossible. The Spirean model of cognition standing behind Nietzsche's epistemology is that of intellectual intuition—a necessary unity of thought and object. The only way that such unity can be reestablished after thought is naturalized is to move the object of knowledge to the judgment itself. But a radically subjectivized antirealism is *functionally indistinguishable from noncognitivism*. Truth is trivially satisfied and so drops out of consideration entirely. *This suggests that the ultimate tendency of Nietzsche's thought is toward a noncognitivist position, under which concepts do not exist.*

6. The Coherence Theory

The other major candidate for Nietzsche's antirealist theory of truth among interpreters has been a position that, I will argue, resembles a coherence theory of truth. This position is usually introduced by commentators in contrast to a traditional theory of justification or truth (Leiter 1994, 347–48; Schacht 1983, 61–62). Maudemarie Clark uses foundationalism: "Following this reading, Nietzsche uses the metaphor of perspective to express his rejection of Cartesian foundationalism. Perspectivism amounts to the claim that we cannot and need not justify our beliefs by paring them down to a set of unquestionable beliefs all rational beings must share. This means that all justification is contextual, dependent on the other beliefs held unchallengeable for the moment, but themselves capable of only a similarly contextual justification" (1990, 130). The heart of this argument is the insight that, as Donald Davidson puts it, "nothing can count as a reason for holding a belief except another belief" (1983, 426). One cannot justify a belief by means of its relationship to things in the world because things in the world cannot enter into relationships of justification at all (Leiter 1994, 342–43). Things in the world just sit there, stupidly and silently, without saying anything. Or, alternatively, one *can* justify a belief by means of its relationship to the world (for example, when saying that one's belief that grass is green is justified because the greenness of grass has a strong tendency to cause one to believe that it is green), but such a justification is, once again, the justification of a belief by another belief. It is not any relationship between actual grass and one's belief that justifies one's belief, but a belief about the relationship.

Because we are causally separated from so many of the things about which we make judgments, philosophers have rarely been tempted to expect some sort of direct confrontation between our judgments and all the things they are about. But the temptation has been very strong in connection with a subset of these things, namely, sensations. The coherentist will reject such an account of judgments about sensations because sensations still are unable to enter into relationships of justification. Sensations, like material objects, just sit there, until we make a judgment about them. And when we do make the judgment, it is the judgment and not the sensation that will enter into the relationship of justification.

One motivation for arguing that when making a judgment about a sensation there is a direct confrontation between judgment and object is that such judgments would provide natural termini for chains of justification for more complex empirical judgments. They would be the justificatory *foundation* for our knowledge by virtue of their intrinsic credibility. Without intrinsically credible judgments, justification would either involve an infinite regress (which, it is argued, would mean that justification is impossible, since justification has to stop somewhere) or an appeal to the coherence of one's system of judgments. The second alternative is criticized by the foundationalist as not being able to exclude the possibility that our system of judgments, although forming a coherent unity, has no connection with reality. Judgments about sensations are attractive as foundations because sensations are what "link our judgments with the world."

But the coherentist can claim that within our coherent collection of judgments there are *epistemic* judgments (judgments *about* judgments) that claim that our judgments about the world are, in general, caused by their objects via our sensations. Accordingly, the coherentist can make just as much sense of the connection between our judgments and the world as the foundationalist. The coherentist will deny, however, that judgments about sensations are intrinsically credible, for judgments about sensations need to be justified by these epistemic judgments about them.

Indeed, the coherentist will claim that the foundationalist actually appeals to epistemic judgments when arguing that judgments about sensations are intrinsically credible and link us to the world. Accordingly, although the foundationalist claims to treat judgments about sensations as foundational, the foundationalist in fact justifies judgments about sensations by other judgments in coherentist fashion (Williams 1980, 247–51). The foundationalist is a coherentist *malgré lui*.

It is taken to follow from these considerations that the justification of a judgment is one of its coherence with other judgments in a systematic whole. The subsequent move from such a coherence theory of justification to a coherence theory of *truth* follows from an application of the principle of cognitive sensitivity. Since how we make our judgments does not require a concern with "the world" as the foundationalist understands it, there is no need to think of our judgments as bound by truth-conditions that concern this world. If one were to insist, however, that our judgments are nevertheless bound by such hyperbolic truth conditions, *skepticism* would follow, for the way we come to our judgments is unrelated to what makes our judgments true.

The theory of truth that Clark attributes to Nietzsche is clearly motivated by the principle of cognitive sensitivity. Clark sees Nietzsche as embracing a form of antirealism under which truth is dependent upon "our cognitive interests" or "our best standards of rational acceptability" (1990, 49). The phrase "best standards of rational acceptability" is meant to capture what leads us to judge as we do. What such an antirealism rejects, according to Clark, is the idea that "a theory that gave us everything else we could want from a theory (e.g. simplicity, coherence, explanatory power, predictive success) might nevertheless fail to be true" (86). According to Clark, truth cannot outstrip our best standards of rational acceptability because "to conceive of something is to conceive of it as satisfying some description or another, which is to think of it as being conceptualizable in some way or another" (46–47). In other words, the idea of a thing that outstrips our best standards of rational acceptability simply *plays no role* in the way we conceive of the world and thus cannot be a means by which we our conceptions of the world are true or false (109–17; see also Leiter 1994, 348–49).

But under Clark's interpretation of Nietzsche's epistemology, there remain cognitive constraints upon our judgments. Truth can outstrip what *we* do in the way of judging, although it cannot outstrip what *anyone* could *ever* do in the way of judging. Clark argues that the antirealist of the Nietzschean variety "should admit that truth is independent of our cognitive capacities—that our capacities might not be sufficient, even in principle, to determine what the truth is in some cases—and insist only that truth cannot be independent of our cognitive interests, of our best standards of rational acceptability. This neo-Kantian position on truth is the one that I shall attribute to Nietzsche" (1990, 60). Thus, for Clark, Nietzsche accepts that there are norms with respect to which our beliefs could fail to be true. First of all, we could simply lack the cognitive capacities to come to a correct determination about what the world is like. We could, for example, lack the adequate sensory apparati or enough money to perform the requisite experiments. In addition, even if we had the necessary capacities, we could fail to satisfy "our best standards of rational acceptability." We could fail to apply correct standards of simplicity, coherence, explanatory power, or predictive success.

To the extent that Clark's theory is antirealist, it resonates a good deal with those antirealist comments that can be found in Nietzsche's works. As we have seen, Nietzsche clearly suggests that there is no possibility of a direct confrontation between the world and our means of interpreting it. He also sometimes suggests that truth consists of the relationship between our judgments (e.g. *KSA* 11:34[247]), in a manner that sounds similar to a form of coherentism: "An isolated judgment is never 'true'—only in the connection and relation of many judgments is there any surety" (*WP* 530). Another possibility is: "'Truth': this, according to my way of thinking, does not necessarily denote the antithesis of error, but in the most fundamental cases only the posture of various errors in relation to one another" (*WP* 535).

But is there any reason to believe that Nietzsche reduces truth to "our best standards of rational acceptability"? Unlike Danto, who can at least present passages where Nietzsche suggests that truth be reduced to pragmatic considerations, Clark's primary argument for attributing her position to Nietzsche is its ability to account for those passages in which he praises science and sensory experience and criticizes Christian interpretations of reality (1990, 103–5). Clark reads standards of rational acceptability into Nietzsche's epistemology because Nietzsche's criticism of Christianity and praise of science "becomes trivial unless we interpret him as claiming that his own perspective is cognitively superior to the religio-moral perspective on history" (140). *Some* standard of cognitive superiority is needed, it seems, and "our best standards of rational acceptability" seem to capture how Nietzsche actually assesses judgments.

But Clark's reading of Nietzsche is just as vulnerable to the principle of cognitive sensitivity as are realism and the pragmatic theory. Assume that there are indeed standards of rational acceptability that our current theories fail to meet, such failure being recognizable, say, at the end of human history after human beings have developed cognitive capabilities significantly better than our own. How is it that these standards are *our* standards, when we currently make judgments in a manner that is insensitive to them? What is the difference between Clark's standards and those of the realist, insofar as both outstrip what we do when making our judgments?

The only standard governing our judgments that meets the principle of cognitive sensitivity is one that is completely reducible to our *current* reasons for making the judgments that we do. But this standard is one that our judgments cannot fail to satisfy. The result is an antirealist position under which our judgments are always true—a position that, as we have seen, is functionally indistinguishable from noncognitivism.

To put the matter crudely but perhaps more intuitively, Clark's position appears to still allow for the existence of *oughts* (standards of rational accept-ability) that condemn what *is* (our current dispositions to judge). But *oughts* that outstrip what *is* are contrary to the principle of cognitive sensitivity. For the only things that can affect what *is* are things that also *are,* not things that *ought* to be. Only if we assume that oughts non-naturalistically influence what is can they be made compatible with the principle of cognitive sensi-tivity. But it is precisely antinaturalism that Nietzsche is arguing against.[7]

7. Nietzsche on the Law of Noncontradiction

Perhaps the best evidence against a cognitivist interpretation of Nietzsche can be found in his comments concerning the law of noncontradiction. If any-thing is essential to the view that our judgments are cognitively constrained it is an obligation not to contradict. If our use of terms is rule-bound at all— if we actually think—then something cannot *both* fall *and* not fall under a term. To allow that something can be both *p* and *not-p* is to deny that *p* has rules for its application. Nietzsche himself notes that "the conceptual ban on contradiction proceeds from the belief that we are able to form concepts" (*WP* 516).

In the face of what he recognizes are the noncognitivist consequences of rejecting the law of noncontradiction, *Nietzsche goes ahead and rejects it.* Our resistance to contradiction is not the result of cognitive obligation but in-stead a merely psychological inability to contradict: "Not being able to con-tradict is proof of an incapacity, not of 'truth'" (*WP* 515). "We are unable to affirm and deny one and the same thing: this is a subjective empirical law, not the expression of any 'necessity' but only of an inability" (*WP* 516).

Explaining resistance to contradiction purely in terms of a psychological disinclination is precisely what one would expect from a philosopher who denies that our application of terms is rule-governed. Imagine someone con-sistently refusing to apply *not-frob* to something if *frob* had already been applied to it. Because the term *frob* has no criteria for correct or incorrect application, this refusal to contradict could not be the result of a respect for one's cognitive obligation and would have to be seen as a merely subjective disinclination.[8]

8. Nietzsche on Consciousness

Nietzsche's comments concerning consciousness and the self provide further support for a noncognitivist reading of his epistemology. These comments have posed problems for interpreters. On the one hand, Nietzsche suggests that mental events have no causal relationship with one another or with our subsequent actions. He argues, for example, that pleasure and pain, rather than being the causes of our reactions, are entirely epiphenomenal (e.g. *BGE* 225; *WP* 701–2). "Everything would have taken the same course, according to exactly the same sequence of causes and effects, if these states 'pleasure and displeasure' had been absent, and . . . one is simply deceiving oneself if one thinks they cause anything at all: they are *epiphenomena* [Begleiterscheinungen] with a quite different object than to evoke reactions; they are themselves effects within the instituted process of reaction" (*WP* 478). Indeed, Nietzsche makes this same point concerning *all* mental events (e.g. *TI* 6:3), including acts of willing or intending: "In summa: everything of which we become conscious is a terminal phenomenon [Enderscheinungen], an end—and causes nothing; every successive phenomenon in consciousness is completely atomistic—And we have sought to understand the world through the reverse conception—as if nothing were real and effective but thinking, feeling, willing!" (*WP* 478).

On the other hand, Nietzsche's naturalistic approach to human behavior involves describing causal relationships between psychological events. For example, he suggests that *ressentiment* is caused by perceived inadequacy (*GM* 3:14–16).[9] Such comments are to be found not merely when Nietzsche engages in what one might call "first-order" or unreflective psychological observation. Even in passages where he is clearly philosophically reflective, Nietzsche argues that such causal relationships exist, although details are sometimes hidden from us: "'Causality' eludes us; to suppose a direct causal link between thoughts, as logic does—that is the consequence of the crudest and clumsiest observation. Between two thoughts all kinds of affects play their game: but their motions are too fast, therefore, we fail to recognize them, we deny them—" (*WP* 477). If affects connect one thought to another (see also *GS2d* 360), then the thoughts *are* causally related—*through the affects*. For example, imagine that my affects are such that the idea of Michael Bolton inevitably leads me to have the idea of acts of horrible violence. It would not be improper to say that the idea of Michael Bolton causes in me the ideas of violence, provided that one recognizes that the causal relation proceeds through an emotional association. In the passage quoted above, it appears that all Nietzsche is concerned with denying is the existence of a "direct causal link" [*ein unmittelbares ursächliches Band*], not the existence of *any* causal link.

A further reason to question whether Nietzsche genuinely believes that there are no causal relations between mental events is the sheer implausibility of such a view.[10] Hales and Welshon provide a good account of just how radical it really is: "If epiphenomenalism is true of all psychological events, then no pain ever causes flinching, no caress ever causes pleasure, no insult ever causes cringing, no memory ever causes remorse or joy, no desire/belief pair ever causes action, no direction of attention to some hitherto ignored detail ever occurs, no one ever intentionally hits another in anger or soothes an unhappy child, no one intentionally crosses the street" (2000, 144).

Hales and Welshon are correct that a denial of causal relations between mental events is a dramatic position to take. But we should not be surprised that Nietzsche takes it. After all, under his view of absolute becoming each event is radically contingent and dissociated from every other event. And this theory applies just as much to mental as to nonmental events. Nietzsche is quite explicit that the same falsifications occur when we make judgments about inner experience as when we make judgments about outer experience (*WP* 475–77). If judgments about outer experience falsify absolute becoming by assuming causal connections between events, then so do judgments about inner experience.

That Nietzsche's theory of absolute becoming should apply to inner experience is doubly appropriate, since our falsifications of outer experience fundamentally depend upon an earlier falsification of inner experience. In chapter 3 I spelled out the role that the image of human agency plays for causal explanation of the external world. In order to see change as causally necessitated, we must insert first causes into the world. The image of the first cause that we rely upon is that of a human agent—a self or substance that is the uncaused generator of change (e.g. *GS* 109; *WP* 627). "The popular belief in cause and effect is founded on the presupposition that free will is the cause of every effect: it is only from this that we derive the feeling of causality. Thus there is also in it the feeling that every cause is *not* an effect but always only a cause" (*WP* 667).

Nietzsche's denial that such free agency can actually be found in internal experience (e.g. *GS* 127; *TI* 6:3; *KSA* 10:12[34]; *WP* 664) is fundamental to his critique of causal reasoning.[11]

> We have absolutely no experience of a cause; psychologically considered, we derive the entire concept from the subjective conviction that *we* are causes, namely, that the arm moves—but that is an error. We separate ourselves, the doers, from the deed, and we make use of this pattern everywhere—we seek a doer for every event. What is it we have done? We have misunderstood the feeling of strength, tension, resistance, a muscular feeling that is already the beginning of the act, as the cause, or we have taken the will to do this or that for a cause because the action follows upon it. (*WP* 551)

"The subject": interpreted from within ourselves, so that the ego counts as a substance, as the cause of all deeds, as a doer. The logical metaphysical postulates, the belief in substance, accident, attribute, etc., derive their convincing force from our habit of regarding all our deeds as consequences of our will— so that the ego, as substance, does not vanish in the multiplicity of change— But there is no such thing as will. (*WP* 488)

The view that there is no doer, only deeds, is Nietzsche's theory of absolute becoming applied to inner experience. It is surprising that so many commentators have sanguinely accepted this view. For to say that there are only deeds does not only mean that there is no underlying soul or transcendental subject. It also means rejecting any causal connection between these deeds, and any enduring substance (including a physical substance) through which this causal connection could proceed. To see inner experience from the perspective of absolute becoming is to treat every act as radically contingent—as arising out of nothing.

But if inner experience is absolute becoming, what are we to make of Nietzsche's inveterate naturalization of human behavior—his requirement that every aspect of human behavior be explainable causally? These two positions are less in conflict than they seem. The theory of absolute becoming and the view that every cause must itself have a cause are both *antithetic* positions. Both reject the idea that first causes or free will can be inserted into the world of becoming. To the extent that one requires that every cause of human behavior itself have a cause, one strips the self of its agency just as much as a theory of absolute becoming. Although finding the cause for an effect means looking for the doer standing behind the deed, *always* demanding a doer for the deed pushes the doer further and further back outside the agent to the beginning of time, such that all one encounters *in experience* is deeds and no doers. As a result, both of Nietzsche's two perspectives on inner experience treat human action as a radically contingent happening.

9. Rule-Skepticism

But it seems clear that Nietzsche is rejecting something else in his discussion of consciousness besides a thetic image of inner experience. For even when he assumes that causal connections can exist in inner experience, he appears concerned to argue that they are not what we think they are. In particular, he argues that the causal connections between thoughts are not *direct* but proceed through affects. This fact, he thinks, undermines logic (e.g. *WP* 478). "'Causality' eludes us; to suppose a direct causal link between thoughts, as logic does—that is the consequence of the crudest and clumsiest observation. Between two thoughts all kinds of affects play their game: but their motions are too fast, therefore, we fail to recognize them, we deny them—" (*WP* 477). "The sequence of thoughts, feelings, ideas in consciousness does not signify that this sequence is a causal sequence; but apparently it is so, to the highest degree. Upon this *appearance* we have founded our whole idea of spirit, reason, logic, etc. . . . and projected these *into* things and *behind* things!" (*WP* 524).

How are we to understand these curious remarks? The fact that these direct causal relations are required for *logic* is significant. As we have already seen, Nietzsche, under the influence of Spir, tends to speak of requirements for objectively valid thought as the presuppositions of logic. Like Spir, he considers self-identical substances to be required for logic because such substances are needed to attribute qualities to objects in an objectively valid fashion. Without such substances, we merely contingently associate qualities in the mind in a manner that says nothing about the world. Accordingly, Nietzsche must consider direct causal relations between thoughts to be necessary for objectively valid thought. This connection between mental causality and cognition is brought out in *Beyond Good and Evil:* "From where do I get the concept of thinking? Why do I believe in cause and effect? What gives me the right to speak of an ego, and even of an ego as cause, and finally of an ego as the cause of thoughts?" (16).

But why would anyone think that direct causal links between thoughts are required for objective validity? Insofar as these links are understood naturalistically, it would appear that objective validity still cannot exist. I believe that what Nietzsche means by direct causal links is what we can call *cognitive compulsion,* that is, the idea that one thought brings about a second because the second *ought* to follow. And Nietzsche is right that cognitive compulsion is undermined by the idea that it is only our *affects* that take us from one thought to another. For if our affects take us from one thought to another, we are not sensitive to any concepts binding our thoughts with respect to which our sequence of thoughts could be in error. In order to make this point clearer, I want to sketch what I believe are closely related issues concerning rule-skepticism in the thought of the later Wittgenstein as interpreted by Saul Kripke.[12]

In his *Wittgenstein on Rules and Private Language,* Kripke calls rule-skepticism "perhaps the central problem of the *Philosophical Investigations*" (1982, 7). The rule-skeptic questions whether we can establish rules for our behavior (with respect to which our behavior is correct or incorrect) because there is no fact that determines what the rules we supposedly established are. Since concepts can be thought of as rules for associating objects, the rule-skeptic's argument is intimately connected to our ability to establish concepts (see Wittgenstein 1978, 3). But it is more comprehensive, for it undermines the idea that we can act intentionally at all—that we can intend, will, or desire to do one thing rather than another.

Kripke begins his discussion of rule-skepticism with the question of whether I can know that one response rather than another is in accordance with my *past* establishment of a rule, for example, whether "125" is the correct response to the problem "68 + 57 = __" given my past understanding of the function "+."[13] Kripke denies that there is any fact that I can point to to show that "125" and not "5" is in accordance with the rule I intended to follow. It is important to realize that the accuracy of my memory is not in question here. Every fact about me when I supposedly intended the rule is fully accessible to me now. And yet, Kripke argues, none of these facts tells me that I should respond with "125" rather than "5." But because there is no such fact, the preliminary question gives way to the more fundamental question of whether there *is* a rule that I intended to follow at all (and whether I can intend to follow rules now). How can there be such intentions if it can never be determined whether I am acting in accordance with them?

But is this answer to the preliminary question correct? Isn't there something about me in the past that, if accurately recollected, will guide me to the response of "125"? Kripke begins by assuming that the problem "68 + 57 = __" is one I have never answered before. Nor did I give myself *specific* instructions concerning the proper answer to this problem. For example, I never said to myself, "Answer '125' to '68 + 57 = __'!" (Even if this is not true of "68 + 57 = __", it is true of an infinite number of other problems.) Rather, my answer is determined, I believe, by my general *understanding* of the rule for the function "+." This understanding makes the response "125" appropriate. It is, as Wittgenstein says, "as if [the responses] were in some unique way predetermined, anticipated—as only the act of meaning can anticipate reality" (1953, §188).

Certainly there is nothing to stop me from understanding my *past behavior* with respect to the "+" function (e.g. my responses "2 + 3 = 5," "5 + 7 = 12") as deriving from my intention to use a bizarre rule whose outcome is "5" in this case. (Let us call this bizarre rule "quus.") After all, I have not explicitly given myself instructions to respond with "125" in this particular case, and this past behavior is just as much in accordance with my having intended quus as with my having intended plus.[14]

Kripke next looks at the *occurrent mental states* I had when I first took myself to have understood the term. He argues that facts of this sort must be *interpreted* in order to suggest anything, and they can just as easily be interpreted such that they suggest that I should respond with "5" as "125." Certainly this is true for the symbol "+" itself. I can interpret this symbol as suggesting that I respond in a quus fashion as easily as a plus fashion. But the same can be said for any instructions, either put verbally or in images, that I might have had at the time. For I have to figure out what I meant by these instructions, and nothing in the instructions themselves will favor a plus interpretation over a quus interpretation.

It seems that *any* response to "68 + 57 = __" can be suggested by the occurrent mental states I had in the past, given the right interpretation. So no fact about my occurrent mental states in the past can by itself tell me what rule I intended. But then what is there to my thinking that I intend a rule for "+" (or anything else) *right now*? To say to myself, for example, "I know what '+' means to me now, anyway—it means *plus*" is merely to bring into being another set of indeterminate occurrent mental states. I can go from these states to anything at all. They will put up not the least bit of resistance if I take them to suggest that I respond with "5."[15] As Kripke puts it:

> Sometimes when I have contemplated the situation, I have had something of an eerie feeling. Even now as I write, I feel confident that there is something in my mind—the meaning I attach to the "plus" sign—that *instructs* me what I ought to do in all future cases. . . . But when I concentrate on what is now in my mind, what instructions can be found there? How can I be said to be acting on the basis of these instructions when I act in the future? . . . What can there be in my mind that I make use of when I act in the future? It seems that the entire idea of meaning vanishes into thin air. (1982, 21–22)

The comprehensive nature of this argument against rule following is made clearer when we recognize that the stipulation that the response "125" is not one that I explicitly instructed myself to perform is superfluous. Even in cases where I apparently explicitly instruct myself to respond with "125," nothing about that instruction (even when it is "Say '125'!") can uniquely determine the response "125." I could interpret such an instruction as suggesting that I respond with "5." Even mental events that we would consider explicitly *intending* or *willing* cannot uniquely determine responses at all. There is, it seems, no way I can meaningfully suggest to myself that I do one thing rather than another.

Facts about my occurrent mental states fail to answer the rule-skeptic because there is nothing about them that suggests that I say "125." But what about answering the rule-skeptic by appealing to what actually brings me to say "125," namely, the presence in me of a disposition or drive to respond with "125"? What rule I intended for "+" would be determined by my disposition to respond to problems in which "+" occurs. Intending would not be an occurrent mental state but a tendency to act in a certain way.

The problem with the dispositional account is that it seems to follow from it that I cannot respond improperly. Because the rule binding my responses is my current tendency to respond, performance is equated with correctness. Let's say that a day after first learning how to add I hastily perform a calculation and "accidentally" put "5" rather than "125" down as the answer to "68 + 57 = __." According to this theory, I will have answered correctly.[16]

It should be clear that the dispositional theory is simply the Humean theory of concepts all over again. The Humean account of causal judgments was inadequate because it too equates performance with correctness. Hume famously argues that after having viewed many games of billiards, there is nothing irrational to conclude anything I want about what follows when one billiard ball hits another. If causal judgments are reduced to the disposition to associate events, then whatever events I am disposed to associate are in accordance with my "concept" of causation. Performance is equated with correctness. Even when my dispositions change—say I am now inclined to associate striking a match with the appearance of a genie when I was previously inclined to associate it with the match's lighting—my new judgment cannot be thought to be irrational, in the sense of being contrary to my concept of causal connection. For I no longer *have* the violated concept; I now have a different concept of causal connection with which my judgments concerning genies are completely in accordance.

Although Wittgenstein was perhaps the first philosopher to put the problem of rule following in as comprehensive a form, the essence of the rule-skeptic's problem can already be found in Kant, Spir, and Nietzsche. It is that a naturalistic explanation of our behavior—for example, an explanation appealing to our dispositions—renders concepts superfluous. We appear perfectly able to explain our answer to the question "68 + 57 = __" by means of natural facts about us without understanding these responses as involving sensitivity to the concept *plus*. Because the naturalistic facts do not require rule following, they are compatible with our having *any* concept. If we reject the principle of cognitive sensitivity and insist that we have concepts even though they make no difference to what we do, we will become skeptics—we will never know whether "5" or "125" is the answer to "68 + 57 = __." If, however, we accept the principle of cognitive sensitivity, we will deny that we have any concepts at all.

Thus it is not surprising that Nietzsche thinks that direct causal links between mental events are required for thought. If what brings us from one thought to another is merely affective or dispositional, then the idea that our thoughts have content at all is undermined. For the flow of thoughts takes place in a manner that is insensitive to any alleged content. Requiring that the causal relationship between thoughts be *direct* means requiring that only the *content* of the first thought determines our subsequent responses. And that means rejecting a naturalistic account of how our thoughts proceed. A theory of direct causation between thoughts is similar to the Kantian transcendental account in forbidding that the flow of thoughts proceeds through empirical laws of association.

10. Pain and Desire

Seeing Nietzsche as accepting the rule-skeptic's argument can also help make sense of some of his curious comments about pain. Pain seems to be a powerful counterexample to rule-skepticism, for it appears to be a mental state that carries *within it* the interpretation of what is the appropriate response, namely aversion. That aversion is the appropriate response to pain cannot, it seems, be questioned. This is not to deny that we can think it appropriate not to recoil from pain for other reasons. But when we do so, we go against what pain itself *recommends*.

It is precisely pain's apparent ability to suggest a state beyond itself that leads Spir to argue that it embodies the fundamental contradiction between man's timeless self and his existence within the sensory flow of plurality and becoming (1877, 1:222–23). As we have already seen, Spir argues that our inability to bring plurality and the temporal flow of sensation into the timeless unity of thought leads to a fruitless and never-ending search within experience for simple self-identical substances and first causes. Analogously, man's existence as a timeless being in the empirical world leads to the futile and never-ending search for repose (1:224–25). Our quest for release from pain and for stable satisfaction is our search for a release from time.

Given the strongly Schopenhauerian and ascetic spirit standing behind Spir's account of pain, it is not surprising that Nietzsche is determined to show that there is no "direct" causal relation between pain and aversion. This is an attack on the idea that pain is able to reach out to the future and *recommend* anything at all without the intervention of an underlying arbitrary disposition. For it is in its apparent ability to reach out normatively to the future that pain shows that the self is essentially a timeless unity standing above the temporal flow of sensations. To put Nietzsche's argument in a Kripkean form: Nietzsche is challenging Spir to show that pain does not "mean" that one should *approach* that which causes pain rather than avoid it. Perhaps in avoiding pain our contingent dispositions have *misinterpreted* pain to mean avoidance, just as in Kripke's argument our dispositions have misinterpreted "68 + 57 = __" to mean "125."

Thus Nietzsche argues that pain and pleasure can be considered to suggest action only when they are given certain *interpretations* (*GS* 127; *KSA* 7:7[148 and 201]; *WP* 669). Fire feels painful and so brings about avoidance not in itself but only in conjunction with a disposition to avoid fire. Because fire feels painful only because I am disposed to avoid fire, it is entirely superfluous to appeal to the painfulness of fire as the reason why I avoid it. If I were disposed to embrace the fire, I would call the same experience with fire pleasurable and offer this pleasure as the reason I embraced it. In attacking the idea that pain directly causes aversion, Nietzsche is attacking one of the most enduring reasons to think that there is an overarching intentional unity to the self with respect to which one's arbitrary and contingent dispositions can be in error. Without the normative unity provided by motives such as the avoidance of pain, no answer can be given to the question of why I did something other than the simple fact that I did it.

For the same reason, Nietzsche attacks the idea that intentions directly cause responses (*KSA* 9:6[254]; *TI* 6:3). Although we think that intending suffices for action, there is nothing we can do or say or point to by means of which a distinction between what we do and what we wanted to do can get off the ground. No occurrent mental state that might be called "intending to raise my arm" can make my raising my arm in any sense the thing that I am aiming for. For I could (given the appropriate dispositions) interpret all these as indicating that I should raise my foot. No matter what effort I put into determining one thing rather than the other to be the thing I want, all this could, without the least bit of resistance, be followed by any action at all. Whatever I might give as a reason I want one thing rather than another will only *be* a reason in the context of an interpretation, that is, in the context of those dispositions that will bring me to action. And therefore, in the end, there is nothing to my assessing whether what I do is in accordance with what I want to do. There is simply an equation of performance with correctness. I simply "want" what happens.

Of course, there is such a thing as catching myself doing something that I "don't want to do," just as there is such a thing as catching myself responding to a rule in a way that I "did not intend." But these phenomena exist only in the context of dispositions that cannot themselves be checked for correctness. For when I try to determine whether these dispositions are correct or not, I must rely on the dispositions themselves to do the determination. But this only means that after all the "checking" of whether what I am doing is in accordance with what I want, I simply assume that the standard by means of which I do the checking is correct. And so we are back to the equation of performance with correctness.

Thus Nietzsche tends to treat all apparent intentionality as the product of drives that are themselves unconstrained (*WP* 692). There is no such thing as purposive action, except for a deflationary purposiveness that is the expression of the organization of our current drives:

> That the apparent "purposiveness" . . . is merely the consequence of the will to power manifest in all events; that becoming stronger involves an ordering process which looks like a sketchy purposiveness; that apparent ends are not intentional but, as soon as dominion is established over a lesser power, an order of rank, of organization is bound to produce the appearance of an order of means and ends. . . . Against apparent "purposiveness":—the latter only an expression for an order of spheres of power and their interplay. (*WP* 552)

For the same reason, Nietzsche seeks to reduce intentionality to the organizational character of the body (e.g. *WP* 643, 660):

> Does the belief in common fictions really *change* men? Or is the entire realm of ideas and evaluations itself only an expression of unknown changes? *Are* there really will, purposes, thoughts, values? Is the whole of conscious life perhaps only a reflected image? And even when evaluation seems to determine the nature of a man, fundamentally something quite different is happening! In short: supposing that purposiveness in the work of nature could be explained without the assumption of an ego that posits purposes: could *our* positing of purposes, our willing, etc., not perhaps be also only a language of signs for something altogether different, namely something that does not will and is unconscious? Only the faintest reflection of that natural expediency in the organic but not different from it? Put briefly: perhaps the entire evolution of the spirit is a question of the body. (*WP* 676)

This position is Nietzsche's noncognitivism. Because we are unable to create intentions that normatively compel responses, we have no concepts. What appears to be cognitive constraint is actually the relationship between cognitively unconstrained drives (*Z* 1:4; *BGE* 16). "Thinking," Nietzsche argues, "is merely a relation of . . . drives to each other" (*BGE* 36). The apparently conceptual unification of objects under a term is merely affective: "The tiny amount of emotion to which the 'word' gives rise, as we contemplate similar images for which *one* word exists—this weak emotion is the common element, the basis of the concept" (*WP* 506).

By attacking the Spirean image of consciousness as a normative unity,

Nietzsche believes he is also attacking the foundation for Schopenhauerean asceticism. Spir sees endless pain and desire as man's penance for being born in time. Although he thinks our life in time is inescapable, Spir's position naturally generates the ideal of release from pain and desire through a life in timelessness. Such a life is precisely the goal of Schopenhauerean asceticism. By rejecting the existence of consciousness as a normative unity, Nietzsche believes that he has removed the foundation for a Schopenhauerean condemnation of time.

11. The Self

Once we see that the movement from one thought to another or from thought to action has no normative coherence, we are inclined to feel that the self as a whole has receded. Nietzsche voices such worries in connection with memory: "One must revise one's ideas about *memory:* here lies the chief temptation to assume a 'soul,' which, outside time, reproduces, recognizes, etc. But that which is experienced lives on 'in the memory'; I cannot help it if it 'comes back,' the will is inactive in this case, as in the coming of any thought. Something happens of which I become conscious: now something similar comes—who called it? roused it?" (*WP* 502). Our notion of a self is tied to cognitive continuity, that is, the idea that what action we perform or what thought we have can be correct or incorrect with respect to self-generated norms that endure over time. But because there is no soul "outside time" no such norms can exist.

It is precisely to preserve cognitive continuity that Kant argues for the existence of a transcendental subject. Kant is aware that if our mental life takes place in (or only in) the empirical world (including in the mental world that is the subject of empirical psychology) we can have only affective or impulsive motivations to make judgments and so cannot judge with sensitivity to rules. No thought would be able to make a later thought appropriate or inappropriate. For this reason, Kant thinks that transcendental freedom is a requirement for the very existence of rules (Allison 1983, 371n.26).

Nietzsche, as we have seen, agrees with Kant and Spir that we can think only if we have a non-natural self. But he rejects such a self and thus the existence of thought: "The 'spirit,' something that thinks: where possible even 'absolute, pure spirit'—this conception is a second derivative of that false introspection which believes in 'thinking': first an act is imagined which simply does not occur, 'thinking,' and secondly a subject-substratum in which every act of thinking, and nothing else, has its origin: that is to say, both the deed and the doer are fictions" (*WP* 477). "Must all philosophy not ultimately bring to light the precondition upon which the process of reason depends?—our belief in the 'ego' as substance, as the sole reality from which we ascribe reality to things in general? . . . Here we come to a limit: our thinking itself involves this belief . . . to let it go means: being no longer able to think" (*WP* 487).

One way of describing the lack of cognitive continuity that Nietzsche sees in our mental life is that we have no reflective distance from our impulses necessary to assess them in accordance with rules. While we appear to be able to stand back and assess our impulses before plunging into action, this assessment is itself merely the expression of free-floating and unrestrained impulses from which we cannot have reflective distance. Any assessment is already an unconstrained plunging into action. True intentionality, Nietzsche and Kant argue, requires reflective distance from *all* our impulses. Nietzsche only adds that such a reflective distance cannot occur. We simply are our deeds.

There is a strong analogy between Nietzsche's account of the self and the emotivist's. For the cognitivist in ethics, moral reflection provides continuity to the self; such reflection involves adopting a perspective from which our changing desires can be assessed according to consistent criteria. But if determining whether something is good is merely the expression of these desires, as the emotivist claims, then there is no continuity to the self over and above the merely contingent stability of one's de facto desires. The most we can do is assess our desires from the perspective of other desires. Which desire wins out and plays the role of assessor is a matter of chance. It is precisely because emotivism rejects the possibility of a stronger notion of personal identity that it has been so often criticized:

> A key characteristic of the emotivist self is its lack of any ultimate criteria. . . . Whatever criteria or principles or evaluative allegiances the emotivist self may profess, they are to be construed as expressions of attitudes, preferences and choices which are themselves not governed by criterion, principle or value, since they underlie and are prior to all allegiance to criterion, principle or value. But from this it follows that the emotivist self can have no rational history in its transitions from one state of moral commitment to another. Inner conflicts are *au fond* the confrontation of one contingent arbitrariness by another. (MacIntyre 1984, 33)

Nietzsche takes this picture and applies it beyond the self of moral reflection to the self as a whole. There is no rational history in our transition from one state to another.

12. Conclusion

I have argued so far that Nietzsche denies that thought is compatible with a naturalistic account of the self, a view that he shares with Kant and that is evident not merely in his epistemology but also in his philosophy of mind. It is his acceptance of Kant's theory of cognition, combined with his unwillingness to give up naturalism, that drives him to noncognitivism.

Such a noncognitivist reading has been resisted by English-language interpreters of Nietzsche.[17] The first reason for this resistance is that without cognitive constraint, we appear to have no reason to judge one way rather than another. Noncognitivism seems incompatible with Nietzsche's passionate advocation of certain judgments over others. Indeed, Nietzsche often praises and attacks judgments in cognitivist terms—he argues that his accounts of man and the world are true and those of the Christian are false. A second (and related) problem with a noncognitivist reading of Nietzsche is self-reference: Even if Nietzsche's advocation of certain judgments over others can be made sense of in noncognitivist terms, what about his advocation of noncognitivism itself? Mustn't that judgment be true in more than a deflationary sense? I shall deal with these objections in the next chapter.

5. Nihilism, Hedonism, and the Self-Reference Problem

IN THIS CHAPTER I will respond to two objections to a noncognitivist interpretation of Nietzsche's epistemology. The first is that if conceptual constraint does not exist, there is no reason to judge one way rather than another, and Nietzsche has no reason to engage in his well-known critiques of Christianity and Christian ethics. I will argue that Nietzsche himself has a response to this objection that bears a strong resemblance to emotivists' responses to their critics. An important part of this response is the affirmation of the noncognitive drives standing behind our judgments. Such self-affirmation is one of the goals of Nietzsche's epistemology.

The second objection concerns the so-called self-reference problem, that is to say, the problem of the place Nietzsche's epistemological statements have within his epistemology itself. We have already encountered the self-reference problem a number of times in this essay.

The self-reference problem is tied to some of the most fundamental issues of philosophical method. Indeed, I believe that any genuinely comprehensive philosophical method will generate the problem (cf. Danto 1980, 230–31). It is not peculiar to Nietzsche's mode of philosophizing and is not a reason to reject his philosophical conclusions. Nor is it a reason to favor one interpretation of Nietzsche's epistemology over another, since all of the plausible alternatives suffer from the problem.

I will argue that Nietzsche presents self-referentially inconsistent positions for two reasons. The first is that he is driven to them by what he takes to be philosophically persuasive arguments. The second is that these positions play an important role in his goal of epistemological self-affirmation by providing a perspective from which this self-affirmation can proceed.

1. The "Phenomenological Objection"

The noncognitivist position that I attribute to Nietzsche is one in which our judgments do not apply concepts and therefore cannot be true or false. Past interpreters of Nietzsche have been disinclined to see him as a noncognitivist for three reasons. The first is that Nietzsche himself presents certain of his own views as true and those of others (Christians, for example) as false (Clark 1990, 140; Leiter 1994, 337–38; Wilcox 1974, 186). The second is that Nietzsche adopts a naturalistic and empiricist approach to philosophy that is incompatible with the principle that "anything goes" in the way of belief (Clark 1990, 104–7; Leiter 1994, 337–38). The third, which we will discuss later in this chapter, is that noncognitivism is self-referentially inconsistent.

It should be clear by this point that the second reason—Nietzsche's naturalism and praise of the testimony of the senses—is hardly an unambiguous reason to think that he is a cognitivist, for his naturalism and empiricism are the foundations for his argument *against* cognitivism. It is precisely because Nietzsche naturalizes thought that he believes that truth cannot exist.

In this respect Nietzsche's thought is much like Hume's. Hume uses a naturalistic account of causal judgments to argue against the objective validity of such judgment. It is fair to worry about how Hume can reconcile his critique of causal reasoning with the fact that his naturalism is itself a form of causal reasoning. This simply means that Hume's thought suffers from the self-reference problem. But it is not fair to appeal to Hume's naturalism to argue that he does not question the objective validity of causal judgments. To come to such a conclusion would mean missing the whole point of Hume's discussion of causal reasoning.

The same can be said about Nietzsche. His commitment to naturalism and empiricism is difficult to situate within his critique of objectively valid judgment. But since his naturalism and empiricism are also the foundations of that very critique, the most we can conclude is that his thought may be self-referentially inconsistent.

The first reason to resist a noncognitivist reading of Nietzsche is more serious. Noncognitivism seems incompatible with our feeling that we can make a *mistake* when judging—that there is a difference between seeming to be right about the world and actually being right. If Nietzsche is a noncognitivist, it is hard to see why he should make any effort to ensure that his judgments are correct. Nietzsche's denial of sin becomes, as Clark puts it, "trivial" (1990, 140). Noncognitivism leads to a form of judgmental nihilism that is foreign to Nietzsche's thought.

This criticism bears a strong resemblance to David Wiggins's "phenomenological objection" to emotivism in "Truth, Invention and the Meaning of Life." Wiggins takes emotivism to be well represented in Richard Taylor's discussion of the myth of Sisyphus (Taylor 1970, chap. 18). Sisyphus, condemned to roll a stone up to the top of a hill only to see it roll back down again, seems to be the perfect image of someone whose life is without meaning. But Taylor argues that Sisyphus's life could be given meaning if we were to implant within him "'a strange and irrational impulse . . . to roll stones. . . . However it may appear to us, Sisyphus' . . . life is now filled with mission and meaning. . . . He has been led to embrace [his life]. Not, however, by reason or persuasion, but by nothing more rational than the potency of a new substance in his veins'" (Taylor qtd. in Wiggins 1976, 336). The substance in Sisyphus's veins is a disposition of the will of the sort featured in an emotivist account of evaluation. Given this disposition, Sisyphus will say that rolling stones has value and that a life consisting of rolling stones up hills has meaning. Furthermore, Sisyphus's evaluations are correct, it seems, because, according to the emotivist, to say that something has value is to express one's desires with respect to the object said to have value—and Sisyphus has been given the requisite desires.

Wiggins argues that we could never accept such an account of evaluation, for we do not feel that our desires are the ultimate arbiters of whether something has value or not. If we thought so, we would have no reason to choose one action rather than another, since any reason, as long as it is one we want, will be as good as any other:

> By the non-cognitivist's lights, it seems that whatever the will chooses to treat as a good reason to engage itself is, for the will, a good reason. But the will itself, taking the inner view, picks and chooses, deliberates, weighs concerns. It craves objective reasons; and often it could not go forward unless it thought it had them. . . . [Non-cognitivism] cannot adopt the inner perspective because, according to the picture which the non-cognitivist paints of these things, the inner view has to be unaware of the outer one and has to enjoy essentially illusory notions of objectivity, importance and significance. (341–42)

Insofar as evaluators consider themselves capable of error when making an evaluation, they must consider their evaluations to employ concepts, in the sense that their application of evaluative terms must be something about which they could make a mistake.

Clark's argument seems strongly analogous to Wiggins's. She argues that there must be cognitive standards that outstrip what we currently do in the way of judging because, if such standards do not exist, we will have no reason to judge one way rather than another, since whatever we *believe* is a correct judgment will *be* a correct judgment. Although she does not attribute to Nietzsche a full-blown realism, under which the correct application of concepts is a matter that is fully divorced from our current dispositions, she nevertheless argues that Nietzsche thinks that the standards for correct judgment cannot be understood solely in terms of what we are currently inclined to do.

2. The Emotivist Response

But emotivists can accommodate our condemning certain judgments about value as mistaken, provided that the condemnation is understood as the expression of our current desires. They are not obligated, therefore, to say that Sisyphus's judgments about the value of his activities are correct. Indeed, if they said these were correct, they would be ignoring their *own* attitudes toward Sisyphus's activities. Stevenson argues along these lines: "A methodological inquiry, when it attempts to find the [reasons] that will justify a given [evaluation], does not stand apart from an evaluative inquiry but simply continues it, yielding ordinary value judgments that are expressed in a different terminology. The so-called non-cognitive view, then, with regard to ordinary value judgments, is equally so with regard to justifications" (1963, 86).

For the same reason, emotivists will deny that they have any reason to accept Taylor's hedonistic view that whatever the will considers a good reason for action is a good reason. They can say that something has a value that is independent of their desires, provided, once again, that such a statement is understood as the expression of a current desire for that thing—in particular, an *unconditional* desire, that is, a pro-attitude toward any possible world in which that thing exists, whether or not they or anyone else desires that thing in the possible world (see Parfit 1984, 151–54).[1] My desire to be kind is unconditional. I have a pro-attitude toward worlds in which I am kind—even when I don't want to be kind in those worlds. As a result, when I imagine a possible world in which I am forced to be kind, I will say that kindness is good in that world.[2] To speak of value that is independent of desires is not a sign that one employs evaluative concepts that outstrip one's current desires—it is merely the expression of one's current desires.

A *conditional* desire, in contrast, is a pro-attitude only toward those worlds in which the desired thing exists *and* I desire it in that world. My desire to drink coffee is a conditional desire—I do not favor worlds in which I am forced to drink coffee.[3] Evaluations that are the expression of conditional desires will indeed be hedonistic because they will condition value upon the presence of a desire for that which is valued. But the emotivist does not have to accept that all desires are conditional.

That there is a connection between evaluations and unconditional desires is supported by the fact that many quintessentially moral choices—in particular, those that ensure the frustration of future desires—are motivated by unconditional desires. Knowing that tomorrow I will have an overriding desire to be unkind, my unconditional desire to be kind can lead me to aid those who I know will frustrate me tomorrow. If my desire to be kind were merely conditional, such aid would be irrational. Furthermore, if I have unconditional desires, I will also spend some effort nurturing those desires and ensuring that they remain in existence. I have a reason to ensure that my desire to be kind continues to exist, since if it disappears I will not be likely to bring about something I think is of value even if I don't desire it, namely, kindness.

I do not have the same interest in perpetuating my conditional desires. If my desire for coffee disappears, it will not be the case that I will fail to bring about something good, for drinking coffee is good only if I desire it. If I have only conditional desires I will have little reason to monitor my desires or prefer certain desires over others. Whatever desires I actually have doesn't matter because whatever I consider a good reason for action is a good reason.

The emotivist's general strategy is to translate every feeling of cognitive constraint—every feeling that we have evaluative concepts and thus can make a mistake with respect to value—into an aspect of our current affective makeup. Indeed, the emotivist argues that to the extent that our feelings of being cognitively constrained make a difference to our behavior at all—to the extent that they lead us to make certain choices rather than others, to condemn others' judgments or our own past or future judgments, to carefully monitor our desires, or to expend effort getting our evaluative judgments "right"— a translation of these feelings into our current affective makeup *must* be possible. To say that the feeling of cognitive constraint makes a difference to us without such a difference proceeding through our affective makeup is to commit oneself to a non-natural account of human behavior.

Accordingly, the phenomenological objection is no reason to think that evaluations are cognitive. Sensitivity to value is not needed to explain why we make the evaluative judgments that we do because our evaluations would go on in exactly the same way if values were annihilated, provided that our current affective makeup remained the same:

> Think of one world into whose fabric values are objectively built; and think of another in which those values have been annihilated. And remember that in both worlds the people in them go on being concerned about the same things— there is no difference in the "subjective" concern which people have for things, only in the "objective" value. Now I ask, What is the difference between the states of affairs in these two worlds? Can any other answer be given except

"None whatever"? How, therefore, can we torment ourselves with doubts about which of them our own world resembles? (Hare 1972, 47)

This argument should be familiar because it is the very same that we have found standing behind Nietzsche's epistemology. Given the principle of cognitive sensitivity, once a judgment is naturalized, considerations of its truth drop out entirely. We can fully explain why we judge the way we do in terms of naturalistic facts without understanding the judgment as bound by the norm of truth.

Just as emotivists can accommodate any feeling that we can make a mistake with respect to value by translating this feeling into our current affective makeup, so can they reject the feeling that we *cannot* make a mistake with respect to value by arguing that it is not supported by our affective makeup. This is the standard emotivist argument against the nihilist, that is, against someone who claims that it follows from the fact that judgments of value are not true or false that life is meaningless. If this feeling that life is meaningless makes a difference to our action—if it leads us to lie in bed, read Camus, and chain smoke—it must be translatable into our affective makeup. Nihilism is itself the expression of our affects or, more correctly, of affective poverty. But there is no reason that we must suffer from affective poverty simply because we accept emotivism. Indeed, there is something incoherent about claiming that life has *no* value, since that would mean one lacked *any* affective attitudes to express. If that were true, one would have no reason to articulate one's nihilism (see Hare 1972, 36).

Because emotivists see all evaluation as proceeding from the perspective of our current desires, they reject the idea that these desires can themselves be genuinely evaluated. Although it is common for us to condemn *some* of our current desires in the light of others with which we identify ourselves more closely, it is not possible to take an evaluative stance with respect to our affective makeup as a whole. For there is *nowhere one can stand* to make such an evaluative judgment. This means that the emotivist theory of the meaning of life is not hedonistic; it is instead the view that no judgment about the meaning of life can be made. All we can do is make judgments *within* life, those expressions of our affective attitudes by means of which we access the value of things in our life. To talk about meaning at all is not to stand back and describe but to respond affectively. What the value of something is *outside* of this affective response, outside of life, cannot be answered; indeed, it cannot be asked.

Thus emotivism is fully compatible with an "internal perspective" under which we can make mistakes with respect to value and struggle to get our evaluative judgments right. Nevertheless, emotivists sometimes find themselves making voluntarist statements that are incompatible with this internal perspective. For example, they often say that we can *choose* what is of value, or that value is something we can *make.* Insofar as our affective attitudes are usually directed *away* from ourselves and our choices, we should say that we *cannot* choose what is of value, for what is of value is an issue independent of ourselves and our choices. Someone who *did* say we could choose what is of value would, once again, be someone who had conditional rather than unconditional desires.

3. Nietzsche on the Moral "Ought"

There are strong analogies between the emotivist's and Nietzsche's accounts of the feeling that our evaluations are cognitively constrained. Nietzsche often argues that our ability to condemn our desires on the basis of value is reducible to a subset of our desires expressing their attitudes toward other desires (e.g. *D* 109; *BGE* 19; *GS* 116; *WP* 966): "The problem 'thou shalt': an inclination that cannot explain itself, similar to the sexual drive, shall not fall under the general condemnation of the drives; on the contrary, it shall be their evaluation and judge!" (*WP* 275). "[One's] morality bears decided and decisive witness to *who he is*—that is, in what order the innermost drives of his nature stand in relation to each other" (*BGE* 6). Although it appears as if the ability to condemn a desire is the product of cognitive reflection on one's affective makeup as a whole, Nietzsche insists that "the will to overcome an affect is ultimately only the will of another, or several other affects" (*BGE* 117).

Just as Nietzsche naturalizes the cognitive self, so he advocates a "moralistic naturalism" (*WP* 299), which emphasizes the causal connection between our desires and our evaluations: "The more our desire for a thing grows, the more value we ascribe to that thing" (*WP* 336). "Value words are banners raised where a new bliss has been found—a new feeling" (*WP* 714). "Moral evaluation is an exegesis, a way of interpreting. The exegesis itself is a symptom of certain physiological conditions, likewise of a particular spiritual level of prevalent judgment: Who interprets?—Our affects" (*WP* 254).

Rather than standing above one's desires, the evaluative self is simply a "social structure of the drives and affects" (*BGE* 12). Self-control comes into being not through recognizing objective values but by organizing desires on the basis of a highest goal. It is this organization that distinguishes a strong from a weak will: "The multitude and disgregation of impulses and the lack of any systematic order among them result in a 'weak will'; their coordination under a single predominant impulse results in a 'strong will': in the first case it is the oscillation and lack of gravity; in the latter, the precision and clarity of direction" (*WP* 46).

Like the emotivist, Nietzsche denies that the relationship between evaluation and desire is a reason to be a hedonist. This is because hedonism is incompatible with projects that can increase one's level of frustration, that is to say, projects motivated by unconditional desires (see *Z* 4:20; *TI* 1:12; *WP* 781, 790, 909, 928, 930). Hedonism "is how a kind of man speaks who no longer dares to posit a will, a purpose, a meaning" (*WP* 35). Since the desires hedonists have are not of relevance to them, as long as these desires are satisfied, hedonists undertake no strategies to maintain certain desires even if they are frustrated. They are unconcerned about affective drift and so are lacking in that self-control that is Nietzsche's criterion of a strong will.

Furthermore, like the emotivist, Nietzsche denies that *life can be evaluated* (*GS* 310; *WP* 675). Because life evaluates through us when we speak of values, the value of life itself cannot be determined: "Judgments, value judgments concerning life, for or against, can in the last resort never be true. . . . One must reach out and try to grasp this astonishing *finesse, that the value of life cannot be estimated.* Not by a living man, because he is party to the dispute, indeed its object, and not the judge of it; not by a dead one, for another reason" (*TI* 2:2). "One would have to be situated *outside* life . . . to be permitted to touch on the problem of the *value* of life at all: sufficient reason for understanding that this problem is for us an inaccessible problem. When we speak of values we do so under the inspiration and from the perspective of life: life evaluates through us *when* we establish values" (*TI* 5:5).

Like the emotivist, Nietzsche argues that nihilism is contradictory (*WP* 36). Since nihilism is itself an evaluation, it must be the expression of an affect or, more precisely, of affective impoverishment. Nihilism is "a sign of the lack of strength to posit for oneself, productively, a goal, a why, a faith" (*WP* 23). But because nihilists still find reasons to bemoan the loss of meaning, they must have the affective basis upon which it can be seen as a loss: "According to [the nihilist's] view, our existence (action, suffering, willing, feeling) has no meaning: the pathos of 'in vain' is the nihilist's pathos—at the same time, as pathos, an inconsistency on the part of the nihilist" (*WP* 585A).

4. Nietzsche on Evaluative Justification

Emotivism gives a full account of our *feeling* of the normativity of value without relying upon the notion of cognitive constraint and answerability to truth. Any justification of our evaluative judgments that could possibly mean anything to us is explicable in terms of the expression of unquestioned and unjustified affective attitudes. As a result, emotivists generally assign no essential role to reflection about one's evaluative responses. We are able to see value only by engaging our affective attitudes, and such expression requires that the attitudes expressed are *not* reflected upon.

This is not to say that emotivists think that evaluative justification is never called for. It is a proper response to the disgregation of affective attitudes, whether within the community or an individual. It initiates a battle between desires through which order among them may be established. But if there is no conflict between desires, then there is no reason to justify one's evaluative judgments. In particular, justification cannot bring about a form of evaluative awareness that can escape a free-floating dependence upon our attitudes. Not only is there nothing about justification that constitutes the essence of a life of value, its presence indicates that the structure of affects by means of which a life of value comes into being is threatened.

All of this has strong parallels in Nietzsche's thought. Far from being the *essence* of value for Nietzsche, justification is indicative of evaluative instability and insecurity. After all, "it would arouse doubts in us concerning a man if we heard he needed *reasons* for remaining decent: certainly we would avoid him" (*WP* 131). Nietzsche goes so far as to speak of the incompatibility of justification and value (see Poellner 1995, 203–7):

> "How should one act?"—If one considers that one is dealing with a sovereignly developed type that has "acted" for countless millennia, and in which everything has become instinct, expediency, automatism, fatality, then the urgency of this moral question must actually seem ridiculous. . . . "How should one act?" is not a cause but an effect. Morality follows, the ideal comes at the end.— On the other hand, the appearance of moral scruples (in other words: the becoming-conscious of the values by which one acts) betrays a certain sickliness; strong ages and peoples do not reflect on their rights, on the principles on which they act, on their instincts and reasons. Becoming conscious is a sign that real morality, i.e., instinctive certainty in actions, is going to the devil—Every time a new world of consciousness is created, the moralists are a sign of damage, impoverishment, disorganization. (*WP* 423)

Nietzsche is probably not saying that evaluative justification is itself unfortunate, only that it is a necessary consequence of those unfortunate circumstances in which value is threatened. If we are confronted with affective chaos, then Nietzsche would not, it seems, recommend that we abstain from evaluative justification as a means of overcoming such chaos. Indeed, his goal of a revaluation of all values is a demand for us to justify our attitudes in response to that affective disorganization and impoverishment that has resulted from an attachment to Christian values.

What Nietzsche finds objectionable is the placing of evaluative justification, argument, and reflection at the *center* of a moral life. This means valuing a side effect of the personal disorganization that threatens value. For this reason, the high estimation of rationality among the ancient Greeks after Socrates was a symptom of the decline of Greek culture: "Positing proofs as the presupposition for personal excellence in virtue signified nothing less than the disintegration of Greek instincts" (*WP* 430). Equating *reason* and *virtue* is indicative of an affective chaos that sees value in its own symptoms. Nietzsche sees in Socrates and post-Socratic philosophers "a decline of the instincts: otherwise they could not have blundered so far as to posit the *conscious* state as *more valuable*" (*WP* 439). Their attempt to overcome evaluative instability perpetuated such instability (*TI* 2:11). For Nietzsche, value (and, with it, selfhood and freedom) comes into being precisely when reason and justification end. Such a view turns the Kantian metaphysic of morals on its head, as Nietzsche is well aware (*WP* 786).

5. Nihilism and Submissiveness

So far, we have understood Nietzsche as rejecting nihilism because it has its source in affective impoverishment. But he also argues that it is motivated by the desire to *submit to an authority*. Imagine that someone is frustrated after having recognized that there is no such thing as evaluative truth and feels that we have no reason to do one thing rather than another without such truth. A plausible explanation of why this nihilist thinks that life is valueless is that the nihilist's sovereign desire was to submit to an *external authority*, and such an authority can no longer be found:[4]

> The nihilistic question "for what?" is rooted in the old habit of supposing that the goal must be put up, given, demanded *from outside*—by some *superhuman authority*. Having unlearned faith in that, one still follows the old habit and seeks another authority that can *speak unconditionally* and *command* goals and tasks. The authority of *conscience* now steps up front . . . to compensate for the loss of a *personal* authority. Or the authority of *reason*. Or the *social instinct* (the herd). Or *history* with an immanent spirit and a goal within, so one can entrust oneself to it. One wants to get around the will, the willing of a goal, the risk of positing a goal *for oneself*; one wants to rid oneself of the responsibility (one would accept fatalism). (*WP* 20)

> The complete renunciation of making one's own evaluations, and the firm desire to see everyone else renounce them too. "The value of an action is de-

termined: everyone is subject to this valuation." We see: an authority speaks—who speaks?—One may forgive human pride if it sought to make this authority as high as possible in order to feel as little humiliated as possible under it. Therefore—God speaks! (*WP* 275)

For Nietzsche, "refined servility clings to the categorical imperative" (*GS* 5). The feeling of evaluative objectivity, rather than being a healthy expression of one's sovereign desires, can instead be the expression of a desire to submit to an evaluative commander (*GS* 335; *GS*2d, 347; *KSA* 11:43[36]; *WP* 346, 585).

But the submissive believer in evaluative objectivity cannot be honest about the role that the desire to submit plays in these evaluations. Objective values (for example, the duty to keep one's promises) are supposed to be non-instrumental. One keeps one's promises not because doing so is likely to satisfy another goal one has but because it is something to be pursued in its own right. But someone who keeps promises *because* of a command to do so does not treat promise keeping as having noninstrumental value—rather, it has value only as a means of satisfying the value of submission.

If this person were aware of the role that the desire to submit plays in such evaluations, the feeling of evaluative objectivity would evaporate. Evaluations feel cognitively compelled because of the compulsion of obedience. Recognizing that commands compel obedience only given the desire to submit would mean recognizing that one is responsible for one's evaluative responses. One responds only because one thinks submission is of value, and the value of submission cannot have its source in the commander.

To maintain the feeling of objectivity, one must deny that evaluative commanders compel responses in one only to the extent that there is the desire to listen to them, that their firmness is really the firmness of one's desire to obey. Objective values must instead bring about responses in a completely nonaffective manner. For this reason, Nietzsche sees a close connection between antinaturalist accounts of evaluation and submissiveness.

6. The Creation of Values

In short, the feeling of cognitive constraint in evaluation has two possible sources for Nietzsche. On the one hand, it can arise from a suppressed will to submit to a commander. On the other hand, it can be the side effect of having a goal or overriding purpose that gives structure to one's character. While the first type of feeling evaporates when one recognizes the inescapably affective nature of any judgment of value, the second does not.

Since Nietzsche clearly allows for the second type of feeling of objectivity, one would expect him to argue that his naturalization of evaluation leaves everything about our evaluations where they are—that it is solely a descriptive account that has no consequences for what is or is not of value. But Nietzsche emphatically does *not* take this position. Indeed, if there is any leitmotif in Nietzsche's ethics, it is that the naturalization of our evaluations has evaluative consequences. Many of these consequences proceed from specific psychological, historic, and genetic analyses of our evaluations. But Nietzsche also believes that the recognition of the affectivity of evaluation can itself make a difference to what we think is of value.

Sometimes the evaluative conclusions Nietzsche draws from the affectivity of evaluation sound voluntarist (*BGE* 211; *WP* 979). "Evaluation is creation. . . . Valuating is itself the value and jewel of all valued things. Only through evaluation is there value: and without evaluation the nut of existence would be hollow" (*Z* 1:15). But voluntarism sees things as having value only *because* we value them, and, as we have seen, such a view is incompatible with our values themselves. If I am true to my unconditional desire to be courageous, I will say that what is of value about courageousness is *courageousness,* not my desiring courageousness, unconditionally or otherwise. I have an unconditional desire for courageousness only when I say that courageousness would be good even if I didn't have an unconditional desire for it. Nietzsche's apparent voluntarism is in tension with the relationship between evaluations and unconditional desires that he himself emphasizes.

How are we to render these statements about the value of valuation compatible with the continued presence of unconditional desires? One possibility is that Nietzsche's apparent voluntarism is some *nonaffective* perspective on our evaluative activities as a whole—a higher-order evaluation of life from outside life that is compatible with but does not stand on the same level as our first-order affective evaluations. But so many passages can be found where Nietzsche rejects the possibility of nonaffective evaluation,[5] it is surely better to see him as affirming desire from the perspective of desire. The naturalization of our evaluations is of importance because it allows the desires that stand behind our evaluations to gain a new perspective on *themselves*—to look at themselves from sideways on (cf. Schacht 1983, 394–402).

The ability of our desires to look at themselves opens up a number of possibilities for changes in our evaluative attitudes. Most obviously, those evaluations, such as asceticism, that must see themselves as nonaffective will not survive this process of self-reflection. But the naturalistic origins of our evaluations also present us with a new fact to which we may adopt an evaluative attitude. Just because some evaluations of evaluation—such as nihilism or voluntarism—are self-contradictory or undermine the very evaluations they praise does not mean that we must avoid all evaluative stances toward evaluation. For example, when one realizes that evaluation comes into being through self-organization, one can praise self-organization without self-contradiction. There is nothing wrong with suggesting that we nurture within ourselves those unconditional desires in the light of which new values can be seen: "To 'give style' to one's character—a great and rare art! . . . It will be the strong and domineering natures that enjoy their finest gaiety in such constraint and perfection under a law of their own" (*GS* 290). Although it is a tricky matter to do so successfully, praise of self-organization is compatible with our seeing the world as having values that are independent of such self-organization.

7. Epistemological Hedonism

So far I have argued that Nietzsche's naturalization of evaluative judgment bears strong resemblance to the emotivists'. And like the emotivists, Nietzsche denies that hedonism or nihilism follow from such an approach. A fully naturalized account of evaluative judgment as having its source in our desires does not mean that the only thing of value is the satisfaction of desires or that we have no reason to evaluate one way rather than another. The heart of Nietzsche's argument against hedonism and nihilism is his recognition that our moral desires are unconditional or goal-oriented, in the sense that they aim at states of affairs other than the satisfaction of our desires themselves.

Let us now draw some analogies between these issues in Nietzsche's metaethics and Clark's criticism of a noncognitivist reading of Nietzsche's epistemology. Clark argues that such a reading makes Nietzsche's denial of sin, as well as any other substantive claim that he makes about the world, "trivial" (1990, 140).[6] This is similar to Wiggins's argument against emotivism. The emotivist's response to Wiggins is to translate every feeling of cognitive constraint in evaluation, as well as every feeling of a lack of cognitive constraint, into a particular affective makeup. Once this translation is complete, Wiggins's criticism amounts to the implausible claim that accepting emotivism makes one's affective makeup more hedonistic by increasing the number of conditional desires. For only those with conditional desires treat evaluation as trivial; only they are so easy on themselves that they think that what the will considers to be a good reason for action *is* a good reason.

There is no reason that the same strategy cannot be employed against Clark. Unless Clark is willing to accept a non-naturalistic account of our feeling of cognitive constraint, she must admit that this feeling is reducible to our current dispositional makeup. My feeling that I *must* put □ under the concept square, no matter what I might *want* to do, must be reducible to what I am currently disposed to do. We can think of this as an unconditional cognitive disposition. For the same reason, the view that such a judgment is "trivial" must be the product of a contingent cognitive disposition—a disposition to ensure that one's dispositions are satisfied. But there is no reason to think that contingent cognitive dispositions follow from an acceptance of noncognitivism. Clark is right that *epistemological hedonists*—those who think that they have a reason to put □ under the concept square only if they *want* to—would indeed treat their judgments as trivial. They would have no reason to judge one way rather than another, since whichever way they judged would be correct. They would have no reason to monitor their judgments or nurture certain dispositions to judge. But the unattractiveness of the epistemological hedonist is not an argument against noncognitivism, for there is no reason to think that the acceptance of noncognitivism brings about within us such hedonistic dispositions.

Nietzsche clearly rejects epistemological hedonism, just as he rejects hedonism of an evaluative form. Indeed, he praises judgmental consistency and self-control:

> The greatest danger that always hovered over mankind and still hovers over it is the eruption of madness—which means the eruption of arbitrariness in feeling, seeing, and hearing, the enjoyment of the mind's lack of discipline, the joy in human unreason. Not truth and certainty are the opposite of the world of the madman, but the universality and the universal binding force of a faith; in sum, the non-arbitrary character of judgments. And man's greatest labor so far has been to reach agreement about very many things and to submit to a *law of agreement*—regardless of whether these things are true or false. (*GS* 76)

Nietzsche sees judgment to be the product only of drives that are sufficiently *organized* (*BGE* 36; *WP* 535). "In place of 'epistemology,' a perspective theory of affects (to which belongs a hierarchy of the affects; the affects transfigured; their superior order, their 'spirituality')" (*WP* 462).

The feelings that our judgments are constrained by concepts that reach out to the world, that they can be mistaken, and that we must work to get them right are the expression of unconditional drives. These feelings are compatible with recognizing that the only things constraining us are these drives themselves. If this recognition leads to nihilism, we must have been conceiving of reality as a commander to whom we owed obedience (*WP* 585A).

These analogies between emotivism and Nietzsche's epistemology allow us to make sense of those passages where he encourages us to take responsibility for and rejoice in our world-making: "*Genuine Philosophers . . . are commanders and legislators:* they say, '*thus* it *shall* be!' . . . Their 'knowing' is *creating,* their creation is a legislation, their will to truth is—*will to power*" (*BGE* 211). "No longer the humble expression, 'everything is *merely* subjective,' but 'it is also *our* work!—Let us be proud of it!'" (*WP* 1059). Just as Nietzsche's praise of the creation of values is compatible with our feeling that we have a duty to get things evaluatively right, so his praise of world-making is compatible with the feeling, which Clark emphasizes, that a judgment is not true simply because we think it is. Thus, although Nietzsche appears to be embracing epistemological hedonism in the following criticism of Lange, he is really criticizing Lange's longing for a disposition-transcendent form of judgment, which Nietzsche considers to be a product of a submissive desire to have one's judgments cognitively compelled (cf. Gemes 1992, 49–53):

> Lange: "A *reality,* as man imagines it, and for which he *yearns,* when this image is *disturbed:* an existence that is *absolutely firm, independent of us* and nevertheless perceived by us—such a reality does not exist" [Lange 1882, 822]. *We* are active in it: but in this Lange takes no pride! Thus he does not want anything deceptive, changeable, dependent, unperceivable—those are the instincts of *fearful* beings and ones still ruled by morality. They seek an absolute lord, something loving and speaking the truth—in short, the yearning of idealists derives from the moral-religious perspective of slaves.
>
> To the contrary our artist-sovereign-power [*Künstler-Hoheits-Recht*] could luxuriate in *having created* this world. "Only subjective," but I feel to the contrary: we created it! (*KSA* 11:25[318]).

There is no reason for Clark to attribute to Nietzsche a form of cognitivism to explain why he advocates his own judgments and rejects those of the Christian. Nor is cognitivism needed to explain why Nietzsche tries to get his judgments right. If Nietzsche were to rely upon cognitivism to explain these facts, he would have betrayed his own naturalistic approach to human judgment and expressed an ascetic hatred of the affects that stand behind his judgments. This connection that Nietzsche sees between cognitivism and asceticism is the topic of the next section.

8. Will to Truth and Asceticism

Toward the end of the *Genealogy of Morals* (3:23–27) and in the second edition of *The Gay Science* (344),[7] Nietzsche argues that science is an expression of the ascetic ideal. To understand this argument, it's important to get a clear idea of what he means by the ascetic ideal. Nietzsche himself gives us a number of descriptions of asceticism in the *Genealogy,* not all of them unsympathetic (e.g. *GM* 3:3–10; see also Berkowitz 1995, 91–92). Even the ascetic priest is taken to sometimes have had good effects. One of the reasons that Nietzsche's attitude toward asceticism is so complicated is that he is not solely concerned with the ascetic project per se (which, I will argue, he thinks is incoherent) but also with the effects of engaging in or feigning to engage in this project, which can sometimes be positive.

I will argue that Nietzsche sees a relationship between the will to truth and the ascetic project per se. He sees the will to truth, like asceticism, as an incoherent project, even though it can at times have positive effects for those who adopt it. Accordingly, we need to understand why Nietzsche thinks asceticism is incoherent, which means looking to Schopenhauer, who provides the model of asceticism for Nietzsche.

Schopenhauer's asceticism is closely related to his pessimism. He does not generally argue for pessimism because the world is such a horrible place. This would be a pessimism a posteriori, the truth of which would depend on contingent characteristics of the world our will encounters. Rather, Schopenhauer offers an a priori argument in favor of pessimism on the basis of the nature of the will itself. The essence of the will is lack or need, which is painful as long as it is not satisfied and, when satisfied, is merely negated (Schopenhauer 1969, 1:§58). It is not necessary to determine empirically whether the sum of satisfaction and dissatisfaction is positive or negative. We know a priori that it will be negative. Only by negating the ground of all suffering and satisfaction—that is, the will—can suffering itself be truly ended. Asceticism has such a negation of the will as its goal.

One might think that suicide is the most plausible means of negating the will. But Schopenhauer denies that the true ascetic would choose suicide. (He allows, however, that death might come upon the ascetic as a side effect of his project of self-denial [1:§69].) One reason is that death is merely the negation of the self as phenomenon and not as thing-in-itself. Suicide is futile because desire and suffering will always return in another phenomenal form. By means of this metaphysical device Schopenhauer excludes the possibility that suicide might perform the role the ascetic desires. More important for our purposes, however, is that Schopenhauer also argues that the act of suicide, far from being a denial or negation of the will, is actually its affirmation and expression. The suicide responds to the world's inability to satisfy a desire—the motive for self-destruction is this unsatisfied desire, not a rejection of desire. To wish to escape pain and suffering, as the suicide does, is to continue to will. What is needed is a complete defiance of the will, and this can proceed only through embracing pain and suffering.

Considerations of this sort lead Schopenhauer to claim that asceticism is the appearance of transcendental freedom in the empirical world (1:§55). Because the ascetic's actions are not motivated by desire, they stand outside of and violate the empirical laws of psychology (as well as all other empirical laws by which they might be described). Asceticism is, strictly speaking, uncaused; it comes upon one as "grace," a product of pure thought: "The will, having arrived to a knowledge of its own real nature, receives from this a *quieter,* by means of which the motives are deprived of their effect" (1:§70).

Thus, although the ascetic project can be understood as "a negative evaluation of natural human existence" (Clark 1990, 162), what is most significant about ascetics is how they take themselves to be *motivated* to hate natural human existence. This hatred is taken to such extremes that they cannot accept that it springs from natural human existence. It must instead have its source in the metaphysical self.

Like Nietzsche, we are inclined to reject this account of the motivations (or, rather, lack of motivations) behind asceticism. As Nietzsche puts it: "*A will to nothingness,* an aversion to life, a rebellion against the most fundamental presuppositions of life . . . is and remains a *will!*" (*GM* 3:28). Ascetics' radical pessimism, their hatred of the very lack in desire, must be an expression of desire. As Nietzsche puts it in *Thus Spoke Zarathustra:* "World-weary! And you have not yet even parted from the earth! I have always found you still greedy for the earth, still in love with your own weariness of the earth! Your lip does not hang down without a reason—a little earthly wish still sits upon it! And in your eye—does not a little cloud of unforgotten earthly joy swim there?" (*Z* 3:12:17). Because ascetics are motivated by desire, they are fundamentally committed to the very thing from which they seek to be released.[8] It is for this reason that Nietzsche sees the ascetic project as necessarily unsuccessful: "Such a self-contradiction as the ascetic appears to represent, '*life against life,*' is, physiologically considered and not merely physiologically, a simple absurdity" (*GM* 3:13).[9]

Because ascetics cannot be aware of their true motivations, they must see asceticism as a form of cognitive constraint—a means of control over desires that has its source outside of one's affective makeup. Thus, we should expect those who hold non-naturalistic views of the self, such as Spir, to be more inclined toward asceticism. As we have seen, Spir argues that pain and the eternal lack of fulfillment of one's desires show that our timeless essence has been corrupted by becoming and plurality.[10] Pain and desire are the products of our partaking of both becoming and being. In pain and desire, we seek the repose of being, but because this project occurs within becoming it can never be fulfilled. Our timeless self, however, offers us a perspective from which we can assess and condemn a life within time.

It is not surprising, then, that Nietzsche sees the will to truth to be ascetic in nature. The essence of asceticism is that it is a condemnation of our empirical nature, which (falsely) takes itself to stand outside our empirical nature. Those who believe in the existence of objectively valid judgment likewise think that we can inhabit a nonempirical standpoint from which we can assess our empirical selves. The ability to apply concepts requires a radically non-natural subject—a self outside time that can assess and correct the entirety of one's dispositional makeup. Because objectively valid judgment requires a non-naturalistic interpretation of the self, "the truthful man, in the audacious and ultimate sense presupposed by the faith in science, *thereby affirms another world* than that of life, nature and history" (GS2d 344; GM 3:24).

Furthermore, Nietzsche's argument against the ascetic and against the "truthful man" is the same—by consistently naturalizing human behavior, Nietzsche shows that their allegedly non-natural perspective is merely another natural fact. Because both asceticism and the will to truth require non-natural motivations, they can be refuted by showing that they are themselves events within nature.

But why does Nietzsche argue that *science* is connected with the ascetic ideal? Why isn't the scientist one of those healthy interpreters of the world for whom the feeling of objectivity is merely an expression of ruling drives? In fact, Nietzsche does not argue that all scientists are ascetic—he explicitly excludes from his analysis those "modest and worthy laborers . . . who are happy in their little nooks" (GM 3:23). Nietzsche criticizes only "these last idealists of knowledge in whom alone the intellectual conscience dwells and is incarnate today." Nevertheless, Nietzsche does appear to argue, somewhat implausibly, that a significant number of scientists are such idealists of knowledge. Thus he argues that "it is still a *metaphysical faith* upon which our faith in science rests" (GS2d 344).

9. Clark on the Will to Truth

I have understood a "will to truth" or a "faith in truth" (GM 3:24) to mean more than a will to arrive at judgments that satisfy whatever naturalistic reasons we have to judge the way we do. It is instead a will to arrive at judgments that are *objectively valid* and so capable of being genuinely true (or false). I do so for two reasons. First of all, Nietzsche generally works with a theory of cognition under which true judgment requires objective validity. That much is evident from chapters 2 and 3. Insofar as truth requires objective validity, it would seem that the will to truth would be a will that our judgments be objectively valid. Second, such an understanding of the will to truth makes it easy to see the link between the truthful man and the ascetic. Both see themselves as non-naturalistically motivated and so affirm "*another world* than that of life, nature and history" (*GS*2d 344; *GM* 3:24).

In contrast, Maudemarie Clark understands Nietzsche's target to be the belief in the *absolute value* of truth, in the sense of "an unquestioning acceptance that truth is more important than anything else, for example, happiness, life, love, power" (Clark 1990, 184). Clark cannot understand the will to truth to be the will to arrive at true judgments because, according to her reading of Nietzsche, such a will to truth is unproblematic—one can believe in the possibility of true judgment without denying our empirical character.

Clark offers rather strong prima facie evidence for her case. In *The Gay Science* Nietzsche speaks of the will to truth as the conviction that "*nothing is needed more than truth*, and in relation to it everything else has only second-rate value" (*GS*2d 344). Likewise, when Nietzsche claims in the *Genealogy of Morals* that the "will to truth requires a critique," this critique is not put in terms of whether truth is possible; it is instead one in which "the value of truth . . . [is] experimentally *called into question*" (*GM* 3:24).

But even a superficial reading of Nietzsche's discussion reveals passages that cannot be reconciled with Clark's interpretation. For example, Nietzsche speaks of the will to truth as a "renunciation of all interpretation" (*GM* 3:24). But why should believing that truth has absolute value require that we reject interpretation? Whether our beliefs are fundamentally interpretive speaks instead to the *possibility* of truth, that is to say, the possibility of a form of cognitive constraint on our beliefs that stands outside of our empirical makeup.

Likewise, Nietzsche offers the order of Assassins, with their motto "Nothing is true, everything is permitted," as an example of the will to truth being abrogated (*GM* 3:24). If Clark's reading were correct, the abrogation of the will to truth should be the far less radical position that truth is not the most important thing, not the denial of truth in toto.

But the most difficult problem with Clark's reading is that it renders Nietzsche's argument incoherent. Why is there a connection between a belief in the unconditional value of truth and the ascetic's project of self-denial? Clark argues that taking truth to be an overriding ideal is ascetic because this project will force one to give up "the comforting illusions [e.g. in God] that have made us happy and our lives meaningful" (1990, 184–85). But simply because making truth one's highest value results in self-denial does not mean that one adopts truth as one's highest value in order to bring about this result. Without self-denial as the *purpose* behind the pursuit of truth, there is no reason to see a connection between this goal and asceticism. It is already implausible that a substantial number of scientists treat truth as a highest value. To say on top of this that they do so *because* it allows them to engage in self-denial is simply incredible (Poellner 1995, 123–26).

Second, why is there a connection between the will to truth and ascetics' denigration of affectivity and our empirical nature—their affirmation of "another world than that of life, nature, and history" (*GS*2d 344; *GM* 3:24)? Clark argues that this connection lies in the unconditional or absolute nature of the will to truth. Since being an absolute value "rules out deriving its value from its connection to the natural world, that is, from its suitability for fulfilling interests or purposes we have as natural beings . . . the value of truthfulness must be derived from its presumed connection to another world" (1990, 187). But if that is what Nietzsche finds wrong with the will to truth, it is unfair for him to pick on it alone. Nietzsche's objections seem to apply to absolute values of any sort (Anderson 1996, 328–33).

My interpretation has the cardinal virtue of making Nietzsche's argument sensible. But how do we make sense of those passages where Nietzsche speaks of the will to truth as a belief in the unconditional *value* of truth?

Because he sees judgment as affectively motivated, Nietzsche tends to speak of the decision to judge one way rather than another as ethical. Once judging is seen as an ethical decision, it makes sense to say that believing in objectively valid judgment is equivalent to believing in the unconditional value of judging in certain ways. Let's say I associate the striking of a match with its lighting. If I want that judgment to be objectively valid, my reason for associating the two events must be that a causal relation between them *actually obtains,* not that I want to associate them. It is not implausible to say that the value of uniting these two representations in my mind is thereby treated as unconditional—it overrides any other concerns that I might have. Indeed, these other concerns count as *nothing* in the face of my duty to associate striking and lighting. For if I even *start* considering them, I will have failed to make an objectively valid judgment about the causal relation. The belief in truth is, in the end, the belief in the unconditional value of judging in ways that are true—in the unconditional value of truth. Questioning the unconditional *value* of truth is at the same time an attack on its *possibility.*

10. Nietzsche's "Cognitivism"

We have already seen why Nietzsche would think we have every reason to continue judging even after denying the existence of cognitive constraint—

why it is not the case, as Clark argues, that "Nietzsche's denial of sin becomes trivial unless we interpret him as claiming that his own perspective is cognitively superior to the religio-moral perspective on history" (1990, 140). The fact that our judgments are constrained not by concepts but by our current empirical makeup is not a reason to conclude that we should stop judging or that "anything goes" in the way of belief. Both conclusions can be rejected by rejecting the empirical makeup that motivates them: the first conclusion is the expression of the desire to submit to reality and an ascetic hatred of one's empirical nature, and the second is an expression of a lack of structure to one's drives (cf. Cox 1999, 135–36).

But what are we to make of Nietzsche's favorable use of seemingly cognitivist words such as "knowledge" (*Erkenntniss*) (*BGE* 230; *GS*2d 343; *AOM* 399), "knowers" (*Erkennende*) (*GS*2d 343), and "knowing" (*Wissen*) (*WP* 229)?[11] Even the word "truth" (*Wahrheit*) is sometimes used by Nietzsche positively: "I hope from my heart . . . that these investigators and microscopists of the soul may be fundamentally brave, proud, and magnanimous animals, who know how to keep their hearts as well as their sufferings in bounds and have trained themselves to sacrifice all desirability to truth, *every* truth, even plain, harsh, ugly, repellent, unchristian, immoral truth.—For such truths do exist" (*GM* 1:1).

Of course, noncognitivism does not keep us from appraising our judgments in seemingly cognitivist terms, provided that such appraisal is understood in a deflationary fashion. There is nothing about this language in Nietzsche that is, strictly speaking, *incompatible* with noncognitivism. But given that Nietzsche's use of cognitivist terms seems to pick out a perfectly respectable form of "truthful" judgment, why insist on speaking of it in noncognitivist terms at all? There are, after all, things that Nietzsche himself *calls* "knowledge" and "truth," things that he thinks we have every reason to pursue. Why not understand him as offering a naturalized interpretation of what humanly realizable knowledge and truth are?

The same point can be made concerning Nietzsche's views of the self. Why saddle him with the view that the self does not exist and that there are no rational transitions from one moment to the next when a perfectly respectable *naturalized* form of selfhood and rational history are possible?

In this respect, Nietzsche's position is importantly different from emotivists such as Stevenson, who could meaningfully speak of evaluative sentences as noncognitive because they could contrast them with descriptive sentences (such as "Snow is white") that are true in some stronger sense. Nietzsche can provide us with no examples of judgments that are genuinely cognitive—only a Kantian/Platonic ideal of cognition that can never be realized. Thus it would appear that Nietzsche is attacking only this hypostatized vision of cognition, not questioning the possibility of cognition per se (e.g. Schacht 2000).

It is possible that the prevailing antirealist readings of Nietzsche attribute to him just such a naturalized theory of cognition. Clark, for example, speaks of Nietzsche's antirealism as "rejecting non-natural interpretations of our reasoning abilities" (1990, 106).[12] But it also appears as if she wants to attribute to Nietzsche the view that there are constraints upon our judgments that outstrip our actual dispositions of use. After all, she speaks of truth as tied to "our best standards of rational acceptability" (49), which our actual dispositions can fail to satisfy. Clark *may* be speaking only about the fact that we, as natural beings, have *current* dispositions to be discontented with our judgments and to revise them in the face of sensory evidence—current dispositions that express themselves in statements like "A judgment is not true simply because I am disposed to make it." In other words, Clark may accept that there is no *ought* that outstrips what *is*—that all oughts that assess and condemn what is are simply functions of what is. If so, then the epistemology that she attributes to Nietzsche is the naturalized theory under consideration. But if she is instead claiming that our best standards of rational acceptability bind our judgments in a manner that is not reducible to what is, she has introduced a form of antinaturalism that is not merely foreign to Nietzsche's thought but that is also vulnerable to the very principle of cognitive sensitivity that leads Nietzsche to reject realism in the first place.

But even if it is assumed that the antirealism that has been attributed to Nietzsche by Clark and others is such a naturalized theory, I do not believe that this theory is present in Nietzsche's thought, at least to the extent that the error theory and noncognitivism are. This is because Nietzsche remains attached to an antinaturalist theory of cognition even as he gives us every reason to be contented with and even to rejoice in purely natural forms of judgment. Why?

I believe that there are two reasons. The first is purely philosophical, and the second is tied to the more broadly therapeutic purposes of Nietzsche's philosophizing. I will deal with the first reason in this section and end this chapter with a discussion of the second.

Let's begin with Nietzsche's continued advocation of the error theory. I believe Nietzsche remains attracted to the error theory because he is convinced that antinomial arguments apply to our everyday concept of an empirical object. The antinomies provide the foundation for his claims that the concepts of substance, cause, time, and space falsify. One cannot overcome these arguments simply by accepting humanly realizable forms of judgment, for once they are accepted, we have the resources by means of which the antinomies may be formulated. Even if thought occurs within becoming, becoming itself seems to create the errors of being (*WP* 517).

If Nietzsche's thoughts followed my own on these matters, he would question whether the antinomies are applicable to our everyday concept of an empirical object—whether they are not instead the result of philosophical demands that have no power to undermine a naturalized theory of cognition. But this is a book about Nietzsche, not about me, and I find myself unable to ignore those many passages where Nietzsche criticizes the concepts of substance, cause, space, and time.

Nietzsche's noncognitivism in turn receives support from the error theory. Once it appears that even a purely naturalized form of judgment relies upon concepts of being, Nietzsche finds himself drawn to a Spirean antinaturalist theory of cognition as the standard by means of which our judgments should be measured. For concepts of being are simply the flip side of such a theory of cognition. To require self-identical substances is tied to the requirement that thought be an atemporal, absolutely simple, and necessary unity. Because this antinaturalist ideal of cognition can never be realized, he concludes that thought does not exist at all.

11. The Self-Reference Problem in Noncognitivism

So far we have been discussing the problem of reconciling with Nietzsche's epistemology his ability to make cognitivist comments in a largely nonepistemological context. It is now time to discuss the related but potentially more intractable problem of reconciling with Nietzsche's epistemology his ability to articulate his epistemology itself. This is the so-called self-reference problem, the granddaddy of problems in Nietzsche exegesis.

The self-reference problem is clearly one reason a noncognitivist interpretation of Nietzsche has been avoided. Walter Kaufmann, for example, has argued that a noncognitivist interpretation of Nietzsche's views on consciousness suffers from an "Epimenidean paradox, insofar as a philosopher who writes books to convince other people of the complete ineffectiveness of consciousness is ludicrous" (1974, 267).

But Nietzsche can respond that the fact that our judgments are not cognitive isn't a reason to stop making them. Kaufmann appears to conclude, with Clark, that noncognitivism leaves us with no reason to judge one way rather than another. Against this conclusion I have already argued that Nietzsche provides us with reasons to continue judging and being hard on ourselves as judgers. Indeed, for Nietzsche, any other conclusion would be the expression of an underlying submissiveness or asceticism. Since he thinks we have every reason to continue making judgments about the world after accepting noncognitivism, why wouldn't he include *noncognitivism itself* among those judgments that we have every reason to continue making?

Still, there is something to Kaufmann's worry. Mustn't this affirmation of the naturalistic sources of our judgments take place on a higher-order, cognitivist level? Without such a perspective, isn't this affirmation impossible? After all, how can we affirm the drives standing behind our judgments if we cannot even *think* about them? If noncognitivism is true, what appears to be such affirmation becomes simply another noncognitive attitude, without any relation to the attitudes that it hopes to affirm.

Here is one way of thinking about the problem. Noncognitivism is like an extreme antirealism that shrinks our referential capacities to an extensionless point. Nothing is able to reach out beyond what it actually *is*. There is no reason not to continue talking about the world after realizing this, since talking is, after all, something that *is*. But, by the same token, it does not appear possible to adopt a reflective attitude toward our talking about the world in order to affirm it, for nothing can reach out beyond itself to *reflect* on anything at all. Rather than *affirming* existence, we merely *are* existence. I believe that Nietzsche is worrying about precisely this problem in the following passage: "To appraise being itself! But this appraisal itself is still this being!—and if we say no, we still do what we *are*" (*WP* 675). Although this passage is directed at a negative evaluation of existence, the same criticism can be made of its positive variant. Since we cannot help being what *is,* the only "affirmation" of existence that is possible seems passive and inescapable rather than an active and reflective choice. Turning it into an active and reflective choice seems to require precisely that ability to outstrip what *is* that Nietzsche's naturalism denies us.

12. The Self-Reference Problem in the Error Theory

Nietzsche's error theory likewise appears to suffer from the self-reference problem. Consider his frequent claims that "everything of which we become conscious is arranged, simplified, schematized, interpreted through and through" (*WP* 477). No content can be given to the process of schematizing without providing some account of what exists before the process has been applied. But if Nietzsche's error theory is correct, we cannot think about anything existing before the process, for thinking about anything means applying the process.[13] This problem shows itself in the inevitable tendency of Nietzsche's theory of absolute becoming to contain precisely those aspects of being (such as causality and substance) from which it is supposed to be free.

But, as we have seen, it is not necessary for Nietzsche to offer an ontology of becoming for him to present his error theory. Rather than speaking of thought schematizing the flux of becoming, it is enough for him to point out the antinomial consequences of our idea of an empirical object. If the idea of an empirical object is contradictory, then our judgments about the world *must* be false.

Still, this antinomial argument must itself proceed through the employment of concepts, and, according to Nietzsche's error theory, any application of a concept must falsify, since it is contradictory. Every step in Nietzsche's argument for the error theory, qua employment of a concept, must be false. How can a string of errors add up to a convincing argument?

Nietzsche hopes to provide us with an argument that our judgments about the world, although false, ought to be made anyway: "The falseness of a judgment is for us not necessarily an objection to a judgment. . . . The question is to what extent it is life-promoting, life-preserving, species-preserving, perhaps even species-cultivating" (*BGE* 4). And Nietzsche's error theory itself might be precisely one of those judgments that we have every reason to make. But the very argument that we ought to affirm our erroneous judgments is not, it seems, *about* these erroneous judgments themselves. It is instead about some erroneous entities that do not exist. We may have every reason to continue judging even if our judgments are errors, but any argument we might give for why we have such reasons will, it seems, miss the mark.

13. The Self-Reference Problem in Antirealism

One cannot use the self-referentially inconsistent character of noncognitivism and the error theory to argue for antirealist interpretations of Nietzsche, for these theories suffer from the same problem. In the previous chapter I argued that the most philosophically plausible formulation of the pragmatic theory of truth that Danto attributes to Nietzsche treats it as articulated on a second-order level to which the pragmatic theory itself does not apply (section 4). If the theory occurred on the "first-order" level, it would conflict with first-order judgments concerning the distinction between what is true and what is useful to believe. The pragmatic theorist is not concerned with rejecting this first-order distinction, arguing instead that all our first-order judgments, with their distinction between "reality" and "utility," are true only by virtue of their utility. The utility that the pragmatic theorist appeals to on the second-order level is not that first-order "utility" that exists only because it is useful to believe it does. Rather, the pragmatic theorist reduces truth to actual *realist* utility. Indeed, this is the reason that the pragmatic theory, in the end, fails: If our judgments are able to concern themselves with realist utility, why can't we be realists *tout court*?

It will be useful to put this problem in a general form. Let us say that if antirealism is true, the world depends upon the self. By "the world" I mean everything we are able to describe through antirealistically true judgments. By "the self" I mean the antirealist's subjective conditions for the truth of our judgments. For Danto, the self is utility. For the phenomenalist, it is our sensations. For Clark, it is our best standards of rational acceptability.

If antirealism refers to itself, then the self upon which the world depends is something that occurs within the world. But the antirealist does not want to say that the self upon which the world depends is a self *in the world*. One reason is that this would be incompatible with many claims that we make about the independence of the world from *any* self in the world. This is, in essence, Clark's criticism of Danto's pragmatic theory (see chapter 4, section 4). Because she interprets Danto to be reducing truth to *utility in the world*, she argues that Danto's theory is in conflict with our beliefs concerning the distinction between what is true and what is useful to believe.

Phenomenalism suffers from the same problem. The phenomenalist wants to say that the world is reducible to our sensations, but this claim is incompatible with our belief that the world existed before sentient beings appeared on the scene. To solve this problem, the phenomenalist must claim that the self upon which the world depends is not the same as these sentient beings. Indeed, these sentient beings are themselves dependent upon the phenomenalist self, who is the limit of the world rather than something occurring within it (Williams 1981). But this self, by the phenomenalist's own lights, cannot be referred to.

The same point is true of Clark's theory. Clark wants to argue that the world is dependent upon our best standards of rational acceptability. But if the self that has these standards occurs within the world, then Clark's theory is incompatible with our first-order belief that the world existed before there were beings capable of having standards of rational acceptability. If Clark's antirealism accepts the dependence of the world on such selves within the world, then it is just as revisionist of our everyday beliefs as she claims Danto's pragmatic theory is.[14] The only way to avoid this problem is to interpret the selves upon which the world depends as not occurring within the world, which means that they are not dependent upon our best standards of rational acceptability and so cannot be referred to.

A second reason to believe that antirealism must be articulated on a level to which it does not apply is that the fact that the world depends upon the self is not something that depends upon the self. For no matter what world the self creates, the self cannot create a world that does not depend upon the self. This fact is not something within the world. For the world *really,* not antirealistically, depends upon the self. The phenomenalist, for example, does not want to claim that the fact that the world is reducible to actual or possible sensations is itself reducible to actual or possible sensations.

Analogously, Clark must want to claim that the fact that the world depends upon our best standards of rational acceptability is not something that depends upon our best standards of rational acceptability. For example, she considers the fact that truth is limited by our best standards of rational acceptability to be tied to the antifoundationalist view that no belief is intrinsically credible—that any belief could be defeated contextually by one's other beliefs (1990, 130). But this belief that any belief is defeasible is presumably *not* a belief that is defeasible. Otherwise Clark would have to admit that the day might come when we realize that foundationalism is true and that there are indeed intrinsically credible beliefs. Clark's whole point, it seems, is that that time can *never* come—not only that we reasonably believe that that time can never come on the basis of the beliefs we have now. To articulate the limits of representation she must, paradoxically, outstrip them.

14. Some Attempts to Resolve the Problem

How can one escape the self-reference problem? How can one articulate the limits of representation without outstripping those limits? One approach is to avoid *any* claim about that standing outside of "the world." Rüdiger Bittner, for example, has argued that past readings of Nietzsche's perspectivism fail because they make ontological claims concerning that standing outside of interpretation. For Bittner, "Nietzsche does not sketch out an ontology of becoming; he rejects ontology as a whole" (1987, 82). Accordingly, Bittner argues that one cannot provide an account of interpretation as actions upon or interactions with some *thing;* indeed, not even the view that only interpretations exist can be accepted: "If there are no facts [without interpretation], then nothing 'exists' at all, not even interpretations. One should say: When we, as skeptics, discard the idea that there is something that determines itself as having such and such a property, so we will also no longer think that there is something that has the character of interpretation" (84).[15] One way of thinking of Bittner's approach is that he tries to completely avoid spelling out what the subjective conditions for the truth of our judgments are. For once these subjective conditions are articulated, they become the focal point for realistically true judgments.

But does Bittner succeed? It is not clear that he avoids speaking about that which precedes interpretation. Consider the following passage: "There are not things that by themselves have this or that character. Our life and our world is a productive action, emerging from productive action. A world of pure activity" (88). Bittner should not be able to speak about this pure activity that is responsible for interpretation, for even speaking about this activity presupposes a referential capacity standing outside of interpretation. No matter how attenuated the "self" by means of which we characterize our antirealism becomes, any reference to this self is illegitimate. Without some reference to this self, however, it is impossible to articulate the very antirealist point that Bittner hopes to make.

Günter Abel is aware of the difficulties we have encountered here. He argues, in effect, that an interpretation of the character of interpretation (in terms of a relationship to the noninterpretative self and world) is and must be itself an interpretation (1984, 161). According to Abel, Nietzsche allows for the possibility of a form of reflection on the subject-dependence of the world that arises within and makes use of the world (e.g. 1988a).

Abel's approach appears to be the most popular among those who have addressed the problem. For example, Richard Schacht's account of Nietzsche's epistemology likewise attempts to provide Nietzsche with a higher-order perspective, within which his claims of cognitive limitation can be situated, that nevertheless is compatible with the fact that he relies upon "first-order" judgments to justify his claims of limitation. Schacht suggests that Nietzsche employs a method involving *multiple first-order perspectives* to arrive at this higher-order perspective. The first-order perspectives are "played off against each other" such that "it becomes possible to achieve a meta-level perspective, from which vantage point various lower-order interpretations may be superceded in favor of others less narrow and distorting than they" (1983, 10). This meta-level perspective can have "an epistemically favored status in relation to various other [interpretations] which have been or might be proposed" (96).

A similar account is provided by John Richardson (1996, 3–15, §4.5). A form of higher knowledge is possible when perspectives turn upon one another and so transcend themselves in a manner that is nevertheless immanent to these perspectives. Richardson argues that Nietzsche's "perspectivism" is credible not because it is realistically true but because it coheres best with the particular perspectives about which it speaks. Because it depends in this way upon our perspectives, there is no division (no "transcendental line") between Nietzsche's perspectivism and the more specific perspectives that it accommodates.

But if claims about the subject-dependence of the world are, in some sense, about the world, how are they to be distinguished from those first-order claims about the subject-dependence of the world that antirealists want to reject? After all, the world we create is one in which we see the world as one we do not create. Unless they want to attribute to Nietzsche revisionist first-order views about the world's dependence upon human beings, those who offer such theories owe us an account of how Nietzsche's claims of the world's dependence on the self are to be distinguished from the first-order falsehood that the world depends upon human beings. It is hard to see how they will be able to do so in a manner that does not presuppose the type of talk about that outside of interpretation that Abel, Schacht, and Richardson admit cannot take place.

15. Nietzsche and Naturalized Neo-Kantianism

Nietzsche is well aware of these problems: "Whether existence without interpretation, without 'sense,' does not become 'nonsense'; whether, on the other hand, all existence is not essentially actively engaged in interpretation—that cannot be decided even by the most industrious and most scrupulously conscientious analysis and self-examination of the intellect; for in the course of this analysis the human intellect cannot avoid seeing itself in its own perspectives, and only in these" (*GS*2d 374). One reason Nietzsche aware of these problems is his exposure to those Neo-Kantians, such as Schopenhauer and Friedrich Albert Lange, who tend to provide a naturalistic gloss on Kant's transcendental idealism.[16]

For both Schopenhauer and Lange, the character of the empirical world is, in a sense, dependent upon something *in that world*. Schopenhauer, for example, thinks that Kant's categories have their source in the *brain* (1969, 2:chaps. 2–3). The same naturalization of Kant can be found in Lange's "physico-idealism" (1925, 3:219). Lange spends a good deal of time criticizing the idea that the empirical world depends upon a subject standing outside of nature: "It is assuredly, on the contrary, not only more correct, but it also agrees with Kant's view, to see in this 'mental' organization only the transcendental side of the phenomenal physical organization; the 'thing-in-itself of the brain' as Ueberweg used to say" (3:205n.60).

Both Lange and Schopenhauer attempt to overcome the self-reference problem generated by claims that the world depends upon a self within the world by treating the empirical self upon which the world depends as the empirical self understood independently of the contributions of that very self. Thus Lange claims that, in speaking of "the knowledge of the dependence of the world upon our organs" (3:205), we are giving an explanation in terms of these organs not as phenomena but, in a sense, transcendentally, that is, as independent of the contributions of the organs themselves. Nevertheless, he insists that it is not a separate transcendental subject that is spoken of but the empirical subject considered in a nonempirical manner (cf. Abel 1990, 118).

Lange sees no other choice but to take such a position in order to avoid what he thinks is the incoherence of more purely Kantian forms of transcendental idealism. He argues that one cannot give a coherent account of the subject-dependence of the empirical world without making substantive (especially causal) judgments about that entity upon which the empirical world is said to depend. But under the Kantian approach such a subject is purely transcendental and so is not that about which such substantive judgments can be made. So Lange defends his use of the term "physico-psychical organization" for that upon which the empirical world is said to depend, for it is "a very intelligible and easily conceivable notion, instead of the scarcely comprehensible Kantian idea of transcendental presuppositions of experience." On the one hand, Kant's account is scarcely comprehensible if the categories themselves are thought of as that upon which the character of the world depends, for the categories "are at most [its] simplest expression." If the categories simply are this subject, "the whole 'Critique of Reason' resolves itself into a mere tautology, to the effect that the synthesis *a priori* has its cause in the synthesis *a priori*." On the other hand, "if we wish to denote the true cause of the *a priori*, we cannot speak at all of the 'thing-in-itself,' for the idea of the cause does not reach to this. . . . For the 'thing-in-itself' we must substitute the phenomenon." Thus Lange claims, "We must not . . . talk of the organization of the mind, for this is transcendental, and therefore co-ordinated with other transcendental assumptions. We must rather understand by organization simply, or physico-psychical organization, what to our external sense appears to be that part of the physical organization which stands in the most immediate causal relation with the psychical functions" (1925, 2:193–95n.25).

Many of Nietzsche's criticisms of Kant's transcendental idealism come directly from Lange. Nietzsche, like Lange, argues that the subject upon which the world depends cannot have any content unless it is considered, in some sense, naturalistically:

"How are synthetic judgments *a priori* possible?" Kant asked himself—and what really was his answer? "By virtue of a faculty"—but unfortunately not in five words, but so circumstantially, venerably, and with such a display of German profundity and curlicues that people simply failed to note the comical *naiserie allemande* involved in such an answer. . . . "By virtue of a faculty"—he had said, or at least meant. But is that—an answer? An explanation? or is it merely a repetition of the question? . . . It is high time to replace the Kantian question, "How are synthetic judgments *a priori* possible?" by another question, "Why is belief in such judgments necessary?"—and to comprehend that such judgments must be believed to be true, for the sake of preservation of creatures like ourselves. (*BGE* 11)

But Nietzsche's attempt to give empirical content to such a subject appears to lead him right into the self-reference problem. For he seems to claim that the world created in our judgments is a product of something in that world itself. Such a view is incoherent because the entire world cannot be dependent upon a subject that is a member of that world—for that would mean that the subject itself, as a member of that world, is dependent upon itself. This is a difficulty that Nietzsche himself recognizes (e.g. *KSA* 10:24[35], 11:34[158]; *WP* 473, 486, 543). "What? And others even say the external world is the work of our organs? But then our body, as a part of this external world, would be the work of our organs! But then our organs themselves would be— the work of our organs! It seems to me that this is a complete *reductio ad absurdum*, assuming that the concept of a *causa sui* is something fundamentally absurd. Consequentially, the external world is not the work of our organs—?" (*BGE* 15). There is an inescapable problem in Nietzsche's goal, as he puts it, "to represent man as a limit" (*KSA* 11:25[393]).

16. Quietism?

I do not think, and I do not think that Nietzsche thought, that the self-reference problem can be solved. It is important to keep in mind, however, that, in suffering from the problem, Nietzsche is in good company. Hume,[17] Kripke's rule-skeptic,[18] the phenomenalist (see chapter 5, section 13 sup.), and Clark's antirealist (see chapter 5, section 13 sup.) all suffer from the same problem.[19] Furthermore, I do not think that self-referential inconsistency is in itself a reason to reject Nietzsche's epistemologies. The minute one rejects them and assumes that one has the referential capacities of the realist, one once again has the resources to reformulate arguments in their favor. Rather than simply refuting these positions, the most that their self-referential inconsistency can do is show them to be paradoxical. Since Nietzsche appears to think that the logic of his arguments drives him to these positions, he should not be faulted for presenting them despite their paradoxical nature.

But the question remains why he thinks it is so *important* to present these positions, given that he appears to be aware that they are paradoxical. The more appropriate response would appear to be to recognize them but admit that it cannot be asserted. This *quietist* position, which is in some respects similar to Bittner's approach, can be found in the later Wittgenstein or, at least, some interpretations of the later Wittgenstein, such as those offered by Bernard Williams (1981) and Jonathan Lear (1982). It is a consequence of the following considerations, which one can find, Williams argues, in the early Wittgenstein of the *Tractatus*:

> That the limits of my language are the limits of my world; that there could be no way in which those limits could be staked out from both sides—rather, the limits of language and thought reveal themselves in the fact that certain things are nonsensical; and . . . that the "me" and "my" which occur in both those remarks do not relate to an "I" in the world, and hence we cannot conceive of it as a matter of empirical investigation . . . to determine why my world is the way it is rather than that way, why my language has some features rather than others, etc. Any sense in which such investigations were possible would not be a sense of "my," or indeed, perhaps, of "language," in which the limits of my language were the limits of my world. (Williams 1981, 146)

The sense in which the limits of our language are the limits of our world is one that cannot be characterized, for such characterization must occur *within language* and so only speak about that within the world. And to say something outside language is to not say anything at all.

Rather than arguing, as the early Wittgenstein does, that this subject upon which the world depends is a "metaphysical self," which is "the limit of the world, not a part of it" (1958, §5.632), Nietzsche, like the later Wittgenstein under such interpretations, accepts that such a subject is an element of the empirical world (a community of language speakers, in the later Wittgenstein's case). But he still should have accepted that such claims of dependence cannot be articulated. Any articulation of such dependence would, once again, be a particular judgment arising from the subject and thus a judgment about something within the world whose dependence Nietzsche claims to be describing. And if Nietzsche attempts to outstrip these subjective limitations in order to describe them, this would also not be a judgment about the dependence of the world on the subject but merely a falsehood about the world, or nonsense.

17. Self-Affirmation

But the fact is that Nietzsche does *not* shy away from describing our cognitive limitations, even as he worries about the possibility of doing so without contradiction. I will argue that another reason he does so, aside from the fact that the logic of his argument compels him to, is that these positions provide him with the perspective from which we can affirm the naturalistic bases of our judgments. Nietzsche does not accept quietism because it is a *passive* recognition of our inability to escape our empirical nature. He hopes for a more active affirmation.

This makes Nietzsche's epistemology remarkably similar to his ethics. On the one hand, he does not think that a higher-order evaluation of life is possible. Insofar as evaluations are motivated by our desires, we have no standpoint from which we could assess desiring as a whole. This inability to evaluate life (see *GS* 310; *TI* 2:2, 5:5; *WP* 675) is just as true of a positive affirmation of life as it is of the ascetic's rejection of life. To even begin to evaluate, whether positively or negatively, is to have already said "yes" to life in an unreflective manner: "In all correlations of Yes and No, of preference and rejection, love and hate, all that is expressed is a perspective, an interest of certain types of life: in itself, everything that is says Yes" (*WP* 293).

On the other hand, Nietzsche also thinks that some form of positive and nonpleonastic affirmation of evaluation as a whole is possible. The naturalization of our values opens up the possibility of an *immanent* form of self-affirmation by allowing the desires standing behind our values to adopt a reflective attitude toward themselves (Schacht 1983, 398).

Nietzsche tends to put this self-affirmation of evaluation in terms of our overcoming certain *tests* that threaten the values we see in the world. The naturalization of our evaluations is itself such a test. Rather than looking at the world naively in the light of our desires, once our evaluations are naturalized our desires themselves become the objects of scrutiny. From this perspective the world can appear valueless. The ability to maintain value under such circumstances is a sign of strength and self-affirmation. Maintaining value is possible by affirming the naturalistic sources of evaluation—that is, the organization of our impulses in the service of an overriding goal: "It is a measure of the degree of the strength of the will to what extent one can do without meaning in things, to what extent one can endure to live in a meaningless world *because one organizes a small portion of it oneself*" (*WP* 585A).

Nietzsche's epistemology is fundamentally motivated by the same project of self-affirmation. But affirming the drives standing behind our "descriptive" judgments is more problematic than affirming the desires standing behind our evaluations. Evaluative self-affirmation can take place within a descriptive framework—a naturalized account of human beings—that is not itself submitted to scrutiny. Things are different when we move to epistemological self-affirmation. This project cannot use a naturalized account of human beings as its descriptive framework. Adopting such a framework will mean naively expressing precisely those drives that need to be reflected upon. The situation would be similar to someone who attempts to affirm the desires standing behind his evaluations by looking at them in a descriptive framework that includes the right and the good. Within such a framework, it is likely that evaluations would simply be pleonastically affirmed on the basis of their ability to track these values.

What is needed is a framework that does not include those objects that are "created" through the expression of our judgmental drives. I believe that Nietzsche's conception of the world as will to power or absolute becoming is meant by him to play this role. It is true that Nietzsche often speaks of absolute becoming as an ontological principle—an attempt to get at what the empirical self and other empirical objects are like when denuded of the content that is created by interpretations. Nietzsche argues, for example, that "the world viewed from the inside, the world defined and determined according to its 'intelligible character'—would be 'will to power' and nothing else" (*BGE* 36). This gives rise to a view of the empirical world as resulting from interpretations of will to power quanta upon one another:

> Every center of force adopts a perspective toward the entire remainder, i.e., its own particular valuation, mode of action, and mode of resistance. The "apparent world," therefore, is reduced to a specific mode of action on the world, emanating from a center. Now there is no other mode of action whatever; and the "world" is only a word for the totality of these actions. Reality consists precisely in this particular action and reaction of every individual part toward the whole— . . . There is no "other," no "true," no essential being—for this would be the expression of a world without action and reaction. (*WP* 567)

But understood as an ontological theory, it lapses into incoherence. If the world is the product of centers of will to power in reaction to one another, and there is no world without this interaction, then one cannot speak of the world as being created by these centers of will to power, for these centers are something standing outside everything in the world as it was originally described. Once again, the will to power is the attempt to express the inexpressible (Danto 1980, 96; Davey 1983, 248).

But setting its coherence aside, the theory offers a perspective from which one can nonpleonastically affirm the drives standing behind one's judgments about nature. Consider the tendency to unify all of the Eiffel Tower's qualities together into an object. Within a framework that includes the Eiffel Tower, such a tendency is likely to be pleonastically affirmed on the basis of its tracking the fact that the Eiffel Tower does indeed have all of these qualities. But from the perspective of absolute becoming, there is no Eiffel Tower. If one continues to affirm one's judgments about the Eiffel Tower from within such a framework, it must be because one affirms the self-organization and self-control that stands behind this judgment (see *WP* 15).

Nietzsche's metaphysical speculations are not merely driven by philosophical arguments. He is also attempting to create a metaphysical doctrine that will have the proper effect on the person who entertains it. The difficulty is that the doctrine that would appear to do the trick—a theory of absolute becoming or will to power—is incoherent. Of course, this is precisely what one would expect of a doctrine that would allow one to reflect upon, without presupposing, one's drives to find the world coherent.[20]

There is a long-standing debate concerning whether the will to power is a metaphysical theory (Heidegger 1979–86), an account of why metaphysical theories are impossible (Bittner 1987; Nehamas 1985, chap. 3), an empirical theory about nature (Cox 1999, 75–79; Kaufmann 1974, 204–11), or a fiction whose role is primarily affective and motivational (Clark 1990, chap. 7; Poellner 1995, 301). Each of these interpretations captures part of the truth. That it is a metaphysical theory is suggested by the fact that antinomial arguments provide Nietzsche with philosophical reasons to think that the world is absolute becoming. That it is an antimetaphysical theory is suggested by the fact that Nietzsche presents the theory with an awareness of its incoherence. Rather than being a straightforward description of reality, it is a manifestation of our inability to arrive at such a description. That it is an empirical theory is supported by the fact that the ultimate evidence in favor of absolute becoming is an empirical awareness of plurality and change. And that it is primarily affective and motivational is supported by the role that a theory of absolute becoming can play in epistemological self-affirmation.

I question, however, whether Nietzsche genuinely needs absolute becoming for his project of self-affirmation. Even within a naturalistic framework one can appreciate the self-control and self-discipline that is required for knowing the world. Let's assume that I adopt a naturalistic framework and so accept that the Eiffel Tower, with its plurality of qualities united in one substance, exists. Even within this framework, there is nothing about the existence of the Eiffel Tower that suggests anything about how I, as a natural being, *ought* to be. That I create within myself those states of being that constitute believing that there is an Eiffel Tower—rather than simply thinking that "anything goes" in the way of belief—is still an act of self-control and self-discipline that can be admired in its own right.

Of course, once frameworks are assessed not according to their adequacy as descriptions of reality but rather on the basis of their ability to promote robust self-affirmation, it would presumably be an empirical question whether absolute becoming or a fully naturalistic framework is best for the job. This would be a question of which promotes more focused, resolute, and disciplined investigators of the world. A positive response to the test would mean that one sees *more* reality in the world than one did when one looked at the world naively. The fact that so many have seen Nietzsche's epistemology as a reason to be *less* focused and disciplined indicates, to me at least, that Nietzsche's test is an inferior one or, at least, that the medicine is too strong for most people to take.

Conclusion

WHAT ARE WE TO MAKE of Nietzsche's discussions of truth and knowledge? First of all, he did not have *one* considered epistemological position. His epistemology was still a work in progress at the time of his collapse in 1889. It *is* possible, however, to make valid claims about the principles that generated the epistemological positions in his works.

The first and abiding principle standing behind Nietzsche's epistemologies and his philosophy in general is naturalism. Nietzsche is concerned with the philosophical consequences of situating man within nature, which means seeing man as a finite, temporal, and causally conditioned being.

But despite his naturalist outlook, Nietzsche is also committed to an *antinaturalist* theory of what judgment must be like to have a truth-value. Here Nietzsche is in the tradition of those Neo-Kantian philosophers that were his primary educators on epistemological matters. Actual human judgment, which is a natural phenomenon, doesn't have what it takes to be true or false. But, Nietzsche argues, we assume that these antinaturalist requirements are satisfied when we make a judgment. To judge that grass is green, we must act *as if* grass had been necessarily and atemporally united with the concept green.

Furthermore, like his Neo-Kantian predecessors, Nietzsche argues that the antinaturalistic presuppositions for judgment can be drawn out of the objects judged. Just as we assume that the representing subject is *being,* so we attribute being to the objects we represent. Because these objects partake of both being and becoming, they generate antinomies when submitted to philosophical reflection.

The antinomies are the primary motivation for Nietzsche's error theory and his theory of absolute becoming. Nietzsche offers absolute becoming as an alternative to standard naturalistic descriptions of the world because he believes that the latter surreptitiously posit antinaturalistic entities. Therefore, Nietzsche's theory of absolute becoming is not an a priori alternative to naturalism. It is instead a radically *empirical* theory—a type of *hyper*naturalism that attempts to get at what is presented to us by the senses without the application of these concepts of being. Still, by ridding science of concepts upon which it must rely, Nietzsche's error theory is incompatible with the naturalism that motivates his thought and that expresses itself when he makes less epistemologically self-aware comments about man and nature. To make matters worse, because Nietzsche believes that we must attribute being to even begin thinking, he ends up denying that absolute becoming can ever be thought of.

Nietzsche's error theory also suffers from his inability to explain how errors, qua thoughts, are possible. His naturalism makes him unwilling to accept Spir's view that the antinomies are the result of a self-identical subject forcing the image of being on becoming. Instead he argues that becoming itself creates the deception of being. But to even begin to deceive ourselves in this way, it seems that we must be *thinking,* and—given Nietzsche's apperceptive account of cognition—thinking is impossible within a world of becoming.

If Nietzsche had liberated himself from transcendental philosophy, his epistemology would be much closer to the unproblematic naturalism and empiricism that some in the literature have attributed to him and that can be found in his less epistemologically reflective moments. But, as I think this essay has shown, he remained influenced by transcendental philosophy until the very end.

Nietzsche's commitment to the transcendental tradition can also be seen in his noncognitivism. If, as Nietzsche argues, *all* human judgment must be seen in noncognitive terms—if the contrasting set of cognitive judgments is *empty*—why not instead provide a fully naturalized theory of what cognition is like? Such a naturalized theory of cognition is particularly attractive given that Nietzsche has provided us with reasons to continue making our everyday judgments about the world. I believe that much of the analytic literature on Nietzsche sees him as providing just such a naturalized theory. But whatever the intrinsic attractions of such a theory, I do not believe that it is close to the whole story about Nietzsche's epistemology. For better or worse, he remains committed to the antinaturalist criteria for cognition that he borrowed from Spir and others in the transcendental tradition, criteria that drive him to noncognitivism.

Nevertheless, the ultimate goal of Nietzsche's epistemological reflections is very close to this naturalized theory. In the end Nietzsche wants us to affirm our judgments about the world. Indeed, he presents noncognitivism and the error theory in part because they provide a framework for this self-affirmation. Both theories, by denying us the usual reasons we give ourselves to judge the way we do, make genuine affirmation of our judgments possible.

In particular, Nietzsche's goal is not to abandon scientifically rigorous examination of man and nature—it is to strengthen such examination by affirming the drives that stand behind it. But in seeking higher-order reflection on our judgments, Nietzsche once again shows himself to be in the grip of the transcendental tradition. Naturalistically inclined philosophers today can be distinguished by their desire *not* to adopt such a higher-order perspective. They advocate an unreflective reliance on naturalism that Nietzsche finds unsatisfactory. For that reason alone we should be skeptical about whether Nietzsche's interests are theirs.

Appendix 1: Concordance between *The Will to Power* and *Sämtliche Werke: Kritische Studienausgabe,* with Dates of Composition for Each Passage

The following table correlates each passage from *The Will to Power (WP)* cited in this book with its corresponding passage from *Sämtliche Werke: Kritische Studienausgabe (KSA)*. I have also provided the approximate date of composition. The information for this concordance was drawn from Haase and Salaquarda (1980) and Fuchs (1996).

WP	*KSA*	Date of Composition
15	12:9[41]	Autumn 1887
20	12:9[43]	Autumn 1887
23	12:9[35]	Autumn 1887
35	12:9[107]	Autumn 1887
36	13:11[97]	November 1887–March 1888
46	13:14[219]	Spring 1888
131	11:26[392]	Summer–Autumn 1884
229	13:14[179]	Spring 1888
254	12:2[190]	Autumn 1885–Autumn 1886
259	11:26[119]	Summer–Autumn 1884
275	12:7[6]	End of 1886–Spring 1887
293	13:14[31]	Spring 1888
299	12:9[86]	Autumn 1887
336	12:10[174]	Autumn 1887
346	13:14[143]	Spring 1888
387	13:11[310]	November 1887–March 1888
412	12:7[4]	End of 1886–Spring 1887
422	11:35[44]	May–July 1885
423	13:14[142]	Spring 1888
428	13:14[116]	Spring 1888

WP	KSA	Date of Composition
430	13:14[111]	Spring 1888
436	12:2[93]	Autumn 1885–Autumn 1886
439	13:14[131]	Spring 1888
462	12:9[8]	Autumn 1887
473	12:5[11]	Summer 1886–Autumn 1887
474	13:11[120]	November 1887–March 1888
475	12:2[204]	Autumn 1885–Autumn 1886
476	11:26[49]	Summer–Autumn 1884
477	13:11[113]	November 1887–March 1888
478	13:14[152]	Spring 1888
479	13:15[90]	Spring 1888
480	13:14[122]	Spring 1888
481	12:7[60]	End of 1886–Spring 1887
485	12:10[19]	Autumn 1887
486	12:2[87]	Autumn 1885–Autumn 1886
487	12:7[63]	End of 1886–Spring 1887
488	12:9[98]	Autumn 1887
493	11:34[253]	April–June 1885
494	11:36[19]	June–July 1885
495	11:25[470]	Spring 1884
501	12:5[65]	Summer 1886–Autumn 1887
502	11:40[29]	August–September 1885
506	11:25[168]	Spring 1884
507	12:9[38]	Autumn 1887
512	11:40[13]	August–September 1885
514	13:14[105]	Spring 1888
515	13:14[152]	Spring 1888
516	12:9[97]	Autumn 1887
517	12:9[89]	Autumn 1887
518	12:2[91]	Autumn 1885–Autumn 1886
519	12:7[55]	End of 1886–Spring 1887
520	11:36[23]	June–July 1885
521	12:9[144]	Autumn 1887
524	13:11[145]	November 1887–March 1888
530	12:7[4]	End of 1886–Spring 1887
532	11:40[15]	August–September 1885
533	12:9[91]	Autumn 1887
534	11:34[264]	April–June 1885
535	11:38[4]	June–July 1885
537	12:2[126]	Autumn 1885–Autumn 1886
538	13:18[13]	July–August 1888

WP	KSA	Date of Composition
539	13:14[148]	Spring 1888
542	13:16[21]	Spring–Summer 1888
543	13:11[115]	November 1887–March 1888
544	12:10[159]	Autumn 1887
545	11:36[25]	June–July 1885
546	12:2[145]	Autumn 1885–Autumn 1886
547	12:2[158]	Autumn 1885–Autumn 1886
550	12:2[83]	Autumn 1885–Autumn 1886
551	13:14[98]	Spring 1888
552	12:9[91]	Autumn 1887
555	12:2[154]	Autumn 1885–Autumn 1886
556	12:2[150]	Autumn 1885–Autumn 1886
557	12:2[85]	Autumn 1885–Autumn 1886
558	12:10[202]	Autumn 1887
560	12:9[40]	Autumn 1887
561	12:2[87]	Autumn 1885–Autumn 1886
562	10:24[13]	Winter 1883–84
563	12:5[36]	Summer 1886–Autumn 1887
567	13:14[184]	Spring 1888
568	13:14[93]	Spring 1888
569	12:9[106]	Autumn 1887
574	10:8[25]	Summer 1883
575	12:2[132]	Autumn 1885–Autumn 1886
579	12:8[2]	Summer 1887
583	13:14[103]	Spring 1888
584	13:14[153–54]	Spring 1888
585	12:9[60]	Autumn 1887
585A	12:9[60]	Autumn 1887
589	12:2[147]	Autumn 1885–Autumn 1886
606	12:2[174]	Autumn 1885–Autumn 1886
616	12:2[108]	Autumn 1885–Autumn 1886
617	12:7[54]	End of 1886–Spring 1887
619	11:36[31]	June–July 1885
624	12:7[56]	End of 1886–Spring 1887
627	12:2[83]	Autumn 1885–Autumn 1886
633	13:14[95]	Spring 1888
643	12:2[148]	Autumn 1885–Autumn 1886
660	12:2[76]	Autumn 1885–Autumn 1886
664	10:24[9]	Winter 1883–84
667	10:24[15]	Winter 1883–84
669	13:11[71]	November 1887–March 1888

WP	KSA	Date of Composition
671	10:24[32, 34]	Winter 1883–84
674	13:11[83]	November 1887–March 1888
675	13:11[96]	November 1887–March 1888
676	10:24[16]	Winter 1883–84
692	13:14[121]	Spring 1888
693	13:14[80]	Spring 1888
701	13:11[61]	November 1887–March 1888
702	13:14[174]	Spring 1888
714	10:4[233]	November 1882–February 1883
715	13:11[73]	November 1887–March 1888
781	12:10[127]	Autumn 1887
786	12:10[57]	Autumn 1887
790	13:11[104]	November 1887–March 1888
909	13:15[114]	Spring 1888
928	13:11[353]	November 1887–March 1888
929	13:15[94]	Spring 1888
930	13:11[89]	November 1887–March 1888
966	11:27[59]	Summer–Autumn 1884
979	11:35[47]	May–July 1885
1059	11:26[284]	Summer–Autumn 1884
1062	11:36[15]	June–July 1885
1067	11:38[12]	June–July 1885

Appendix 2: Dates of Composition for Passages from *Sämtliche Werke: Kritische Studienausgabe*

Listed below are the approximate dates of composition for each notebook in *Sämtliche Werke: Kritische Studienausgabe (KSA)* from which I have cited passages.

Volume:Notebook	Date of Composition
7:6	End of 1870
7:7	End of 1870–April 1871
7:19	Summer 1872–Beginning of 1873
7:23	Winter 1872–73
7:26	Spring 1873
7:29	Summer–Autumn 1873
8:9	Summer 1875
9:6	Autumn 1880
9:10	Spring 1880–Spring 1881
9:11	Spring–Autumn 1881
9:12	Autumn 1881
9:21	Summer 1882
10:4	November 1882–February 1883
10:7	Spring–Summer 1883
10:12	Summer 1883
10:24	Winter 1883-84
11:25	Spring 1884
11:26	Summer–Autumn 1884
11:34	April–June 1885
11:35	May–July 1885
11:40	August–September 1885

Volume:Notebook	Date of Composition
11:43	Autumn 1885
12:5	Summer 1886–Autumn 1887
12:7	End of 1886–Spring 1887
12:9	Autumn 1887
13:21	Autumn 1888

Notes

Introduction

1. See, for example, deMan 1979, 116–18; Derrida 1978, 280; Kofman 1977, 201–14.

2. Some examples are Clark 1990; Clark 1998; Hales and Welshon 2000; Leiter 1994; Poellner 1995; Schacht 1983, chap. 2; Schacht 1995, chap. 3.

3. For a detailed look at Nietzsche from the perspective of Platonic and pre-Socratic influences on his thought, see Richardson 1996.

4. Such an antinaturalist account is not equivalent to a nonphysical account, for a nonphysical entity can still be understood as subject to deterministic laws and in causal relation to physical objects and other nonphysical entities. As we shall see, Hume's account of causal judgments, although appealing to the mental, is still fundamentally naturalistic in outlook for this reason.

5. On Nietzsche's naturalism, see Cox 1999, 69–106; Leiter 1998; Schacht 1983, 54–57; Schacht 1988.

6. Elements of evolutionary epistemology in Nietzsche's writings are discussed in Poellner 1995, 138–49.

7. "Object" is being used here liberally to include anything to which a concept might be applied; it does not refer to physical objects per se.

8. That Hume and the British empiricists generally conflate seeing and seeing as is a criticism that goes back to Thomas Reid and T. H. Green. See Rorty 1979, 139–48.

9. By "cognition" I mean judgments that are capable of being true or false. Thus I will argue that Nietzsche holds a naturalized theory of *judgment* but an antinaturalistic theory of *cognition*. He holds a naturalized theory of judgment because he argues that actual human judgment must be explained naturalistically. But he holds an antinaturalistic theory of cognition because, like others in the Neo-Kantian tradition, he believes that judgments with truth-values must be understood in antinaturalist terms.

10. *The Will to Power* is a selection from Nietzsche's notebooks from 1883 to 1888 edited by Peter Gast, Ernst Horneffer, and August Horneffer.

Chapter 1: The Problem of Nietzsche's "Error Theory"

1. Many examples of Nietzsche's error theory can be found in his published works. See, for example, *GS* 107; *BGE* 4, 24, 34; *TI* 3:5. In his notebooks the passages where he expresses the error theory run into the hundreds.

2. Clark and Leiter argue that Nietzsche considers our beliefs to be false only while holding a metaphysically realist theory of truth, which he subsequently rejects (Clark 1990, 95–125; Leiter 1994). Others argue that Nietzsche makes such claims only to indicate what would follow if one accepted a metaphysically realist theory of truth. This is the position taken by Rüdiger Grimm (1977, 26–28; 1979). According to Grimm, all judgments are false according to the "correspondence theory" but can be true or false according to the criterion of truth Nietzsche himself proposes, namely, that of the enhancement of power.

3. It is, of course, possible to question the law of the excluded middle. But the acceptance of a three-valued logic does not solve the problem. We need merely assume three people: one who believes that x is green, one who believes that x is not green, and one who believes that x is neither green nor not green. One of these three must have a true belief.

4. Another example of someone who appears to take this approach is Grimm, who argues that the will to power is "a grand monumental chaos which can only be characterized by negative qualities" (1977, 2).

5. Nietzsche's nominalism is discussed in Abel 1984, 332–33; Abel 1985; Cox 1999, 86–91. Other examples of such nominalism in Nietzsche's notebooks occur in *The Will to Power* (512, 532).

6. See chapter 5, sections 11–16.

7. This is argued for by Harries: "To be aware of a perspective as a perspective and of the limitations imposed by a particular point of view, is to be, at least in thought, already beyond these limitations" (1983, 243).

8. See chapter 4, section 4; chapter 5, section 13.

9. On skeptical tendencies in Nietzsche, see Magnus 1980.

10. More examples of this view can be found in the Nachlaß (*KSA* 9:11[18]; *WP* 551, 569, 584).

11. Hare argues, for example, that "in the ordinary commendatory sense of 'good,' it is self-contradictory to say 'It is a good one, but that is no reason for preferring it,' but that in the ordinary sense of 'yellow' it is never contradictory to say 'It is a yellow one, but that is no reason for preferring it'" (1981, 67; see also 1952, §5.4). A reason to prefer something could be prima facie, of course. Evaluations may recognize reasons for action that are overridden by *other* reasons for action.

12. Hare criticizes Mackie on these lines: "What is wrong with the claim that there can exist authoritative objective prescription is incoherence, not falsity" (1981, 83).

13. One might argue that our partial perspectives on the world are false because we implicitly deny that they are partial. Our perspectives are distorting because they present themselves as exhaustive. But what compels us to think of them this way? Why can't we simply engage in an examination of *part* of the world while conceding that the rest of the world will have to be examined later, or not at all? If this is Nietzsche's argument for his

error theory, then it seems to rest on a presumption that we are all epistemic megalomaniacs. For a similar criticism of this argument, see Clark 1990, 155–58.

14. According to Clark's reading, the change in Nietzsche's views must have taken place between June 1886 (when *Beyond Good and Evil* was given over to C. G. Naumann, his publisher) and July 1887 (when he wrote the *Genealogy of Morals*) or possibly October 1887, when he finished the proofs. In fact, the time frame would have to be even narrower. During this period Nietzsche added a fifth book to the second edition of *The Gay Science*. This fifth book contains entirely new expressions of his error theory (e.g. GS2d 354), which Clark herself places in Nietzsche's "early" period (1990, 117, 127). Nietzsche was still working on the fifth book in April 1887. So the change in Nietzsche's views on truth must have occurred between April and July 1887 or, less likely, between April and October 1887.

15. Clark argues that Nietzsche was confused before the *Genealogy of Morals,* and so expressed contradictory views, and it is only in the *Genealogy* that he comes to realize the consequences of a denial of the intelligibility of the thing-in-itself. For example, in *Human, All Too Human,* Nietzsche explicitly allows that "there could be a metaphysical world," although "one could assert nothing at all of the metaphysical world except that it was a being-other, an inaccessible, incomprehensible being-other; it would be a thing with negative qualities" (9). Clark points to the tension between sections 9 and 16, where Nietzsche claims that the thing-in-itself is "empty of significance," to argue that he was confused pre-*Genealogy.*

16. See the final two parts of *Twilight of the Idols,* "What the Germans Lack" and "Expeditions of an Untimely Man," and much of the first part, "Maxims and Arrows."

17. Clark offers as evidence the fact that Nietzsche places "reason" in quotation marks in *Twilight of the Idols* (3:2). But he later speaks of the "prejudice of reason," "the presuppositions of reason," and "the categories of reason" (3:5) without the use of scare quotes.

18. Clark would presumably argue that the error that Nietzsche speaks of is not *necessary* for causal reasoning but is merely a misinterpretation of causality, albeit one that extends somewhat beyond metaphysics. This would be analogous to her argument that the concept of "substance" that Nietzsche criticizes in *Twilight of the Idols* refers only to a "metaphysical concept of substance as an unchanging substrate" (1990, 107) that is not employed "in common sense beliefs or the sciences" (108).

19. Because Clark identifies Nietzsche's error theory with the phenomenalist version, under which our sensations falsify, she is unable to explain why Nietzsche thinks that logic and mathematics falsify reality. Clark's explanation of Nietzsche's views concerning logic and mathematics is that his phenomenalist error theory led him to reject relatively enduring things as incompatible with the chaos of sensations. This "helps explain why [the early Nietzsche] believes that logic and mathematics falsify reality, for he believes that mathematical and logical truths presuppose the existence of substances, presumably as the bearers of properties, and things to be counted and measured. That logic and math could not have been developed in the absence of a notion of enduring things seems plausible" (Clark 1990, 122).

But Clark fails to explain why Nietzsche thinks that logic and mathematics are inapplicable to a world that consists of only our fleeting sensations. Mustn't it be the case that a sensation is either green or not green? Don't two sensations plus two sensations make four sensations? It may be that logic or mathematics would not have *arisen* if we had not assumed the existence of enduring objects. But Nietzsche's argument is much stronger than that. He claims time and time again that logic, mathematics, or any form of conceptualization *falsifies* the world (including the *inner* world of our sensations).

20. Further examples can be found in "On Truth and Lies in a Nonmoral Sense" (p. 83), *Human, All Too Human* (18), and the Nachlaß (*KSA* 9:6[349], 9:6[412 and 441], 9:11[329–30]; *WP* 532, 544). On this aspect of Nietzsche's epistemology, see D'Iorio 1993, 257n.2; Schlechta and Anders 1962, 161–66.

Chapter 2: Nietzsche's Neo-Kantian Roots

1. All page references to Kant's *Critique of Pure Reason* will follow the convention of preceding page references to the first edition (1781) with "A" and to the second edition (1787) with "B."

2. Indeed, it is not clear that Kant tries to answer the problem of induction in the *Critique of Pure Reason*.

3. On this topic, I have been much influenced by Henry Allison's reading of Kant. See Allison 1983, chap. 7.

4. Another difference between the phenomenalist and the apperceptive approach to judgment concerns their differing conceptions of the thing-in-itself. For the phenomenalist, the thing-in-itself is the unknowable and unrepresentable *cause* of our sensations. It is an ontologically distinct entity. For the transcendental idealist, the thing-in-itself is the very same object we know, but it is that object considered independently of the transcendental conditions for representing it.

5. Given the enormous influence that Spir exerted on Nietzsche's epistemology, it is remarkable that their relationship hasn't been given greater attention. I have been able to find only three philosophical articles discussing Spir's relationship to Nietzsche: Small discusses Spir's influence on Nietzsche's conception of time, absolute becoming, and the eternal recurrence (1994, reprinted in 2001, chap. 1); D'Iorio chronicles Nietzsche's responses to Spir's thought in his Nachlaß (1993); and Dickopp discusses Nietzsche's response to Spir's and Teichmüller's views on the Cartesian cogito (1970). Spir's influence on Nietzsche will also be discussed in Brobjer (n.d.). One possible reason for this lack of discussion of Spir's influence on Nietzsche in English is the fact that, with the exception of a marginal work on ethics (Spir 1954), Spir has never been translated into English. Another reason is the difficulty of finding Spir's works in the United States. I was able to track down only two copies of the second edition of Spir's *Denken und Wirklichkeit* (the one owned by Nietzsche). One is in the Library of Congress, and another is in Harvard's Widener Library.

The little that is said about Spir in the literature on Nietzsche often distorts his views. Hales and Welshon, relying upon Zedlin (1972), call Spir "a sort of neo-Kantian phenomenalist" (2000, 38). Given that Spir entirely denies the role of sensation in our knowledge of the world, the *last* thing that he can be called is a phenomenalist.

6. For further discussion of Nietzsche's interest in Spir's writings, see Janz 1978–79, 1:555, 1:755, 2:82, 2:227, 2:430; D'Iorio 1993. Thomas Brobjer kindly provided me with some of

his transcriptions of Nietzsche's extensive annotations of the second addition of *Denken und Wirklichkeit.*

7. In *Philosophy in the Tragic Age of the Greeks* (15), Nietzsche quotes Spir 1873, 1:264–65, and Spir 1877, 1:209–10. In *Human, All Too Human* (18) he quotes Spir 1877, 2:177.

8. See *KSA* 7:26[1], 7:29[200], 11:35[56 and 61], 11:40[12, 24, and 41], 13:21[1]. In addition, Nietzsche quotes a long passage from Spir 1877, 1:379–80, without mentioning him or *Denken und Wirklichkeit* by name (*KSA* 9:11[329]).

9. See *KSA* 11:25[318 and 424], 11:34[99].

10. The same passage occurs in Spir 1877, 1:209–10.

11. P. F. Strawson makes much the same criticism of Kant: "Consider . . . the view that since space and time are nothing but forms of our sensibility, our awareness of all things in space and time, including ourselves, is awareness of things only as they appear to us and not as they are in themselves. We are aware, then, of ourselves in a temporal guise and hence only as we appear to ourselves and not as we are in ourselves. But what sort of truth about ourselves is it, that we appear to ourselves in temporal guise? Do we really appear to ourselves or only appear to ourselves so to appear to ourselves? It seems that we must either choose the first alternative at once or uselessly delay a uselessly elaborated variant of it. Then is this a temporal fact, a fact about what happens in time, that we really so appear to ourselves? To say this would be to go back on our choice; for all that occurs in time belongs on the side of appearances" (1966, 38–39).

12. For a discussion of this theme in Nietzsche's thought, see Small 2001, 11–12.

13. Richardson spells out the infirmities of an interpretation of Nietzsche's theory of becoming as a claim that the world changes more than we take it to or that our choices about how to individuate objects in some sense do digital violence to an analog world (1996, §2.1.1, esp. p. 88). Richardson opts for an understanding of Nietzsche's becoming-ontology as a quasi-epistemological view, similar to that offered here, which primarily concerns the relationship between the knowing subject and the world (§§2.1.2–2.1.3).

14. Passages in Plato's dialogues are referred to by page and section from the canonical Stephanus edition of his works published in 1578.

15. One of the few extended discussions of Nietzsche's views on logic can be found in Hales and Welshon (2000, 37–56). They do not discuss the principle of noncontradiction, however, although they do read Nietzsche as denying the law of the excluded middle (50–52).

16. For a discussion of passages in "On Truth and Lies in a Nonmoral Sense" and *Twilight of the Idols* where Nietzsche appears to indicate that logic is true by convention (*TL* p. 81; *TI* 3:3), see chapter 3, section 13.

Chapter 3: Nietzsche's "Error Theory" Explained

1. See chapter 1, section 6.

2. On the distinction between diachronic and synchronic self-identity, see Hales and Welshon, who claim that "there is little unambiguous textual evidence that Nietzsche rejected synchronic self-identity" (2000, 55). As I argue below, this claim does not stand up under scrutiny. The two are well ahead of other interpreters of Nietzsche, however, in

at least entertaining the *possibility* that Nietzsche rejects the existence of synchronic self-identity.

3. More examples of the view that reality is contradictory can be found in the Nachlaß (*KSA* 7:26[12], 8:9[1, p. 136], 9:10[E93]; *WP* 579, 584–85).

4. Compare the following passages from the period 1881–82: *KSA* 9:11[149] (*"die ewige Veränderung, der ewige Fluß aller Dinge"*), 9:11[155] (*"ewiger Fluß der Dinge"*), 9:11[162] (*"absoluter Fluss"*), 10:4[76] (*"ewiger Fluss"*), 9:11[84] (*"eine ewige Wechsel der Stoffe"*), 9:11[268] (*"fortwährende Wechsel"*), 9:11[321] (*"ein fortwährendes Werden und Wechseln"*), 9:11[329] (*"der Wechsels, die Relativität"*); *GS* 107 (*"den Fluss des Werdens"*); *GS* 112 (*"den Fluss des Geschehens"*).

5. See *KSA* 7:19[242]: "The essence of definition: a pencil is a long etc. body. A is B. That which is long is at the same time colored. The qualities consist only of relations. A particular object is simply so and so many relations. Relations can never be the essence, only the consequences of the essence. The synthetic judgment describes a thing according to its consequences, i.e. *essence* and *consequences* are *identified*, that is a *metonymy*. Thus in the essence of a synthetic judgment there is a *metonymy*, that is, a *false comparison*."

6. Spir is not the only philosopher to understand substances as violating the principle of identity. The same argument can be found, for example, in absolute idealists such as F. H. Bradley (1969, 40–44).

7. This problem of unifying representations of an object over time is discussed by Nietzsche as well: "Even as an image [a thing] is not complete. There is a presupposition that afterward, the thing in *this* instant that it makes an impression upon us, is the *same* thing that in another instant . . . provides us with a new impression, that is, a second relation to us. A tree that is long, *then* round, then green etc. appears" (*KSA* 9:6[412]). For a tree to be thought of as long and round and green, these representations must be unified over time.

8. For a sophisticated response to this problem, see Allison 1990, 146–57.

9. Although Spir thinks atomism is respectable as a physical theory (1877, 2:113–14), these atoms are *not simple,* even if they cannot be physically divided. They are themselves unities of various qualities and thus conditioned.

10. For a clear exposition of the close relationships between Nietzsche's idea of becoming as *contextuality* and Platonic and Heraclitean conceptions of becoming, see Richardson 1996, 89–109.

11. It is important to see that the primary problem here is not the existence of the infinite. Thus the contemporary mathematical concept of a limit does not solve the problem. One needs space-atoms not because one needs only a finite number of units but because there needs to be a definite unit of space with reference to which things can have a definite size. Space-atoms are no different from the one absolute Newtonian space within which things are to occur—they are the absolute measure of space.

12. See Spir 1877, 2:9–10. For a detailed discussion of Spir's argument, see Small 2001, 4–8.

13. Although Spir's argument is similar to Kant's Second Analogy, Spir argues that Kant fails to achieve his stated goal in the Second Analogy, which is to show that the category of causality applies to sensory intuition. To think of change we must see it as part of one simple self-identical substance, but the very plurality and temporality of change violates

this simplicity and self-identity. Kant's attempt to bridge this gap between thought and sensation through the schematism fails. The empirical world of causal relations is a world of error.

14. Boscovich (1922) argues that atoms with discrete extensions could not exist because change in motion as a result of their collision would involve instantaneous change in velocity, in violation of the principle of continuity of motion. See Poellner 1995, 48–53; Stack 1981; Moles 1990, chap. 5. He argues instead that reality consists of fields of force emanating from central points.

15. For examples where Nietzsche ties his theory of force to his theory of the will to power, see *The Will to Power* (619, 693).

16. A useful study along these lines is Richardson 1996.

17. See also *TL* p. 83; *WP* 501, 515, 532, 551, 568.

18. Maudemarie Clark argues that 3:3 of *Twilight of the Idols* indicates that Nietzsche changed his views concerning logic after *Beyond Good and Evil* (1990, 105). But Nietzsche continues his critique of logic in his Nachlaß during what Clark takes to be his mature period (*WP* 516–17). What is more, he continues to criticize the concept of self-identical substances, upon which his critique of logic relies, both in *Twilight of the Idols* and in his Nachlaß during this period (*TI* 3:5; *WP* 521 and 569). Hales and Welshon (2000, 43) offer a similar criticism of Clark's reading.

19. Such a reading is suggested by this passage: "That *everything recurs* is the closest *approximation of a world of becoming to a world of being:*—high point of the meditation" (*WP* 617).

Chapter 4: Antirealism and Noncognitivism

1. In fact, not all combinations of a naturalistic account of a judgment with a realist account of its truth lead to skepticism. They will not lead to skepticism if we can demonstrate that, despite the fact that we are not *directly* sensitive to the object of a judgment, our making the judgment does mean it is more likely to be true. Assume that when I judge that the air pressure is low, I am only concerned about whether a barometer falls. If I consider my judgment that the air pressure is low to employ concepts concerning *air pressure* rather than *barometers,* I need not be a skeptic, because I can give an independent demonstration that my judgment is indirectly sensitive to air pressure. The reason cognitive compatibilism leads to skepticism for Nietzsche is that the *comprehensiveness* of his epistemological positions excludes the possibility that such an independent demonstration is itself justified.

This same problem arises in connection with traditional skepticism about the external world. Such skepticism begins with a naturalistic account of our judgments about the external world under which these judgments are brought about by our sensations. This means that these judgments are not sensitive to the character of the external world, the skeptic argues. But let's say one attempts to show that they are nevertheless justified, through a demonstration that when we judge on the basis of our sensations, it is likely that we are able to get at the character of independent objects. Such an argument would not succeed, for any demonstration of the relationship between our sensations and the external world would itself be a judgment about the external world. The demonstration would only be justified if it assumed what it intended to prove, namely, that our judgments about the external world are justified.

2. On the extent to which Nietzsche expresses skeptical views, see chapter 1, section 4.

3. Although Stevenson emphasizes what he calls this "emotive meaning" of an evaluative utterance, he nevertheless allows that "ethical definitions involve a wedding of descriptive and emotive meaning" (1944, 210). Stevenson gives the following "working model" of the semantics of the evaluation "This is good": "I approve of this; do so as well" (21). The initial clause is a relatively precise rendering of the descriptive meaning of the expression, and the second is a rendering of its emotive meaning (one that is rather inadequate because moral utterances express one's affective attitudes and lead others to change their attitudes in a manner different from prescriptions).

4. A number of interpreters have argued against Nietzsche's holding a pragmatic theory of truth for this reason. See Clark 1990, 32; Cox 1999, 36, 46–47; Nehamas 1985, 52–53.

5. Clark argues against Danto's reading of Nietzsche on the basis of such passages (1990, 50).

6. For a reading of Nietzsche's pragmatic theory of truth in which enhancement of power is used as an explicit criterion for the truth of a judgment, see Grimm 1979; Grimm 1977, 26–28.

7. It may be that Clark is presenting a form of antirealism in which the standards of rational acceptability that bind our judgments are reducible to our actual current dispositions to judge. But if that is the case, then her position is substantially the same as the noncognitivist's. The only difference between the two is terminological—whether one chooses to call this fully naturalized form of judgment "cognition" or not. I will discuss this issue in section 10 of the next chapter.

8. It is true that at times Nietzsche's skepticism concerning the law of noncontradiction appears to be primarily a claim about the nature of reality, not about our ability to form concepts: "I have the suspicion, that things and thought don't correspond to one another. In logic the law of contradiction rules, which *perhaps* is not valid of things, which are manifold and contradictory" (*KSA* 7:7[110]). But, as we have seen, for Nietzsche, claims about the world being contradiction and flux are intimately related to claims about our ability to conceptualize. For Nietzsche to question whether the law of noncontradiction is adequate to the world is for him to question whether we have objectively valid concepts—whether our uniting of representations in the mind manages to say anything about the world.

9. On this conflict in Nietzsche, see Berkowitz 1995, 80–83; Hales and Welshon 2000, 145.

10. For this reason, Hales and Welshon reinterpret Nietzsche's claims concerning the epiphenomenality of mental events. According to their reinterpretation, Nietzsche allows that psychological events can cause other psychological and nonpsychological events. He merely argues that these causal relations do not proceed through the conscious properties of the psychological events (2000, 147–48). By "conscious properties," they mean those properties that we ascribe to mental events as a result of our second-order awareness of them (134; cf. Schacht 1983, 279–96; Jarmolych 1985). I will argue that we should take Nietzsche at his word—he really means that there are no causal relations between mental events.

Such a position is the straightforward application of Nietzsche's theory of absolute becoming to the mental world.

Those passages where Nietzsche denies only that there are *direct* causal connections between mental events, however, can be understood along lines similar to Hales and Welshon's theory. I will argue in chapter 4, section 9 that these passages are similar to the rule-skeptic's claim that the movement from one thought to another is not conceptually constrained.

11. This topic is discussed by Poellner in detail (1995, 40–46).

12. Although I think Kripke's book does justice to a good deal that is in Wittgenstein, I will not argue for this.

13. The question is not a mathematical one—I am concerned only with whether the response of "125" is in accordance with the rule I *intended* for the function "+," whether or not this rule is equivalent to the arithmetic function of addition.

14. Of course, taking myself to have meant quus rather than plus is incompatible with *other* rules I take myself to have intended at the time. I cannot have intended "+" to mean quus *and* intended "-" to mean minus, if the rules concerning the relationship between the "+" and the "-" symbols are as I currently believe I intended them to be. But the rule-skeptic can simply apply the skeptical argument to my intentions concerning the "-" symbol and the relationship between the "+" and the "-" symbols.

15. This conclusion supports the antiphenomenalist argument, discussed earlier, that one cannot identify having a sensation of green with seeing it *as green.* For the sensation of green will not tell us how to go on without an *interpretation* of it. Given the right interpretation, one can consider grouping this sensation of green with anything.

16. Of course, one might try to associate the rule binding my responses with only *one* disposition I have or had. But how am I to choose *which* disposition this is unless I antecedently know what it is I meant? Such a dispositional account assumes precisely what it intended to prove. For it is the chosen disposition that determines what the rule for "+" is and so what "+" means.

Here is one way of thinking of this problem. Although this chosen disposition was to act as a cognitive constraint upon what I do (it was to be that with respect to which what I do could be in error), my choice of this disposition is itself something that I do. I must assume that what I do is not in error to think that I can correctly choose the disposition that determines the rule binding what I do. If I do make this assumption, I have equated performance and correctness again. If I don't, I'm unable to find the disposition that is supposed to establish what the rule binding me is.

17. There is more receptivity to such a reading in the literature in German. An outstanding example is Djuric 1980. See also Figl 1982, 90; Müller-Lauter 1971, 21.

Chapter 5: Nihilism, Hedonism, and the Self-Reference Problem

1. On these issues I have been much influenced by White 1991, chaps. 7–9, and by personal conversations with White.

2. This general position has been argued for strongly by Simon Blackburn (1985, 5–6). But the argument is older. It can be found, for example, in Stevenson 1963, 93.

3. Unconditional desires are not equivalent to noninstrumental desires. My conditional desire to drink coffee can be noninstrumental—I can have a desire to drink coffee only if I want to but not desire to drink coffee because it satisfies another desire I have. Unconditional desires, it should also be noted, are not necessarily *uncontingent* either. What unconditional desires one has can be just as contingent a matter as what conditional desires one has.

4. For an analogous view that objective values are conceived of as authorities, see Mackie 1977, 43.

5. See section 3 of this chapter.

6. The full sentence is as follows: "Nietzsche's denial of sin becomes trivial unless we interpret him as claiming that his own perspective is cognitively superior to the religio-moral perspective on history" (Clark 1990, 140).

7. Part of section 344 of the second edition of *The Gay Science* is quoted in *On the Genealogy of Morals* (3:24), and it and the entire fifth book of the second edition of *The Gay Science,* as well as the preface to the second edition of *Daybreak,* are referred to there as elaborations of his argument in the *Genealogy.*

8. For an argument that Nietzsche criticizes pity for suffering from a similar evaluative inconsistency, see Green 1992.

9. This does not mean that an ascetic cannot actually hate desire, only that he or she cannot do so without desiring. When Nietzsche says that "a condemnation of life by the living is after all no more than the symptom of a certain kind of life: the question of whether the condemnation is just or unjust has not been raised at all" (*TI* 5:5), he does not suggest that there is no condemnation of life, only that it is itself a product of life.

10. See chapter 4, section 10.

11. Richard Schacht points to such language as a reason to attribute to Nietzsche a form of cognitivism (1995, chap. 3; 2000). Another example of cognitivist language in Nietzsche is his use of the word "truth" (e.g. *AC* 50; *GM* 1:1).

12. Clark suggests such an approach elsewhere as well (1990, 74–78). Leiter's adoption of such an approach is even more explicit. He draws an analogy between Nietzsche's epistemology and the Wittgensteinian view that it "is only against a background of [particular] dispositions that it is possible to employ any intelligible idea of a constraint upon meaning" (1994, 348).

13. This problem arises in Günter Abel's account of Nietzsche's "interpretationism": "But how do we make worlds? The answer is—in processes of interpretation. . . . All interpretation is an organization, omission, subsumption, demarcation, completion, arrangement, simplification, abstraction, regularization, weighing, effacing and deforming. Therefore these processes of interpretation, the function of organizing forces, should not be understood as involving passive reproduction, but as active creation. Interpretations of all kinds are means of organization, means 'to become master of something'" (1987, 115). Similar passages can be found in "Realismus, Pragmatismus, Interpretationismus" (1988b) and "Interpretations-Welten" (1989). But if the world about which we can speak comes into being though such a process of schematization, how can we speak about this very process? We will have to speak about what the process *acts upon* in order to give any talk about the process content. But we cannot speak about that which lies before the pro-

cess is applied, for the very act of speaking about it would mean the application of the process. For a criticism of Abel along these lines, see Lenk 1988; cf. Poellner 1995, 190–91.

14. It sometimes looks like she does want to deny this. See Clark 1990, 50–51.

15. It is for this reason that Bittner (1987, 84–86) criticizes Günter Abel's characterization of Nietzsche's conception of interpretation as a form of "organization, omission, subsumption, demarcation, completion, arrangement, simplification, abstraction, regularization, weighing, effacing and deforming" (Abel 1987, 115) and Abel's occasional assertions that the only things that exist are interpretations.

16. Another example of Nietzsche's awareness of the problem can be found in his Nachlaß (*KSA* 9:6[441]). On Nietzsche's debt to Lange, see Salaquarda 1978; Stack 1983.

17. The very language within which Hume presents his argument that we have no idea of causal connection is causal. Are we supposed to understand this argument itself in noncognitivist terms? Is Hume *not thinking* when giving this argument? Is he merely expressing dispositions to associate?

18. The rule-skeptic questions whether I can know that any response I give is in accordance with the rules governing such responses. But every step in the rule-skeptic's argument itself is one of these rule-governed responses. If we are skeptical about whether our responses are in accordance with these rules, how can rule-skepticism get off the ground? Kripke, anticipating this problem, initially formulates rule-skepticism as a question about whether our current responses are in accordance with *past* rules that we established, without questioning whether they are in accordance with any current rules. It is only after establishing skepticism about past rules that he then applies it to current rules (1982, 11–14).

19. One should not conclude, however, that *all* skeptical arguments suffer from the self-reference problem. Consider skepticism about the external world. Skeptics about the external world do not rely upon a belief about the external world to lodge their argument. All they need to assume is a naturalistic account of our *judgments* about the external world, under which such judgments are seen as brought about by our sensations rather than by any direct contact with the external world. Skepticism follows, because we have no reason to believe that judgments about the external world are correct simply because they are caused by our sensations. There is no problem of self-reference because the naturalistic account of our judgments is not a judgment about the external world. Admittedly, those who think we have knowledge of the external world also accept this account. It is for this reason that they are vulnerable to skepticism, since they cannot reject this premise upon which the skeptical argument relies. But the naturalistic account is not itself a judgment about the external world and so is not undermined by the skeptical argument.

20. Nietzsche's doctrine of the eternal recurrence appears to be an attempt to present a theory of absolute becoming in a way that can be entertained but that nevertheless allows for epistemological self-affirmation. This may be able to explain why Nietzsche claims that the idea of the eternal recurrence "is the closest *approximation of a world of becoming to a world of being:*—high point of the mediation" (*WP* 617). But these issues cannot be pursued further in this work.

Bibliography

Nietzsche's Published Works in English

The following English translations of books that Nietzsche published or intended to be published were used in this work. The approximate final dates of composition, usually the month and year that Nietzsche completed the page proofs for the publisher, are also provided.

The Antichrist. In *The Twilight of the Idols and The Antichrist.* Trans. R. J. Hollingdale. Harmondsworth, U.K.: Penguin, 1968. 122–97. (September 1888.)

Assorted Opinions and Maxims. In *Human, All Too Human.* Trans. R. J. Hollingdale. Cambridge: Cambridge University Press, 1986. 215–299. (1st ed. February 1879; 2d ed. April 1886.)

Beyond Good and Evil. Trans. Walter Kaufmann. New York: Random House, 1966. (June 1886.)

The Birth of Tragedy. In *The Birth of Tragedy and The Case of Wagner.* Trans. Walter Kaufmann. New York: Random House, 1967. 15–151. (1st ed. December 1871; 2d ed. August 1886.)

The Case of Wagner. In *The Birth of Tragedy and The Case of Wagner.* Trans. Walter Kaufmann. New York: Random House, 1967. 153–92. (August 1888.)

Daybreak: Thoughts on the Prejudices of Morality. Trans. R. J. Hollingdale. Cambridge: Cambridge University Press, 1982. (1st ed. May-June 1881; 2d ed. October 1886.)

Ecce Homo. In *On the Genealogy of Morals and Ecce Homo.* Trans. Walter Kaufmann. New York: Random House, 1969. 215–335. (December 1888.)

The Gay Science. Trans. Walter Kaufmann. New York: Random House, 1974. (1st ed. June 1882; 2d ed. April 1887.)

Human, All Too Human: A Book for Free Spirits. In *Human, All Too Human.* Trans. R. J. Hollingdale. Cambridge: Cambridge University Press, 1986. 1–205. (1st ed. April 1878; 2d ed. April 1886.)

On the Genealogy of Morals. In *On the Genealogy of Morals and Ecce Homo.* Trans. Walter

Kaufmann and R. J. Hollingdale. New York: Random House, 1969. 13–163. (October 1887.)

Thus Spoke Zarathustra. Trans. R. J. Hollingdale. Harmondsworth, U.K.: Penguin, 1969. (Part 1, February 1883; Part 2, July 1883; Part 3, February 1884; Part 4, March 1885.)

Twilight of the Idols. In *The Twilight of the Idols and The Antichrist.* Trans. R. J. Hollingdale. Harmondsworth, U.K.: Penguin, 1968. 29–121. (September 1888.)

The Wanderer and His Shadow. In *Human, All Too Human.* Trans. R. J. Hollingdale. Cambridge: Cambridge University Press, 1986. 301–95. (1st ed. December 1879; 2d ed. April 1886.)

Nietzsche's Unpublished Works in English

The following English translations of Nietzsche's unpublished works and notes were used in this work. The approximate dates of composition are provided.

"On Truth and Lies in a Nonmoral Sense." In *Philosophy and Truth: Selections from Nietzsche's Notebooks of the Early 1870s.* Trans. and ed. Daniel Breazeale. Atlantic Highlands, N.J.: Humanities Press, 1979. 79–97. (June 1873.)

Philosophy in the Tragic Age of the Greeks. Trans. Marianne Cowan. Chicago: Regnery, 1962. (April 1873.)

The Will to Power. Trans. Walter Kaufmann and R. J. Hollingdale. New York: Random House, 1968. (See appendix 1 for dates of composition and corresponding passages in *Sämtliche Werke: Kritische Studienausgabe.*)

Nietzsche's Unpublished Works in German

When referring to passages from Nietzsche's Nachlaß that were not included in *The Will to Power* and have not been published in any other English translation, I cite the fifteen-volume *Sämtliche Werke: Kritische Studienausgabe,* ed. Giorgio Colli and Mazzino Montinari (Munich: Deutscher Taschenbuch Verlag, 1980), abbreviated *KSA.* References take the form *KSA* 9:11[329], where the volume appears first, followed by the notebook number and, within brackets, the passage number. For long passages, a page number is also given. All translations of passages citing *KSA* are my own. To determine the approximate date of composition for each notebook, see appendix 2.

Secondary Works

All references to the following works are to page number, unless identified otherwise. All translations of Abel, Bittner, and Spir are my own.

Abel, Günter. 1984. *Nietzsche: Die Dynamik der Willen zur Macht und die ewige Wiederkehr.* Berlin: Walter de Gruyter.

———. 1985. "Nominalismus und Interpretation: Die Überwindung der Metaphysik im Denken Nietzsches." In *Nietzsche und die philosophische Tradition.* Vol. 2. Ed. Josef Simon. Würzburg: Königshausen und Neumann. 35–89.

———. 1987. "Logik und Ästhetik." *Nietzsche-Studien* 16:112–48.

———. 1988a. "Interpretationsphilosophie: Eine Antwort auf Hans Lenk." *Allgemeine Zeitschrift für Philosophie* 13:79–86.

———. 1988b. "Realismus, Pragmatismus, Interpretationismus: Zu neueren Entwicklungen in der Analytischen Philosophie." *Allgemeine Zeitschrift für Philosophie* 13:51–68.

———. 1989. "Interpretations-Welten." *Philosophisches Jahrbuch* 96:1–19.

———. 1990. "Interpretatorische Vernunft und menschlicher Leib." In *Nietzsches Begriff von Philosophie.* Ed. Mihailo Djuric. Würzburg: Königshausen und Neumann. 100–130.

Allison, Henry E. 1983. *Kant's Transcendental Idealism: An Interpretation and Defense.* New Haven, Conn.: Yale University Press.

———. 1990. *Kant's Theory of Freedom.* Cambridge: Cambridge University Press.

Anderson, R. Lanier. 1996. "Overcoming Charity: The Case of Maudemarie Clark's *Nietzsche on Truth and Philosophy.*" *Nietzsche-Studien* 25:307–41.

Bäumler, Alfred. 1937. *Nietzsche der Philosoph und Politiker.* 3d ed. Leipzig: P. Reclam.

Berkowitz, Peter. 1995. *Nietzsche: The Ethics of an Immoralist.* Cambridge, Mass.: Harvard University Press.

Bittner, Rüdiger. 1987. "Nietzsches Begriff der Wahrheit." *Nietzsche-Studien* 16:70–90.

Blackburn, Simon. 1985. "Errors and the Phenomenology of Value." In *Morality and Objectivity: A Tribute to J. L. Mackie.* Ed. Ted Honderich. London: Routledge and Kegan Paul. 1–22.

Boscovich, Roger Joseph. 1922. *A Theory of Natural Philosophy.* Chicago: Open Court Publishing.

Bradley, F. H. 1969. *Appearance and Reality.* 2d ed. Oxford: Oxford University Press.

Brobjer, Thomas H. N.d. "Nietzsche's Knowledge of Philosophy." Ms. copy in the author's possession.

Clark, Maudemarie. 1990. *Nietzsche on Truth and Philosophy.* Cambridge: Cambridge University Press.

———. 1998. "On Knowledge, Truth and Value." In *Willing and Nothingness: Schopenhauer as Nietzsche's Educator.* Ed. Christopher Janaway. Oxford: Oxford University Press. 37–78.

Cox, Cristoph. 1999. *Nietzsche: Naturalism and Interpretation.* Berkeley: University of California Press.

Crescenzi, Luca. 1994. "Verzeichnis der von Nietzsche aus der Universitätsbibliothek in Basel entliehenen Bücher (1869–79)." *Nietzsche-Studien* 23:388–442.

Danto, Arthur C. 1980. *Nietzsche as Philosopher.* New York: Columbia University Press.

Davey, Nicholas. 1983. "Nietzsche's Doctrine of Perspectivism." *Journal of the British Society for Phenomenology* 14:240–57.

Davidson, Donald. 1983. "A Coherence Theory of Truth and Knowledge." In *Kant oder Hegel?* Ed. Dieter Henrich. Stuttgart: Klett-Cotta. 423–38.

———. 1985. "True to the Facts." In *Inquiries into Truth and Interpretation.* Oxford: Oxford University Press. 37–54.

deMan, Paul. 1979. *Allegories of Reading.* New Haven, Conn.: Yale University Press.

Derrida, Jacques. 1978. *Writing and Difference.* Trans. Alan Bass. Chicago: University of Chicago Press.

Dickopp, Karl-Heinz. 1970. "Zum Wandel von Nietzsches Seinsverständnis: Afrikan Spir und Gustav Teichmüller." *Zeitschrift für philosophische Forschung* 24:50–71.

D'Iorio, Paolo. 1993. "La Superstition des Philosophes Critiques: Nietzsche et Afrikan Spir." *Nietzsche-Studien* 22:257–94.

Djuric, Mihailo. 1980. "Das nihilistische Gedankenexperiment mit dem Handeln." *Nietzsche-Studien* 9:142–73.

Figl, Johann. 1982. *Interpretation als philosophisches Prinzip: Friedrich Nietzsches universale Theorie der Auslegung im späten Nachlaß.* Berlin: Walter de Gruyter.

Fuchs, Dieter. 1996. "Ergänzungen und Berichtigungen der Konkordanz WM-KGW." *Nietzsche-Studien* 25:378–79.

Gemes, Ken. 1992. "Nietzsche's Critique of Truth." *Philosophy and Phenomenological Research* 52:47–65.

Green, Michael S. 1992. "Nietzsche on Pity and *Ressentiment.*" *International Studies in Philosophy* 24:63–70.

Grimm, Rüdiger. 1977. *Nietzsche's Theory of Knowledge.* Berlin: Walter de Gruyter.

———. 1979. "Circularity and Self-Reference in Nietzsche." *Metaphilosophy* 10:289–305.

Haack, Susan. 1978. *Philosophy of Logics.* Cambridge: Cambridge University Press.

Haar, Michel. 1977. "Nietzsche and Metaphysical Language." In *The New Nietzsche: Contemporary Styles of Interpretation.* Ed. David B. Allison. New York: Dell. 5–36.

Haase, Marie-Luise, and Jörg Salaquarda. 1980. "Konkordanz der Wille zur Macht." *Nietzsche-Studien* 9:446–90.

Hales, Steven D., and Rex Welshon. 2000. *Nietzsche's Perspectivism.* Urbana: University of Illinois Press.

Hare, R. M. 1952. *The Language of Morals.* Oxford: Oxford University Press.

———. 1972. "Nothing Matters." In *Applications of Moral Philosophy.* Berkeley: University of California Press. 32–47.

———. 1981. *Moral Thinking.* Oxford: Oxford University Press.

Harries, Karsten. 1983. "Copernican Reflections and the Task of Metaphysics." *International Philosophical Quarterly* 23:235–50.

Hegel, G. W. F. 1981. *The Berlin Phenomenology.* Trans. M. Petry. Dordrecht: D. Reidel.

Heidegger, Martin. 1979. *Nietzsche.* Vol. 1: *The Will to Power as Art.* Trans. David Farrell Krell. New York: Harper and Row.

———. 1982. *Nietzsche.* Vol. 4: *Nihilism.* Trans. Frank A. Capuzzi. New York: Harper and Row.

———. 1984. *Nietzsche.* Vol. 2: *The Eternal Recurrence of the Same.* Trans. David Farrell Krell. New York: Harper and Row.

———. 1986. *Nietzsche.* Vol. 3: *The Will to Power as Knowledge and as Metaphysics.* Trans. Joan Stambaugh and Frank A. Capuzzi. New York: Harper and Row.

Hollingdale, R. J. *Nietzsche.* 1973. London: Routledge and Kegan Paul.

———. 1999. *Nietzsche: The Man and His Philosophy.* 2d ed. Cambridge: Cambridge University Press.

Hume, David. 1978. *A Treatise of Human Nature.* Oxford: Clarendon Press.

———. 1983. *Enquiry Concerning the Principle of Morals.* Indianapolis: Hackett.

Janz, Curt Paul. 1978–79. *Friedrich Nietzsche: Eine Biographie in Drei Bänden.* München: Hanser.

Jarmolych, Nina. 1985. "Nietzsche's Concept of Consciousness." *International Studies in Philosophy* 17:69–77.

Kant, Immanuel. 1964. *Groundwork of the Metaphysics of Morals.* Trans. H. J. Paton. New York: Harper and Row.

———. 1965. *Critique of Pure Reason.* Trans. Norman Kemp Smith. New York: St. Martin's.

Kaufmann, Walter. 1974. *Nietzsche: Philosopher, Psychologist, Antichrist.* 4th ed. Princeton, N.J.: Princeton University Press.

Kemp Smith, Norman. 1962. *A Commentary to Kant's "Critique of Pure Reason."* 2d ed. New York: Humanities Press.

Kerner, George C. 1966. *The Revolution in Ethical Theory.* Oxford: Oxford University Press.

Kofman, Sarah. 1977. "Metaphor, Symbol, Metamorphosis." In *The New Nietzsche: Contemporary Styles of Interpretation.* Ed. David B. Allison. New York: Dell. 201–14.

Kripke, Saul. 1982. *Wittgenstein on Rules and Private Language.* Cambridge, Mass.: Harvard University Press.

Lange, Friedrich Albert. 1882. *Geschichte des Materialismus und Kritik seiner Bedeutung in der Gegenwart.* 4th ed. Iserlohn: J. Baedecker Verlag.

———. 1925. *History of Materialism and Criticism of Its Present Importance.* Trans. E. C. Thomas. London: Routledge and Kegan Paul.

Lear, Jonathan. 1982. "Leaving the World Alone." *Journal of Philosophy* 79:382–403.

Leiter, Brian. 1994. "Perspectivism in Nietzsche's *Genealogy of Morals.*" In *Nietzsche, Genealogy, Morality: Essays on Nietzsche's Genealogy of Morals.* Ed. Richard Schacht. Berkeley: University of California Press. 334–57.

———. 1998. "The Paradox of Fatalism and Self-Creation in Nietzsche." In *Willing and Nothingness: Schopenhauer as Nietzsche's Educator.* Ed. Christopher Janaway. Oxford: Oxford University Press. 217–57.

Lenk, Hans. 1988. "Welterfassung als Interpretationskonstrukt: Bemerkungen zum methodologischen und tranzendentalen Interpretationismus." *Allgemeine Zeitschrift für Philosophie* 13:69–78.

Locke, John. 1979. *Essay Concerning Human Understanding.* Oxford: Clarendon.

McDowell, John. 1978. "Are Moral Requirements Hypothetical Imperatives?" *Proceedings of the Aristotelian Society.* Supplemental Volume. 13–29.

MacIntyre, Alasdair. 1984. *After Virtue.* 2d ed. Notre Dame, Ind.: University of Notre Dame Press.

Mackie, John L. 1977. *Ethics: Inventing Right and Wrong.* Harmondsworth, U.K.: Penguin.

Magnus, Bernd. 1980. "Nietzsche's Mitigated Skepticism." *Nietzsche-Studien* 9:260–67.

Mittelman, Willard. 1984. "Perspectivism, Becoming, and Truth." *International Studies in Philosophy* 16:3–22.

Moles, Alistair. 1990. *Nietzsche's Philosophy of Nature and Cosmology.* Berlin: Peter Lang.

Müller-Lauter, Wolfgang. 1971. *Nietzsche: Seine Philosophie der Gegensätze und die Gegensätze seiner Philosophie.* Berlin: Walter de Gruyter.

Nehamas, Alexander. 1985. *Nietzsche: Life as Literature.* Cambridge, Mass.: Harvard University Press.

Parfit, Derek. 1984. *Reasons and Persons.* New York: Oxford University Press.

Pippin, Robert B. 1989. *Hegel's Idealism: The Satisfactions of Self-Consciousness.* Cambridge: Cambridge University Press.

Plato. 1961. *The Collected Dialogues.* Ed. Edith Hamilton and Huntington Cairns. Princeton, N.J.: Princeton University Press.

Poellner, Peter. 1995. *Nietzsche and Metaphysics.* Oxford: Clarendon Press.

Richardson, John. 1996. *Nietzsche's System.* Oxford: Oxford University Press.

Rorty, Richard. 1979. *Philosophy and the Mirror of Nature*. Princeton, N.J.: Princeton University Press.

———. 1989. *Contingency, Irony, and Solidarity*. Cambridge: Cambridge University Press.

Salaquarda, Jörg. 1978. "Nietzsche und Lange." *Nietzsche-Studien* 7:236–60.

Schacht, Richard. 1983. *Nietzsche*. London: Routledge and Kegan Paul.

———. 1988. "Nietzsche's *Gay Science*; or, How to Naturalize Cheerfully." In *Reading Nietzsche*. Ed. Robert Solomon and Kathleen Higgins. New York: Oxford University Press. 68–86.

———. 1995. *Making Sense of Nietzsche: Reflections Timely and Untimely*. Urbana: University of Illinois Press.

———. 2000. "Nietzschean Cognitivism." *Nietzsche-Studien* 29:12–40.

Schlechta, Karl, and Anni Anders. 1962. *Friedrich Nietzsche: Von den verborgenen Anfängen seines Philosophierens*. Stuttgart-Bad Cannstatt: F. Frommann.

Schopenhauer, Arthur. 1969. *The World as Will and Representation*. 2 vols. Trans. E. F. J. Payne. New York: Dover.

Small, Robin. 1994. "Nietzsche, Spir, and Time." *Journal of the History of Philosophy* 32:85–102.

———. 2001. *Nietzsche in Context*. Aldershot, U.K.: Ashgate.

Spir, Afrikan. 1869. *Forschung nach der Gewissheit in der Erkenntniss der Wirklichkeit*. Leipzig: Forster and Findel.

———. 1873. *Denken und Wirklichkeit: Versuch einer Erneuerung der kritischen Philosophie*. 1st ed. 2 vols. Leipzig: J. G. Findel.

———. 1877. *Denken und Wirklichkeit: Versuch einer Erneuerung der kritischen Philosophie*. 2d ed. 2 vols. Leipzig: J. G. Findel.

———. 1954. *Right and Wrong*. Trans. Alexander Frederick Falconer. Edinburgh: Oliver and Boyd.

Stack, George J. 1981. "Nietzsche and Boscovich's Natural Philosophy." *Pacific Philosophical Quarterly* 62:69–87.

———. 1983. *Lange and Nietzsche*. Berlin: Walter de Gruyter.

Stevenson, C. L. 1944. *Ethics and Language*. New Haven, Conn.: Yale University Press.

———. 1963. "Relativism and Nonrelativism in the Theory of Value." In *Facts and Values*. New Haven, Conn.: Yale University Press. 71–93.

Strawson, P. F. 1966. *The Bounds of Sense*. London: Methuen.

Tarski, Alfred. 1944. "The Semantic Conception of Truth." *Philosophy and Phenomenological Research* 4:341–75.

Taylor, Richard. 1970. *Good and Evil*. New York: Macmillan.

White, Stephen. 1991. *The Unity of the Self*. Cambridge, Mass.: MIT Press.

Wiggins, David. 1976. "Truth, Invention and the Meaning of Life." *Proceedings of the British Academy* 63:331–78.

Wilcox, John T. 1974. *Truth and Value in Nietzsche: A Study of His Meta-Ethics and Epistemology*. Ann Arbor: University of Michigan Press.

Williams, Bernard. 1981. "Wittgenstein and Idealism." In *Moral Luck*. Cambridge: Cambridge University Press. 144–63.

Williams, Michael. 1980. "Coherence, Justification and Truth." *Review of Metaphysics* 34:243–72.

———. 1999. *Groundless Belief.* 2d ed. Oxford: Basil Blackwell.

Wittgenstein, Ludwig. 1953. *Philosophical Investigations.* Trans. G. E. M. Anscombe. New York: Macmillan.

———. 1958. *Tractatus Logico-Philosophicus.* Trans. C. K. Ogden. London: Routledge and Kegan Paul.

———. 1978. *Remarks on the Foundations of Mathematics.* Trans. G. E. M. Anscombe. Cambridge, Mass.: MIT Press.

Zedlin, Mary-Barbara. 1972. "Afrikan Alexandrovich Spir." In *Encyclopedia of Philosophy.* Ed. Paul Edwards. New York: Macmillan. 544.

Index

MICHAEL STEVEN GREEN, an assistant professor of law at George Mason University, earned a Ph.D. in philosophy and a J.D. in law from Yale University. He has taught philosophy at the University of Alabama in Huntsville and at Tufts, Wesleyan, and Yale universities.

International Nietzsche Studies

The University of Illinois Press
is a founding member of the
Association of American University Presses.

Composed in 10.5/13 Adobe Minion
with Adobe Minion display
at the University of Illinois Press
Manufactured by Thomson-Shore, Inc.

University of Illinois Press
1325 South Oak Street
Champaign, IL 61820-6903
www.press.uillinois.edu